MIND SIEGE

MIND SIEGE

THE BATTLE FOR TRUTH
IN THE NEW MILLENNIUM

TIM LaHaye
AND DAVID NOEBEL

WORD PUBLISHING
NASHVILLE
A Thomas Nelson Company

Mind Siege

Copyright © 2000 by Tim LaHaye and David Noebel

Published by Word Publishing, a division of Thomas Nelson Company, P. O. Box 141000, Nashville, TN, 37214, in association with the literary agency of Alive Communications, Inc., 7680 Goddard Street, Suite 200, Colorado Springs, CO, 80920

Unless otherwise indicated, Scripture quotations used in this book are from the The New King James Version (NKJV), copyright 1979, 1980, 1982, Thomas Nelson, Inc., Publishers.

Other Scripture references are from the following sources:

The Holy Bible, New International Version (NIV). Copyright © 1973, 1978, 1984, International Bible Society. Used by permission of Zondervan Bible Publishers.

The King James Version of the Bible (KJV)

New American Standard Bible (NASB), © 1960, 1977 by the Lockman Foundation.

Library of Congress-in-Publication Data

LaHaye, Tim F.
   Mind siege : the battle for truth in the new millennium / Tim LaHaye and David Noebel.
   p. cm.
Includes bibliographical references.
ISBN 0-8499-1672-0 (HC)
1. Apologetics. I. Noebel, David A. II. Title.
BT1102.L257 2001
239—dc21   00-049974
                                                 CIP

Printed in the United States of America

0 1 2 3 4 BVG 9 8 7 6 5 4 3 2 1

This is what the LORD says:

"Cursed is the one who trusts in man,
who depends on flesh for his strength
and whose heart turns away from the LORD.
He will be like a bush in the wastelands;
he will not see prosperity when it comes.
He will dwell in the parched places of the desert,
in a salt land where no one lives.

"But blessed is the man who trusts in the LORD,
whose confidence is in him.
He will be like a tree planted by the water
that sends out its roots by the stream.
It does not fear when heat comes;
its leaves are always green.
It has no worries in a year of drought
and never fails to bear fruit."
(Jeremiah 17:5–8, NIV)

DEDICATION

In the tradition of Dr. Benjamin Rush's famous 1788 "An Address to the Ministers of the Gospel of Every Denomination in the United States, Upon Subjects Interesting to Morals," this book is dedicated to the 250,000 American evangelical ministers of the gospel of Jesus Christ. These Christian leaders head the only viable force with a sufficiently large constituency to make a difference in our society and culture: the church!

Dr. Rush offered a plan "for the advancement of morals in the United States." By the same token, we believe the plan offered herein speaks to our present situation.

We pray that each minister of the gospel will see his strategic role in encouraging his congregation to get involved in the struggle for the hearts and minds of our people in general and our children and grandchildren in particular. This struggle is primarily between the biblical Christian and the Secular Humanist worldviews. It involves every aspect of life, including the theological, philosophical, ethical, biological, psychological, sociological, legal, economic, political, historical, artistic, musical, literary, and scientific.

We call on all evangelical Christian ministers in all denominations to inform themselves fully about these two religious worldviews—Christianity and humanism—then to instruct their congregations as well. We challenge them to encourage lay leadership to carry on the battle in all worldview areas and to exhort their young people to take every idea captive to Christ (2 Corinthians 10:5) as they enter each arena of combat.

While this book will concentrate on merely a few areas, such as theological atheism, moral relativism, and political globalism, we are well aware that the battle is being waged in every area of culture.

We pray that, after reading and studying this work, ministers of the gospel will intelligently and actively urge their portion of the 80 million adult believers in America to become informed and responsible Christian citizens. We pray that each minister will encourage his people to read newspapers and watch television news with understanding; recognize humanist left propaganda; get involved with children's education from grade school to graduate school; and vote for pro-moral, pro-American candidates—candidates who actually believe in America's founding documents (the Declaration of Independence, U.S. Constitution, Northwest Ordinance Treaty) and in its mission to the world as a "city on a hill," defending faith in God, morality, human freedom, free enterprise, and limited government.

With such dedication on the part of the Christian public, we could again live in a pro-moral America, instead of the anti-God, anti-Christian, amoral, and liberal-socialist-humanist nation it is rapidly becoming.

CONTENTS

CONTENTS

IT COULD HAPPEN . . .

It's not my fault, I tell you.

How could I have known what was about to take place? It all happened so fast, in a blur . . . One minute everything seemed fine; the next—well, I just don't know. I still can't quite believe it.

But I want you to know the truth. I want to tell you about the events of that week so you don't get the wrong idea.

It's not my fault, I tell you.

School Daze

Since we moved here in 2010, I've worked in the high-tech industry, where the rules shift faster than the speed of light. I know things can change in a blink of an eye, and I was OK with that. I made a decent living, and my family and I enjoyed a comfortable lifestyle. That's why I never paid much attention to politics and all that. Life is so complicated that you have plenty to do just trying to build a good life for yourself. Let those who know what they're doing take care of that political stuff! Besides, I didn't want to tell other people how they ought to live. "Live and let live"—that's always been my motto.

Still, it bothered me the day I heard somebody on the radio talking about how for the last several decades a "dangerous philosophy" officially taught in our schools had been "corrupting" (those were the speaker's words) our children. He described how this philosophy—he called it "Secular Humanism"—was anti-God and anti-Christian and how it was demolishing the morals of our country. I have to admit, what he said upset me a little. And it dovetailed with what I'd been hearing for some time from my neighbor.

So one day I decided to ask my son, Mark, what was going on in his school.

Now, Mark and I don't talk a whole lot—most ninth graders don't think their dads are cool enough—but every once in a while we find a few minutes to chat (especially when I bribe him). After he came home from school one afternoon, I promised that if he'd spend just ten minutes telling me about his day, I'd make it worth his while.

"I don't even know what classes you're taking," I admitted, "and I really want to know. If you'll fill me in, I'll send you and your buddy Jim to the ball game, with enough cash to keep your stomachs filled and your throats wet for three hours."

Mark hesitated, but since both he and Jim love the Cardinals—and the despised Cubs were scheduled to be in town that weekend—he agreed. He held out his hand.

"After I get what I want," I said, shaking my head.

Mark sighed and started to protest but quickly realized he'd get his money only after I got my story.

"OK," he said. "Well, let's see." He thought for a moment, then began. "When the bus pulled up to school about eight this morning, we saw a bunch of loser kids—mostly Christians, I think—gathered around the flagpole. It looked like they had just finished praying. We ignored them, but as soon as we stepped off the bus, they walked over and started handing out some brochures. I didn't take one, but Jim did. The word *Origins* was at the top of the page, and it said something about how evolution didn't make sense and that an orderly universe required an intelligent Designer. We didn't get to read any more, though, because Vice Principal Dewey came running out of his office, screaming like a wild man that we couldn't be exposed to such 'dangerous material.'"

Mark paused, then broke into a big grin.

"What happened next was *really* cool! Just a few seconds later a couple of police cars and a S.W.A.T. van came screeching into the parking lot, and a bunch of cops, armed with automatics, jumped out. They arrested the students with the brochures and threw them into the van. They also grabbed all their materials."

"And that didn't bother you?" I asked, alarmed.

"Nah—why should it?" my son wondered. "Besides, before classes started, Dewey came on the P.A. to explain that police had just arrested a gang of terrorists who had targeted our school. 'Due to their quick and heroic action,' he said, 'Margaret Sanger High School is safe this morning from the forces of destruction.' He went on like that for a long time, droning on about the dangers of 'unscientific religion' and 'the triumph of the human spirit'—boring stuff we hear all the time."

I didn't know what to say. What my son was telling me sounded a little too much like what I had heard on the radio; it made me . . . uncomfortable. Still, I needed to know more.

"Tell me about your classes," I said.

"First hour is biology," Mark explained. "Today we discussed one of the classics: *Bully for Brontosaurus*, by some Harvard dude. Basically, I learned that I am an accident of nature, an evolving animal. As a species we've done better than the brontosaurus because we have bigger brains, but we're really no different from him. Still, even though we're just blobs of protoplasm floating through space, we can 'live with courage as we face the unknown future.' Stupid line, I know, but that's what they tell us."

"You got all that in the first hour?" I asked, hardly believing it.

"Sure. It's not like we haven't heard it before. Mr. Athenos reminded us that the Bible is myth and legend, that Adam and Eve never really existed, and that science proves evolution is not a theory but a fact. Not much different from the last few years."

I could barely stop myself from making a few comments, but I wanted even more to hear about the rest of my son's day. So all I said was, "Umm, well, how about second hour?"

"That's history class," he informed me. "Lately we've been studying to pass the National History Standards. It's kind of depressing to hear about America's oppressive past. I really didn't know that George Washington and Thomas Jefferson and the rest of those guys were a bunch of brutal slave owners."

"Mark," I interrupted, "haven't you learned anything about America's *Christian* heritage?"

"Christian heritage?" Mark asked, genuinely puzzled. "Dad, I don't think you have your facts straight. Those guys were all deists, atheists, or agnostics. This country was founded on the principle of separation of church and state. They didn't want religion oppressing the people like in the Spanish Inquisition."

My head was starting to spin—and we hadn't yet made it out of second period!

"Tell me about third hour," I said shakily, hoping for better news.

"That's gym class," Mark replied, and immediately my spirits picked up. What could go wrong in gym class?

I was about to find out.

"Today we got another sex-ed lecture. We don't get to play ball much anymore," my son sighed, a faraway look in his eyes. "Captain Condom made another appearance and showed us where to get contraceptives in school colors and how to use them. It was a little embarrassing."

"Captain Condom?" I asked. "Who on earth is *that?*"

"Oh, he's a regular," Mark explained. "He's some guy from the government. I think I heard he's a third-year medical student. Today he told us that sex is a purely biological function, like going to the bathroom, and that whatever we decide to do is up to us; there's nothing 'sacred' about sex at all. We're the only ones who can decide when it's right for us, and anyone who says otherwise is a fanatic from the religious right—like the terrorists who got hauled away earlier."

A chill shot down my spine as I watched my son—my tall, handsome, freckle-faced boy—describe all of this in a perfectly matter-of-fact tone. He clearly bought it all. *Everything.* I wondered if he had yet exercised his right to "sexual choice," and I shuddered at the thought. But I really didn't want to know.

I asked him to move on to the next hour.

"English class is *really* boring," he said, "and it's hard for me to pay attention."

"Shakespeare and Dickens a little too much for you, eh?" I asked, jabbing him in his ribs.

"Who?" he inquired. "I don't think either of them wrote *Travels with Rigobertha.* That's what we're reading right now. We study a lot of feminists and don't read too much of the older writers. Why should we spend time with white heterosexual male oppressors? That's what Ms. Irving always tells us."

"Well," I stammered, "do you spend any time diagraming sentences or doing grammar?"

My son laughed out loud.

"DAD!" he roared. "Don't you know that standard English is a myth? What would be the point of studying *that?*" Between his chuckles, I could tell my son truly pitied his old, ignorant dad.

We quickly moved on past the lunch hour and into fifth period: social science.

"We're learning that everything is relative, just as Einstein said," Mark told me. "Good and evil, life and death—everything is relative. Absolute truth does not exist, and the values of a culture get made up to serve the interests of the rich and powerful. We have to create our own reality."

Before I could ask how his teacher arrived at *that* conclusion, Mark informed me that a representative from Planned Parenthood would be making a presentation in class later in the week. The speaker was going to profile Margaret Sanger, the founder of his organization and the woman whose name now graced the high school (having replaced a white male oppressor named James Madison). The speaker would also discuss the cruelty of Christian ethics, an evil system steeped in myth and legend with no tolerance for diversity.

I looked at the clock, certain our ten minutes had expired, but a couple of minutes were left. "Tell me about sixth period," I said weakly.

"I like math much better than I used to," Mark declared with gusto. "Mr. Eldridge told us today that grades are no longer necessary and will not be given. I like him—he never tells anyone that an answer is wrong. Instead he just says, 'Not quite,' and gets us to agree as a class on a workable answer. He says he's most concerned about our self-esteem, and I believe him. He's really cool."

"So . . . what's seven times six?" I asked.

Mark just sat there, staring at me in disbelief, his upper lip curling into a snarl.

"Um, well, OK, how about seventh hour?" I said, trying to warm the chill in the room.

"Study hall," Mark replied with a grunt.

"And . . . what did you study?" I asked meekly.

My son sighed deep and long. "You don't really *study* in study hall," Mark explained. "It's just a time to wind down. Some guys were preparing for their Death Education class and were starting to write their own obituaries, but most of us just talked about the Marilyn Manson reunion tour that's coming here in a couple of weeks. I know it's really old, but I like his 'Antichrist Superstar.'"

Mark noticed the arching of my right eyebrow and demanded, "Why are you looking at me like that? So what if he sings about Satanism, mass murder, and suicide? It's just a show. I'm hoping he'll also sing 'Irresponsible Hate Anthem.' It's *still* so cool! Listen, Dad: 'I am so All-American, I'd sell you suicide / I am totalitarian, I've got abortion in my eyes / . . . I am the animal who will not be himself / . . . it . . . I am the ism, my hate's a prism / Let's just kill everyone and let your god sort them out / . . . it.'"

I couldn't stand to hear another word, so I blurted out, "That's enough for now, Mark." My stomach began to heave. "Here's your money." I took out my billfold and handed him a smart-chip card containing a couple of hundred dollars.

"That's *it?*" he complained.

"I'm sorry," I apologized. "You'll have to sit in the bleachers this time around." Before he could say anything else, I whirled around and made a beeline for the bathroom. As I closed the door, I heard him mutter, "This really sucks."

Yes, I thought, *it does. I just wish there were something I could do about it.*

And then I threw up.

All the News That's Unfit to Print

For several hours I struggled to digest my unsettling conversation with Mark. *Could the guy on the radio have been right?* I wondered. *Surely Mark's school is an exception. Things really can't be that bad.*

Tired of pacing, I plopped down in my favorite easy chair and hit the On button recessed in its arm. "Let's see what I can find to take my mind off all this," I mumbled as the room darkened and a large menu of options glowed to life in front of me. I silently praised God for the high-end entertainment system that dominated our family room: big-stage, holographic TV; multiple speakers capable of rousing a dead man from the tomb; and thousands of channels grouped into scores of categories (sports, news, shopping, movies, home-audience-participation shows—you name it).

I selected "talk shows," hit Scan, and then sank back into my chair to see what topics and guests might be available to lift my spirits.

Immediately the garish logo for *The Billy Waxman Show* popped up, and I found myself staring into the steel blue eyes of Billy himself. "Our next guest is the beautiful and talented Harina Shanaunda," Billy gushed, flashing his pearly whites to an audience that at that moment numbered about 32 million worldwide. "Harina joins us fresh off the set of her new movie, *Tongues of Fire*. Please welcome, Harina Shanaunda!"

The audience roared its approval as the gorgeous superstar emerged through an opening in some backstage curtains and slunk into an over-stuffed couch next to Billy's walnut desk. "Great outfit, Harina," purred Billy, as he took her hand and gave it a sloppy kiss. "Say," he added, "you wouldn't be the new spokesperson for Saran Wrap, would you?"

The crowd howled, appreciating Billy's joke about his guest's see-through gown. Harina smiled, then gracefully stood up, faced the audience, spread her arms wide, and said with a wink, "Saran Wrap would have been a lot cheaper.

As the audience whistled and clapped its delight, the fleshy image hovering in my family room dissolved into another as an alternate channel came up for review. A distinguished-looking, silver-haired man was talking: " . . . really a new day! The sky's the limit, and you can't allow anyone to dictate what is right or wrong for you. That's the basic message of my newest book, and that's why I've called it *No God but You: Choosing to Live Out Your Divine Rights*."

Scan mode had chosen *Book Talk with Winnifred Opera,* and at a touch of another button I learned that her guest was none other than Dr. Joseph Storm, best-selling author of the *Ascent to Heaven* trilogy and founder of the worldwide Pacifica Mental Health Clinics.

"Tell me, Doctor," Winnifred asked. "If what you say is true and it's been scientifically established that there is no deity outside of ourselves, then why does a full *9 percent* of our population still admit that it attends church every Sunday? Why does belief in a transcendent God persist?"

The kindly doctor smiled and lovingly patted Winnifred's hand. With a twinkle in his eye, he asked his host, "Tell me, my good friend, is it true what the tabloids say about you and your most recent diet book—that since its publication, you have, well, struggled somewhat with maintaining a healthy diet?"

Winnifred made no effort to hide her surprise. "Doctor! I don't see what—"

"Now, my dear, please don't take offense," said Dr. Storm in a calm, reassuring tone. "I simply use this as an illustration. I have read your book, and it is excellent. It is both wise and entertaining. You believe its message, do you not?"

"Well, of course. But I still don't see—"

"The point is simply this," broke in the smiling doctor. "You and I both agree that the principles in your book would make life better for millions. And yet, it is so very easy to slip back—if only for a moment!—into old, bad habits. Is this not so?"

"Certainly, Doctor."

"And so it is in all of life. Even though we know there is no God, when life becomes difficult, we too easily slip back into old, bad habits of belief. Yet as we grow and mature, these slips become less frequent and damaging. Why, twenty years ago nearly *50* percent of our population attended church every Sunday and thus nurtured an irrational belief in God! But as you have mentioned, that figure is now at *9* percent and dropping rapidly. It is much easier to treat the insanity of 9 percent of the population than 50 percent, true? Just as it is easier to deal with ten unwanted pounds than twenty?"

Winnifred laughed and nodded her head. "Right! Exactly right on both counts! Now, Doctor, can you tell me—"

But scan mode cut her off midsentence. The ghostly image of Maury Povich was beginning to take shape as the logo for *Classic Talk* flashed above. But I had lost my appetite for talk. I snuffed Maury and returned to the main menu, where I selected "news" instead. This time I avoided scan mode and chose WWN, the Worldwide News Channel.

Holographs of the massive buildings attached to the United Nations instantly hovered just a few feet in front of me. The sharp image of veteran newscaster, Sheila Wolf, walked into the scene, and as the camera zoomed in for a closeup, she announced, "Just moments ago WWN learned that plans for the long anticipated 'modernization' of the UN are about to be made public. We take you now into the General Assembly of the UN, where Secretary General Raul Hernandez is ready to address the delegates with a historic announcement."

As WWN cameras ushered me into the great hall, where for decades nations had been trying to hammer out their differences, I felt as if I were suddenly sitting among some of the most powerful men and women in the world. Leaders representing every nation on earth sat waiting in breathless expectation as the secretary general approached the podium. The room fell silent and still as Hernandez scanned the august body. He seemed to revel in the amazing diversity and potential there and nodded gravely to several of his closest associates. In a few moments he cleared his throat and, with barely a trace of a Central American accent on his tongue, he began in English: "My friends, this is a great day for our planet. Today marks a new and glorious turning point in our struggle for universal freedom and human rights. For too long we have treated each other as competitors and rivals instead of what we truly are, brothers and sisters engaged in a common fight for dignity and human nobility. Today is a great day in our history, for all that is about to change."

A murmur of anticipation spread through the crowd as the secretary's words were rendered into dozens of languages, but when a few excited members began to clap, Hernandez silenced them with a wave of his hand.

"Hear me, distinguished members, colleagues, and friends! Hear me! To mark the extraordinary progress toward world peace that we have achieved in the past few years, I am proud to announce today that this body will no longer be known as the United Nations. That title represents the past, when individual nations took center stage and petty nationalistic concerns dominated and divided us. Those days are gone!

"As of this moment, I welcome you all—as equals—to work with me for global prosperity and harmony through the greatest vehicle humankind has ever conceived to ascend to its rightful place of majesty. I give you the World Alliance!"

At that instant an enormous hologram displaying the breathtaking symbol of the newly announced WA burst into the air above the delegates, slowly rotating and glittering with gold and bright streaks of blue and green and red. An instant of awed silence erupted into minutes of sustained, thunderous applause.

The secretary general broke into a wide smile and stepped back from the podium, joining his colleagues in energetically putting his hands together. When it appeared the uproar would never cease, Hernandez again approached the podium and put up his hands to ask for quiet. Only begrudgingly did the vast audience comply.

I admit it: I, too, was moved by the ceremony. I could hardly take my eyes off the glowing symbol of the new WA as it floated majestically in my family room.

But what did it mean?

"My friends," the secretary began again, "my dear friends, this would not have been possible without the enormous sacrifices many of you have made over the past decades. Never could we have arrived at this great day without having first put aside our childish differences, both national and religious. Yet we have done so! And so here we stand, a world united, a world at peace, a world headed into a future of unparalleled brotherhood and prosperity.

"Let us never return to the times of ignorance when superstitious dogma and irrational prejudice poisoned our better selves. Humanity has come of age! No longer do we need the confused myths and legends that kept our forefathers in deep darkness. Instead I invite you to step boldly into the light of human reason, unaided by any fictitious deity. Today, my brothers and sisters, *we have become adults!*"

As the enraptured audience burst into another avalanche of cheers and unbridled joy, I reached for the control panel on my armchair and hit the Off button. The UN—or, now the WA—disappeared, and once again my family room took shape around me. My heart had leaped at all this talk of brotherhood and peace and harmony. And the newly unveiled symbol of the WA certainly dazzled my eyes. But what did the secretary mean by the phrases "superstitious dogma" and "fictitious deity"? When he said that today we had "become adults," did he mean that only children could believe in God?

Just what *did* he mean?

As I pondered this, I pushed another button on my armchair console, and instantly the latest condensed edition of *The Daily News and Courier* began printing out. I could have accessed the same thing on holographic television, of course, but after hearing the secretary's speech, I wanted that thing *off*.

As I scanned the front page, one headline in particular jumped out at me: "Christians legally insane, expert testifies."

What on earth . . . ?

My jaw dropped open as I read the little article, tucked between "Pro wrestler set to run for Senate" and "Local woman wins $1 billion in transgender suit." But there it was, as big as life:

Washington, D.C. (AP) — World-renowned psychiatrist Edwin B. Simpson testified today that what he termed "fundamentalist Christians" should be considered legally insane. In testimony before a special Senate subcommittee investigating international terrorism, Simpson insisted that those who profess faith in a transcendent God, who believe they are "saved" through Jesus Christ, and who interpret the Bible in a literal fashion should by definition be classified as insane.

"When one ardently believes in the existence of a nonentity, tries repeatedly to communicate with this mythical being, and attempts to discern current instructions from an ancient book of legends, there exists nothing less than a state of complete legal insanity," Simpson testified. "Such persons should immediately be confined to a mental ward and stripped of their privileges as parents. How can we call ourselves civilized and yet permit our children to be exposed to such hurtful and deranged mental constructs?"

Once more I felt my stomach tightening into a knot, just as it had hours earlier during my conversation with Mark. I let the paper fall from my hands to the floor. I didn't want to read the comics. I didn't want to check the box scores. And I didn't want to turn the television back on.

What I really wanted at that moment was to go to bed, turn out the lights, say a little prayer for my family and nation, and trust that things would be better in the morning.

I mean, what else could I do?

Take a Number, Mr. 439776

Thank the Lord, Tuesday slipped by much more comfortably than Monday did, and I was able to relax a little. By Wednesday morning I had nearly forgotten about all the unpleasantness—that is, until I saw my neighbor just as I was going to work.

"Mornin', Bruce!" he called out from his garage. "We'll see you tonight at six-thirty, right?"

I'm not at my sharpest early in the day, so for a moment I didn't know what to say. *What is he talking about?* I wondered.

"You haven't forgotten, have you?" Rick asked. "Remember? We've been talking about this for the last few weeks."

"Uh, well," I stammered.

"Oh, come on! You were telling me how you wished you could do something to ensure a good future for your kids, and I suggested you get involved in the political process. You hemmed and hawed, but finally you said you'd come with me to the next city council meeting. That's tonight. You *do* remember, don't you?"

Ah, yes. It all came flooding back. Rick was right. I *had* promised to attend the meeting with him. It was the only way I could get him to shut up.

You have to understand something about Rick Hawthorne. He's a good neighbor and a respected fellow member of our church, Redeemer

Evangelical, but he's . . . well, a little too extreme on some things, if you know what I mean. A little too vocal about his views. When he starts talking politics, he makes me squirm.

Take, for example, the conversation where I promised to attend the city council meeting. We were standing outside the church foyer one Sunday morning after services, and Rick launched into one of his "We all ought to be involved in politics" diatribes. He went on and on about how we were losing our freedoms and how we needed to be doing something besides complaining. Rick has run for the city council a couple of times, but he's never won. (I didn't tell him I forgot to vote both times.)

Anyway, after he asked both Mrs. Olson and Fred Buckhalter some pointed questions about their involvement in city politics, he turned to me. "Bruce," he said, "you're my neighbor. You know how I feel about all this. But do you really know what's going on at city hall? When was the last time you attended one of its meetings?"

I stuttered something about a busy schedule and my live-and-let-live philosophy, but he clamped his eyes on me like a pit bull fastened on a piece of raw meat. "You've told me you're concerned about your kids' futures," he said, "so why don't you come with me to the next council meeting and see for yourself what that future is starting to look like? Well? How about it?"

Everybody was looking at me, and I was starting to sweat as I stood there in the noon sun. So I agreed. "OK," I said, "I'll go."

"Great!" Rick replied. "Two weeks from Wednesday, seven o'clock. I'll drive. We should leave about six-thirty. OK?"

"OK," I said, managing a smile but feeling as miserable as a grizzly caught in a rusty bear trap.

And now the awful day had arrived.

My good humor plunged as I contemplated a ruined evening with an opinionated neighbor at a public meeting. But I had promised, and Rick hadn't forgotten. "See you tonight!" he called out as he jumped into his car and drove away.

"Yeah," I replied weakly, "tonight."

I confess I didn't get much work done that day as I groused about the crummy few hours that were rushing toward me. Before I knew it,

I was home, showered, fed, and sitting unhappily in Rick's car on the way to city hall.

"You picked a good night to come," Rick was saying. "The council is considering a number of rules and ordinances that ought to concern the Christian community. And yet most of us don't even know what's up for discussion."

I let him go on like that for the entire twenty-minute trip downtown. He never seemed to notice that I kept my mouth shut the whole time—and I wasn't telling him that silence was my plan for the whole evening. *Just keep quiet and let the professionals do their work in peace,* I thought.

We arrived at the council's chambers five minutes before the meeting started. While the large room could seat perhaps 250 spectators, only a handful of citizens had shown up. It quickly became obvious that Rick was a regular attender. When he walked into the room, a couple of people in the audience nodded their greetings, a handful scowled, and the council president and one of the council members muttered some not-so-silent profanities.

Rick just smiled and took a seat.

Amid last-minute discussions and much paper rustling, council president Josh Williams finally banged his gavel, called the meeting to order, then asked everyone to stand and recite the pledge of allegiance:

> I pledge allegiance to the world
> To care for earth, sea, and air,
> To honor every living thing
> With peace and justice everywhere.

"What was *that?*" I whispered to Rick as we all sat back down. "That doesn't sound anything like the pledge I learned as a kid."

"You haven't heard it before?" Rick asked, surprised. "That's the pledge our kids are learning these days. President Williams has been reciting those words since the third grade. And did you notice? The American flag is kept at the back of the room, while the UN flag—or is it the WA flag now?—stands right up front."

I looked around and saw that everything was arranged exactly as Rick had said. "How long has *this* been going on?" I asked.

My friend paused, shook his head, and said, "You really haven't been paying attention, have you?"

I said nothing, but I determined that on this night I *would* keep my eyes and ears open. Not that there was much to note in the first quarter-hour or so. The council approved the minutes and took care of several other housekeeping items—pretty routine, it seemed. Finally the council moved on to bigger issues. First on the agenda: discussion concerning the city's Right Step program.

"What's that?" I asked Rick.

"Right Step is our city's version of what used to be called Affirmative Action," he explained. "Several years ago the city started giving preferential treatment in hiring and contracting to members of racial groups that in the past had been discriminated against. For some time now, though, the emphasis of Right Step has shifted toward preferential treatment of the gay and lesbian community. Tonight the council is scheduled to discuss how it can attract more gays and lesbians into key administrative positions."

"Wait a minute," I interrupted. "Do you mean that our city is treating gays and lesbians just like it does certain racial groups?"

Rick stared at me again with that impatient look that shouted both disbelief and pity. "Bruce, where have you been?" he asked. "For *years* now gay and lesbian couples have enjoyed all the rights and privileges of heterosexual couples. It used to be that they had to show they were a 'couple.' But now even that is considered passé. Who's to say a union of two weeks is any less deserving of government endorsement than one of fifty years? That's the official reasoning."

This was all news to me. But I hadn't heard anything yet.

"The discussion tonight goes even beyond that," Rick continued. "They're trying to figure out how to recruit as many homosexuals as possible into city government. The real debate concerns how much more they're willing to pay them and how many bennies they're willing to give."

"Just for being gay?" I asked.

Rick didn't answer but slowly shook his head again and turned his attention to the meeting.

I kept silent as I listened to council members debate suitable compensation packages for those recruited under Right Step. Nobody opposed the basic idea; they only disagreed on how much of the city's resources to allocate. The final consensus seemed to be the more, the better.

I struggled to keep up as the discussion shifted to other items on the agenda: an official declaration of support for the new World Alliance; funding for the Civic Arts Consortium's summer exhibit, "On Our Own: Adrift in a Silent Universe"; and the usual array of citizen complaints about potholes, barking dogs, and abandoned cars.

As the meeting wound down around ten-thirty, President Williams wearily acknowledged that it was time to hear from concerned citizens. Rick had told me the open-mike segment was a time-honored tradition in our little community. In fact, when the council had tried to jettison it a couple of years before, the largest crowd in living memory had showed up to protest—every citizen red-faced, loud, and angry. The floor mike stayed in place.

Rick rose to his feet and approached the microphone.

Without the least attempt to mask his disgust, President Williams said, "The chair recognizes Rick Hawthorne."

Rick disregarded the snub and spoke directly into the microphone in a confident, respectful tone. "My name is Rick Hawthorne, and I live at 1327 Sycamore Street. Mr. President, I'd like to comment briefly tonight on two issues: our city's Right Step program and the council's decision to support this week's development at the UN. I'd like to address the second concern first."

Williams rolled his eyes and slumped in his chair, while the other members of the council started talking among themselves. Two of them actually turned their backs as Rick began.

"Distinguished council members, I do not think it's a good idea for our city to endorse this week's actions at the UN. The creation of a World Alliance is just another major step toward a one-world socialistic state in which individual citizens become nothing more than numbers in a huge, godless machine."

I was sure I heard one of the council members mutter, "I wish *his* number were up!"

Rick continued, undaunted. "For the past several years we have been giving away our freedoms, one by one. This country was founded on the conviction that religious liberty is among the most precious rights we possess, but in his speech the secretary general made it sound as if traditional religions, including Christianity, were diseases that need to be eradicated. I believe we have forgotten what U.S. President Harry S Truman told us many years ago: 'The fundamental basis of this nation's law was given to Moses on the Mount. The fundamental basis of our Bill of Rights comes from the teachings we get from Exodus and St. Matthew, from Isaiah and St. Paul. I don't think we emphasize that enough these days. If we don't have the proper fundamental moral background, we will finally wind up with a totalitarian government which does not believe in rights for anybody except the state.'"

"Are you done yet, Rick?" an exasperated President Williams complained. "We all want to go home."

"Just one more comment," Rick answered patiently. "I also want to register my strong disagreement with this council's decision to pursue as many gay and lesbian administrators as possible, based solely on their sexual behavior and regardless of their competency."

"That's *it!*" bellowed councilwoman Evelyn Dirks, jumping to her feet while thrusting her bony finger at my neighbor. Her outburst jerked me a full two inches out of my seat.

"Hawthorne, you *know* we could bring you up on hate-speech charges for what you just said! And we're sick to death of your moralizing. You, a hatemonger and Nazi sympathizer and a member in good standing of that vile group on the hill, the Redeemer Fundamentalist Church—terrorists all!"

Neither President Williams nor any other council member spoke up to quiet the bitter explosion; they just sat there, smiles lighting their faces. They were clearly enjoying this.

"I've learned just this week, *Hawthorne*," continued Dirks, "that your hate group refused to hire Ben Clinton as your pianist, even though he applied for the position, is a fine musician, and is a leading member of our vibrant gay community. As his representative, therefore, I have begun legal proceedings to strip your group of its religious exemptions and have asked the city attorney to seek the heaviest penalties allowed by law against your organization and its evil leadership. We won't tolerate your hate spreading any further!"

Rick tried to respond, but the whole council stood as one and drowned him out with ecstatic applause and hoots of support for Dirks. Several members of the audience immediately joined them. Rick, seeing his predicament, quickly retreated to his seat, snatched up his coat, and motioned for me to follow as he strode out of the room. When I felt several pairs of irate eyes focusing on *me*, I, too, stood up, muttered, "I'm sorry about Rick," and almost sprinted from the building.

Oh, why did I come tonight? I berated myself. *That's what I get for messing around in politics. I should have stayed home and minded my own business!*

As I climbed into Rick's car, for once he wasn't saying anything. He sat at the wheel, silent and shaken by this unexpected turn of events.

Well, at least he's finally shut his mouth, I thought. *I wish he'd done it sooner. Nothing good ever comes from sticking your nose where it doesn't belong.*

Still, I had to admit that I admired his courage. As I stared at the sweat beading up on his forehead, I couldn't help but wonder how this night might have turned out differently had Rick and others like him been elected to the council.

What a shame, I thought. *It's too bad he couldn't have raised more support.*

Limits and Other Foul-Letter Words

After all the upheaval of the week, I was more than ready for the weekend. I've always loved Saturday. It's the one day of the week when I can kick back, take it easy, maybe putter around in the garden, take a long afternoon nap, or catch up on my mail. I try not to schedule anything major for Saturday; that's my day to relax.

This Saturday was no different. It was nearly ten o'clock by the time

I got up, and I wouldn't have stirred even then had the delicious aromas of blueberry pancakes, sizzling sausage, and freshly squeezed orange juice not wafted into the bedroom. The heavenly odor drew me irresistibly into the kitchen, where I found my wife, Sally, carefully taking the hot treats out of the Chef'sMate and placing them on the table.

"I thought this might get you up," she said as I stumbled around the corner. "The smell of sausage and blueberry pancakes works better on you than any alarm clock."

I kissed her on the cheek and plopped down at the table. Yawning broadly, I asked, "Where are the kids?"

"It's Saturday, dear," she reminded me. "They've got their own plans. Mark left with Jim for the ball game, and Lauren spent the night at Gina's. I don't expect her home until this afternoon. It's just you and me, babe." She smiled, then walked behind me and started rubbing my shoulders.

I let out a soft moan.

"You're pretty tight," she said. "Are you still upset about this week?"

"Can we not talk about that?" I asked. "I just want a day to relax."

My good wife massaged my shoulders for a few moments more, then moved to the other side of the table and sat down. We ate breakfast largely in silence—a comfortable silence born of years of easygoing intimacy. As the last gulp of orange juice slid down my throat, I noticed a small mound of unopened mail that had accumulated on the counter.

"I suppose I should go through that pile," I said, nodding my head toward the mail.

"I don't know why you don't throw all that stuff away as soon as it comes," Sally said. "It's never anything but junk mail. Now that our grandparents are dead, nobody sends letters anymore. And we pay all our bills automatically. So why do you insist on sifting through it?" She wasn't scolding, just curious. My habit never made much sense to her. Nevertheless, she grabbed the pile and set it in front of me.

"You never know," I replied. "Wouldn't you feel bad if I threw out a $50 million grand-prize sweepstakes winner?"

"Then we'd never know, would we?" she asked.

I ignored her and started sorting. As she predicted, mostly junk. But soon one classy-looking envelope caught my eye. I picked it up and read aloud part of the return address. "It's from the president and board of directors of the American Civil Liberties Union," I said.

"So?"

"So why would they write us?"

"I don't know. Who are they?"

"Not sure. Let's look."

I tore open the envelope and found a four-page letter and a card that looked like an official certificate of membership. In elegant script the card said, "The president, executive director, and board of directors of the American Civil Liberties Union are honored to invite *Bruce Van Horn* to full-vested membership in the American Civil Liberties Union with all the rights and privileges of membership."

Intriguing, I thought. So I started reading the letter. "Dear Friend of Freedom," it began, then informed me I was being invited to join the most "essential and unique citizen organization" in existence. It said that the ACLU had handled more cases in the Supreme Court than anyone except the government and that it led the fight in "the never-ending ebb and flow of the battle to maintain freedom over authoritarianism."

After the painful events of my week, *that* sounded pretty good! I kept reading.

I learned that I was part of "the saving remnant" of society and that I could join the fight against "the forces of backlash and reaction." I discovered that the ACLU opposed "anti-liberty" forces and that it talked a lot about protecting and enlarging "personal freedoms" and "individual rights."

Wow! I thought. *After what I've seen in the past few days, this seems almost like an invitation from God Himself!* On the spot I decided to send a generous donation.

Only one thing bothered me about the appeal letter. While it made a big deal out of the ACLU's fight for freedom and individual rights, it made an even bigger deal out of naming its enemy. You couldn't miss it. The real enemy was "the far right," "right-wing extremists," "right-wing efforts," and "the extreme right."

I wasn't sure, but I thought "the far right" was a term the media often used to identify conservatives, especially Christians. But I dismissed the thought even as it occurred to me. *Couldn't be the same thing*, I told myself. *Christians have always fought for liberty and freedom. They must be talking about some other group.*

That decided, I got up, headed for the family room, turned on the television, transferred funds to the ACLU, and patted myself on the back for doing my bit for freedom and liberty.

The rest of the day I basked in the glow of my civic-mindedness. I hummed while washing my car, whistled through some weed pulling, and smiled in my sleep as I napped in the shade of our backyard sugar maple. I was still in a good mood that night as Sally and I got ready to attend the theater.

We'd been looking forward to this performance for months. We don't often get into the city to see a show, especially not one straight from Broadway. And the tickets weren't easy to get! But I pulled a few strings at the office and managed to grab two balcony seats for opening night.

As we pulled into the parking structure next to the Performing Arts Center, I noticed that the message board below the theater marquee said *"Straight from Broadway, thanks to the ACLU!"* That piqued my curiosity. I couldn't wait to see how *my* donation had made this performance possible. (Well, if not this particular victory, it *would* enable similar ones in the future!)

We had arrived before the theater's doors opened, so we stood outside in the cooling evening air along with hundreds of other patrons eager to see the show. Soon we struck up a conversation with the couple in front of us.

"Are you as excited to see this play as we are?" Sally asked.

"Actually, we saw it performed in New York just last month," replied a thirty-something woman, dressed to kill in an elegant black gown, jeweled tiara, and exquisite pearl necklace. "But we wanted to see this performance as well, to see if they . . . *changed* anything . . . for the sake of—well, Midwesterners."

Sally and I shot each other a look that must have betrayed our ignorance. The woman noticed our perplexity and continued, *"Surely* you've been following the controversy."

We shook our heads no.

With a sideways glance at her companion as if to say, "Can you *believe* these bumpkins?" the woman continued. "It's been in *all* the media. There wasn't much controversy in New York, of course, because we tend to embrace all the arts, especially works of genius like *An Evening in Paradise*. The furor didn't really begin until the producers decided to make this into a traveling show."

She paused, and when neither Sally nor I responded, she resumed her condescending lecture. "Yes. Well, in New York, of course, audiences are not . . . *scandalized* . . . by frank scenes of homoeroticism, pederasty, and bestiality. We take these to be a part of nature and therefore beautiful. But in places such as . . . well, *here* . . . you see, that's often not the case."

Sally nudged me at the waist and whispered in my ear, "What's pederasty?" As unobtrusively as I could, I whispered back, "I think it's sex between men and boys. And bestiality is—" My wife cut me off, shuddered, but said nothing.

The woman was too busy smirking in the direction of her sharply dressed partner to see our exchange, and for that I was grateful. But I can't say that I appreciated her tone. She seemed to relish this impromptu tête-à-tête with Midwestern plebeians.

"Robert and I flew out here this afternoon to make sure the full, uncut play is presented," she declared, embracing him with her eyes. "Some extreme right-wing elements in this . . . *Bible*-belt region of yours tried to censor it, claiming violation of 'community standards of decency.'" At this she and her previously silent companion laughed. "But thankfully . . . oh, please, pardon me. Let me compose myself . . . Thankfully, the ACLU stepped in and got the courts to enjoin any such pandering to cultural terrorists."

Now she had my full attention.

"The ACLU?" I asked. "You mean, the American Civil Liberties Union?"

The woman stared at me as if a satellite dish had sprouted from my head.

"Why . . . yes," she replied. "I don't know of any other." And with a wave of her white-gloved hand, she turned her back on us and began speaking in low tones to her companion. Yet I was quite sure she hadn't forgotten about us. The intermittent trembling of her shoulders told me that our brief conversation continued to amuse her.

I don't think Sally ever noticed the slight. She nudged me forward a few paces, out of earshot of our sophisticated friends, and in a voice choking with worry asked, "Bruce, what have we gotten ourselves into? I thought *An Evening in Paradise* was an old-fashioned love story! Isn't that what the critics meant by 'a modern love for the ages'?"

I didn't know what to say. I had worked so hard to get the tickets I hadn't spent much time checking out the play itself. It had received rave reviews; it starred the original Broadway cast. How could I have known the kind of deprivation that would be displayed *live* on stage?

"Bruce," my wife announced firmly, "Bruce, I want to go home. I don't feel well."

Without hesitation I agreed. "Yes, I think we should leave," I declared. I took her arm, and together we briskly walked away from the theater and toward the parking garage. In the dying light of dusk I noticed another billboard overhead advertising the glories of *An Evening in Paradise*. With great remorse I noted that across the top of the ad in fiery red letters appeared the words: "STRAIGHT FROM BROADWAY, THANKS TO THE ACLU!"

And I shuddered to realize that the day had cost me a lot more than the price of two unused theater tickets.

Shut Up and Sing

Rarely had I anticipated a church service as much as I did that Sunday. I was glad our Lord had told us, "Come to me, all you who are weary and burdened, and I will give you rest," for I felt more weary and burdened than I ever had. I *needed* His rest!

I wanted the whole family to attend church together that morning, but Mark was still in bed after his long day at the ball game with Jim, and I didn't want to wake him. Lauren had decided to stay another night at Gina's, and since that seemed fine with Gina's parents, I let her. So once more it was just Sally and I who donned our Sunday best for worship (unfortunately, that happened a lot in our family).

It was deathly quiet as we got ready, and I knew the silence was due to more than the mere absence of boisterous kids. Neither Sally nor I could get *An Evening in Paradise* out of our minds. But neither of us wanted to talk about it either.

We drove to church in a sullen hush, speaking only when the ushers greeted us at the door.

"Good morning, Bruce! Nice to see ya!" said Ed McFarlane.

"My, don't you look pretty today, Sally!" said Barbara McFarlane.

We exchanged pleasantries, then Sally and I headed to the right side of the sanctuary, tenth pew back—our usual place. Before taking a seat, I grabbed a program and scanned it for the order of service and the day's Scripture text. Pastor Ron always provided a page or two of fill-in-the-blank notes so his audience could better follow his sermon. As I read the Bible passage printed next to the pastor's notes, it dawned on me that I might have avoided a lot of anguish that week had I taken the time to study those ancient words for myself:

> This is what the LORD says:
> "Cursed is the one who trusts in man,
>> who depends on flesh for his strength
>> and whose heart turns away from the LORD.
> He will be like a bush in the wastelands;
>> he will not see prosperity when it comes.
> He will dwell in the parched places of the desert,
>> in a salt land where no one lives.
> "But blessed is the man who trusts in the LORD,
>> whose confidence is in him.
> He will be like a tree planted by the water
>> that sends out its roots by the stream.
> It does not fear when heat comes;
>> its leaves are always green.

It has no worries in a year of drought
and never fails to bear fruit."
(JEREMIAH 17:5–8, NIV)

Cursed is the one who trusts in man, I repeated in my mind. *Sounds to me like that's exactly this country's problem.*

And then it hit me.

Is that what the guy on the radio was talking about? Is that what he meant by . . . what did he call it? "Secular Humanism"? Scientific Humanism? Planetary Humanism? Is this nation in so much trouble because our leaders decided to trust in man?

Images of the past week flooded my mind. I knew I was supposed to be preparing for worship, but I couldn't stop the pictures. There was my handsome son, describing in blasé terms how he was merely an evolved animal, how the Bible was all a myth, how God didn't exist, and how he needed to choose for himself what was right and wrong.

And I heard the Bible telling me, "He will be like a bush in the wastelands."

There stood Harina Shanaunda in her see-through dress . . . Dr. Joseph Storm and his book *No God but You* . . . Secretary General Raul Hernandez announcing the formation of the World Alliance and proclaiming that we had matured beyond a childish need for God . . . the "expert" testifying before a Senate subcommittee that all Christians should be considered legally insane.

And I heard the Bible telling me that they "will not see prosperity when it comes."

I saw our fellow citizens pledging allegiance to the world at the city council meeting. I saw the council, through Right Step, planning to recruit as many homosexuals as possible into city government. I saw a furious Evelyn Dirks ranting that Christians were hatemongers and Nazi sympathizers and threatening to shut down our church.

And I heard the Bible telling me that we "will dwell in the parched places of the desert, in a salt land where no one lives."

Could it really be true? Were we beginning to see the fulfillment of Jeremiah's dark prophecy?

But I had no more time to ponder our nation's precarious position, for the booming strains of our Call to Worship had begun. The disturbing pictures in my mind dissipated as I drank in the familiar chords of "A Mighty Fortress Is Our God." While the Call to Worship at our church is purely instrumental, I followed along mentally with the lyrics I had learned as a child:

> A mighty fortress is our God,
> A bulwark never failing;
> Our helper He amid the flood
> Of mortal ills prevailing.
> For still our ancient foe
> Doth seek to work us woe—
> His craft and power are great,
> And, armed with cruel hate,
> On earth is not his equal.

The full orchestra joined in at the second stanza, and as the music swelled, I closed my eyes, and in my mind I repeated, "Did we in our own strength confide, our striving would be losing—"

And then utter chaos broke out.

The hymn broke off with a flurry of sour notes and squeaking horns, and I looked up to see our minister of music being restrained by a uniformed police officer. Some orchestra members sat in their chairs, paralyzed and wide-eyed, while others had dropped their instruments and were scrambling to flee the area.

Before Pastor Ron could get to the pulpit to ask what was going on, he, too, was forcibly restrained and hauled from the sanctuary by a team of officers. Fear and confusion rippled through the audience, and those who tried to run out the exits found them blocked by police.

Suddenly my eyes noticed movement toward the center of the sanctuary where I saw a middle-aged woman striding right down the center aisle—not toward the exit, but straight toward the pulpit. The police made no effort to stop her progress but, in fact, seemed to make way for her. She climbed the few steps of the platform, walked behind the pulpit, and turned to address the congregation. I gasped when I saw her face.

It was councilwoman Evelyn Dirks.

"There is no need for alarm," she commanded as she gripped the sides of the pulpit. "Please! May I have your attention, please! No one is going to be hurt, but I need your attention. Please!"

Two uniformed officers joined Dirks on the platform, and I was amazed how quickly the congregation hushed. With the exception of a few crying babies and a handful of frightened toddlers, everyone in the audience seemed to freeze on the spot.

Dirks smiled.

"Thank you," she said. "I do apologize for the inconvenience this morning, but it was unavoidable. I am Evelyn Dirks, councilperson representing the fourth precinct and recently appointed liaison to the World Alliance. While none of us has any desire to dictate to anyone else how they should express their privately held religious beliefs, recent official investigations have revealed that the leadership of this org—er, *church*—has been co-oped by certain known terrorist groups."

A murmur of surprise and alarm rumbled through the audience, but no one dared speak.

Dirks smiled again.

"We had to act quickly before any further damage could be done," she continued. "But we want to assure you that the terrorists will be dealt with quickly and fairly according to law. This morning, however, we want you to continue your meet—er, your worship service—with a minimum of disruption. To accommodate that goal, the Very Reverend Philip Spencer from the Humanist Society of Friends has graciously consented on short notice to lead you. Reverend Spencer."

A short, balding man wearing an oversized black robe waddled up to the pulpit and vigorously shook Dirks's hand. The councilwoman left the stage immediately, and the Reverend Spencer turned to face his new congregation.

"My dear friends," he began in a deep, therapeutic voice, "let us not allow the evil of a few to overshadow the good of most, but instead let us rejoice that justice and right shall prevail and intolerance and wrong shall be crushed. Amen?"

Not a peep sounded from the congregation, but the Reverend Spencer remained undeterred.

"Amen," he repeated. "This morning I would like to ponder with you the tremendously liberating words spoken by a true prophet of our age. This man, a trustworthy herald of the New World Order, gave us the truth and set us free when he said, 'For his great achievements man, utilizing the resources and the laws of Nature, yet without Divine aid, can take full credit. Similarly, for his shortcomings he must take full responsibility. Humanism assigns to man nothing less than the task of being his own savior and redeemer.'

"My fellow seekers of truth, I would like to help you unpack these precious words in the next few moments before us . . ."

I admit that I didn't hear much more of what was said that morning. I *never* thought it would come to this. I never dreamed that my pastors could get dragged away as terrorists or that our service could be disrupted by police. I never imagined that instead of praise choruses or hymns we would be "encouraged" to sing Top 40 tunes and little ditties extolling the virtues of human genius. (When one man sitting in the pew ahead of us started talking to his wife instead of singing, a police officer standing nearby leaned over, poked the man in his ribs with a long club, and barked, "Shut up and sing, buddy!")

And the worst thing of all is—I just can't imagine how it happened.

Do you see now why I said it wasn't my fault? Do you understand why I wanted to tell you the whole story of that awful week so you wouldn't get the wrong idea?

How could I have known that powerful people in the media and education and government were out to exclude God from every arena of life?

How could I have known that they intended to corrupt the morals of my children and lead them into a cesspool of debauched sex and drugs?

How could I have known that they would make evangelism a hate crime and declare Christians legally insane? How was I to know they'd take my kids away from me and put me in this mental institution? How could I have known?

It's not my fault, I tell you.

INTRODUCTION

Of the sons of Issachar who had understanding of the times,
to know what Israel ought to do, their chiefs were two hundred;
and all their brethren were at their command.
1 CHRONICLES 12:32

Bruce Van Horn is a fictional character, but many of us are more like him than we care to admit. Most of us do not realize what Secular Humanism really is and how it is destroying our culture, families, and country—and one day will destroy the entire world.

It is no overstatement to declare that most of today's evils can be traced to Secular Humanism, which already has taken over our government, the United Nations, education, television, and most of the other power centers of life. Secular Humanism—whether it calls itself Marxist Humanism, Cosmic Humanism, Scientific Humanism, Planetary Humanism, Postmodern Humanism, or sports some other label—is driven by a flaming hatred for Jesus Christ that seeks to eradicate the Christian worldview from the media, the government, and especially public education. Secularists scorn creationism, design in nature, man in the image of God, the Fall, traditional or biblical morality, the natural family of father and mother, and the religious and political faith of the majority of America's Founding Fathers.

The awful truth is that the last major obstacle for the humanists to conquer is the church of Jesus Christ . . . and they intend to remedy that.

Unfortunately, the mainline churches—especially the denominations and seminaries affiliated with the National and World Council of Churches—have eaten, swallowed, and digested tons of humanist dogma: evolution, socialism, Marxism, higher criticism of the Bible, moral relativism, amoral sex education, nontraditional families, liberation theology, process theology, gay theology, feminist theology, black theology, world government, and global citizenship, to name but a few.

Therefore, unless the 80 million evangelical Christians in our nation wake up to whom the enemy really is, humanists will soon accomplish their goal of world domination.

A Sewer by Any Other Name

Brad Scott in his *Streams of Confusion* lists several ideas that threaten the well-being of the twenty-first century: man makes right, not God; every man possesses an innate moral sense; man is good by nature but corrupted by society; happiness is the measure and goal of a good life; man, too, is an animal; material and economic causes alone produce social change; only slaves and fools restrain their wills and desires; there is no God, only unconscious, mechanistic causation; Christianity is primitive and even Christ is flawed; life is meaningless; free will is an illusion; everything is relative; and all we need is love. All of these rotten ideas spew directly from the foul-smelling sewer of Secular Humanism.

Yet Secular Humanism, postmodernism, New Age thought, and a thousand other ideologies just like them are really little more than repackaged versions of the ancient satanic doctrine that ruined Eden. Remember how the devil convinced Eve to eat of the forbidden fruit? "You will be like God," the serpent hissed, "knowing good and evil" (Genesis 3:5). Ever since that fateful day, the unchanging goal of rebellious mankind has been to sit—all by himself—on God's throne.

Don't believe it? Then just listen to the mantras being intoned these days:

Secular Humanism says, "There is no deity to help us; we must help ourselves."

Postmodernism says, "There is no absolute truth; we must create our own."

New Age thought says, "There is no Christian deity; I am my own God."

Call these worldviews what you will, their central and controlling thought remains the same: We human beings will be like God. We will know good and evil for ourselves and on our own terms.

This catastrophic lie has plagued us from the beginning of human history until now, and the Bible makes it clear that it will continue to deceive the world until the end. The Antichrist, the man the Bible pictures as the very embodiment of human rebellion, will first and foremost be a worshiper of himself. The prophet Daniel says of him:

> The king will do as he pleases. He will exalt and magnify himself above every god and will say unheard-of things against the God of gods. He will be successful until the time of wrath is completed, for what has been determined must take place. He will show no regard for the gods of his fathers . . . nor will he regard any god, but will exalt himself above them all. (Daniel 11:36–37, NIV)

This epitome of secular Humanists "will oppose and will exalt himself over everything that is called God or is worshiped, so that he sets himself up in God's temple, proclaiming himself to be God," says the apostle Paul (2 Thessalonians 2:4, NIV).

Do you see it? The same lie that destroyed Eden? Puny man saying, "I am God!"

In every age and in every place, this remains forever the temptation—to believe the devil's lie and to imagine that we have become God.

The *Oxford English Dictionary* contains thousands of obscure words that don't get much use these days, but we think one word buried in its massive bulk deserves to get out more often. Oxford defines *anthropolatry* simply as "man-worship; the giving of divine honours to a human being."

Anthropolaters—that's what unredeemed men and women inevitably become. Secular Humanists, New Agers, postmoderns, and all their cousins may not realize it, but every one of them is blindly roaring down the same dead-end highway called "Man Worship."

But on second thought, it's a good deal more personal than that.

At first the temptation is to see mankind as God. Then it becomes us as God. And finally it's me as God. So the progression moves from worship of man, to worship of us, to worship of me.

In the end, all anthropolaters become *I*-dolaters. "*I* am God." Like little antichrists, they exalt and magnify themselves above all gods and set themselves up in the temple of their minds, proclaiming themselves to be God.

That's the gargantuan error this book is written to combat. We want to provide a resource that will help all of us to turn away from anthropolatry, to steer clear of *I*-dolatry. This book examines and explains Secular Humanism in simple terms so that the man on the street and in the pew can both understand its danger and be motivated to oppose it. Yet we don't want merely to oppose Secular Humanism or postmodernism or any other current mutation of the devil's original lie. Therefore you will find positive suggestions on what you can do to triumph over this evil and to help return our families, churches, schools, and country to moral and spiritual sanity. This is not a book of gloom and doom but a wake-up call for all evangelical Christians to

- herald Messiah's message;
- be lights in the world (Matthew 5:16; Philippians 2:15);
- raise the moral climate of our culture (Matthew 5:13; 25:35–36; Romans 12–14; Colossians 3:12–23; Jude 22–23).

And most of all, we want to assist the church in rightly worshiping the only living and true God, the God of Abraham, Isaac, and Jacob, the Father of our Lord Jesus Christ.

To Him alone be the glory!

The Battle Is On

While each generation has to face its own challenges (Acts 13:36), the ideas and beliefs battling for the minds of every generation have much in common. Each generation has to decide if Christ is superior to Nietzsche; if God is smarter than Plato; if freedom is better than totalitarianism; if private property is superior to socialism; if creationism is superior to evolution; if purpose and design are superior to chance; if truth is better than falsehood; if beauty is better than ugliness; if love is better than hate; if good is better than evil; if right is better than wrong; if heaven is better than hell; if moral absolutes are better than moral relativism; if adoption is better than abortion; if self-control is better than licentiousness; if individual responsibility is better than victimization; if patriotism is better than globalism.

The Christian is obligated to bring mistaken ideas and beliefs to Christ for His light. As Paul says, "Do not be conformed to this world, but be transformed by the renewing of your mind, that you may prove what is that good and acceptable and perfect will of God" (Romans 12:2).

Christians cannot remain neutral and forgo this battle for the heart and mind. Elijah took on the state religion of Baal and Asherah at Mount Carmel in 1 Kings 18. Jesus Christ took on the Greeks (Pan) and the Romans (Caesar) at Mount Hermon in Matthew 16–17. And Paul took on the Greek philosophers (Epicurean and Stoics) at Mount Mars in Acts 17. All engaged the battle. None raised the white flag to surrender.

We must do no less, otherwise every idea that Christians hold dear, as well as the institutions based on these ideas (home, church, state), will be lost.

Second Corinthians 10:5 makes the Christian response very clear. It is our responsibility to overthrow "arguments and every high thing that exalts itself against the knowledge of God, bringing every thought into captivity to the obedience of Christ."

Christians must capture every idea and bring each one into the obedience of Christ—or else those ideas will capture them, damage their minds and souls, and ultimately destroy their lives.

May the materials presented in the following pages provide Christians—and especially Christian young people—with the ammunition necessary to wage the battle for the mind intelligently, strategically, tactically, and prayerfully.

It's Not Too Late!

When I wrote *Battle for the Mind* in 1980, I discovered what it felt like to be a prophet without honor in his own country. Indeed, when I insisted that Secular Humanism was a distinct threat to America and its Judeo-Christian founding and the well-being of the Christian church, I was accused by the national media of creating a bogeyman.

But now, twenty years later and with the recent publication of

Humanist Manifesto 2000, it looks as if I may have been right all along. Humanism continues to be a threat well into the twenty-first century.

Nevertheless, we believe there is still time to defeat the humanist agenda and to reverse our country's moral decline. America does not have to remain on its current course of becoming Sodom and Gomorrah. We believe God will yet bless this nation and give us another great revival, which we call Great Awakening IV. It will come, however, only if we get serious about our Christian beliefs, aims, world-view, and actions. It will happen only when we become informed about what and who is the destroyer of our hearts and minds. We must learn how to combat a new, subtle form of evil, one that has Western civilization by the throat.

As our fictional friend Bruce Van Horn discovered too late, life is mainly about the battle for your mind: whether you will live by man's wisdom or God's wisdom (1 Corinthians 1:17–25). The wisdom of man has taken the multifaceted form of Secular Humanism, while the wisdom of God is revealed in the Bible and displayed throughout creation (Genesis 1:28; Romans 1:18–20).

Which of these two options *you* choose will affect the way you live now and ultimately where you will spend eternity.

PART ONE:
THE CONFLICT

1

YOUR INCREDIBLE BRAIN, YOUR MAGNIFICENT MIND

Who has put wisdom in the mind?
Or who has given understanding to the heart?
JOB 38:36

Your brain is the most complex mechanism in the world and the most influential organ of your body. It enables your mind to think, remember, love, hate, feel, reason, imagine, and analyze.[1]

The average brain weighs about three pounds and contains 12 billion cells, each of which is connected to 10,000 other brain cells. That's 120 *trillion* brain connections!

Some have compared the human brain to a sophisticated computer, but technology hasn't come close to duplicating its capabilities. Dr. Gehard Dirks, who holds fifty patents on the IBM computer, said that he acquired most of his ideas from studying the functions of the human brain.

Your brain supervises everything you do, from the involuntary beat of your heart to the conscious decisions of your life. It controls hearing, sight, smell, speech, eating, resting, learning, prejudices, and everything else that makes you behave as you do. Scientists tell us that the brain is our most important organ because it determines the function of the other organs and systems, including the pituitary gland, heart, and nervous system. Your unique traits, temperament, and even physical growth patterns are all controlled by your brain.

We have little or no conscious control over many of these traits, and even today, scientists disagree over the extent to which we rule ourselves. Yet most experts insist that we can regulate far more mental activity than we realize. One thing is certain: What we choose to see and hear and how we think (our philosophy of life) are the most significant influences on our lives, and they greatly affect all three major aspects of the mind: intellect, emotion, and will.

Your Intellect

A major portion of your three-pound brain houses your intellect. It, too, is influenced by inherited temperament. That helps to explain why some people by nature are analytical perfectionists with good retention capabilities, while others are prone to be goal-oriented people lovers who struggle with organization and concentration.

Your intellect has phenomenal potential. Scientists inform us that the average person uses less than 10 percent of his brain's capability. If that is true, then most people die with 10 to 11 *billion* brain cells still unused.

The vast majority of what we know about the intellect has been discovered during the past 100 years, yet scientists anticipate that even greater discoveries await us. Thinking and memory are the chief functions of the intellect, but it also affects our intuition, conscience, sexuality, and much more. Recent studies indicate a difference between the minds of men and women, providing scientific support for the traditional claim that the sexes think differently. For example, boys and girls from primitive cultures responded differently when introduced to modern toys. Without the benefit of cultural conditioning, the boys gravitated to trucks and toy soldiers while the girls were drawn to dishes and dolls.

Since the eyes and ears are the two most important channels for communicating with the brain, how you employ these information gatherers largely determines how you think. And be sure of this: How you think *will* determine the way you live! It remains true, as the writer of Proverbs long ago observed, "As he thinks in his heart, so is he" (23:7).

The way you think is the result of the intellect you inherited, plus your training, plus what you have seen, read, done, and heard. Your inherited temperament also has a significant influence on your personality, helping to determine how you do things.[2] For example, if you are an introvert, it is probably because you were born with an introvert's temperament. Although you can become more aggressive than your heritage might suggest, you will never be a spontaneous extrovert.

The philosophy of life that you adopt on the basis of what you have programmed into your mind through your reason, your senses, and your study determines the way you look at life. Whether we call this a worldview or simply the way we perceive life, nothing but life itself is more important. It will affect your morals, work drive, integrity, and life investment.

Until this generation, parents were the most influential force in helping children to develop a personal philosophy of life. That is no longer true. Modern technology has given us the Internet and WebTV and has opened countless other ways to expose young minds to incredibly enticing sounds, colors, and visual images. Through countless seductive channels, thousands of parents already have lost their children's intellects to atheistic educators, sensual entertainers, liberal clergy, Elmer Gantry–type politicians, and a host of other anti-God, amoral influences.

Ever since God first explained to Adam and Eve how to think so they could live successful, fulfilled, obedient, and happy lives, there has been a constant battle over who will control human thought processes—man or God. Sooner or later, every human being makes that decision.

Because your thought processes are largely the result of the stimuli your brain has received from various senses, only by being careful can you win the battle for control of your intellect and your children's intellects.

Emotional Center

The second significant part of your brain is what the Bible calls your "heart," your emotional center. It's not heart-shaped, as romantics tend to visualize it, but in reality looks more like a walnut. Tied neurologically to every organ of your body, it activates both feeling and movement. If your emotional center is disturbed, you will be upset all over.

Emotionally induced illnesses—which doctors claim account for 65 to 80 percent of all modern sickness—originate in the heart. A person who feels angry, fearful, or tense will suffer from all kinds of physical ailments, from high blood pressure to ulcers to strokes. One list describes 51 diseases caused by an emotional center gone haywire.

A man I knew went to the doctor because of a racing heart. He discovered that fears in his mind had caused his body to simulate a heart attack. By learning to govern his fears, the man was able to slow down his racing heart.

Your emotional center is influenced by many factors, beginning with your inherited temperament. That explains why some people are excitable by nature, while others are passive or indifferent. Life experiences, education, beliefs, and, most significantly, the mind also influence how we feel.

To illustrate the relationship of the mind to the emotions, visualize a man who owns two thousand shares of AT&T, purchased at $100 a share. How does he feel as he reads his morning paper to find that his shares have dropped to $10? He feels angry, depressed—even suicidal. Once he grasps the loss of his fortune, his "heart" or emotions get involved. Now visualize the same man as he calls his broker and discovers that the newspaper made a typographical error; actually, each share is now worth $1000. A smile brightens his face and he feels relieved, even exhilarated.

The mind is to the emotions what food is to the body. For that reason, what the mind feeds upon becomes the most influential force in your life.

One of the great myths of our time is that feelings are spontaneous. Actually, they are created by what you put into your mind. Computer experts repeatedly warn us that we get out of a computer only what we program into it. The same can be said for the mind. Whatever the eyes and ears pick up, the mind processes. The other senses—smell, taste, and touch—also influence our thinking but do not have as significant an impact on our mind.

Consider the unmarried, twenty-one-year-old college student who admitted to me a serious problem with sexual thoughts. I wasn't surprised by the young man's confession since he was at the zenith of his sexual drive. In an attempt to help him learn how to control his passions, I asked, "What have you been reading and seeing lately?" After mumbling a few vague references to newspapers and magazines, he finally acknowledged a more-than-passing acquaintance with *Playboy* and certain pornographic books. When pressed about movies, he admitted that he had been watching X-rated movies on cable television.

I then pointed out that such a large intake of pornography was like pouring gasoline on a fire.

The old truism "You are what you read" could be enlarged to "You are what you see." What the eyes feast upon forms an impression on the mind, which in turn feeds the emotions. Just as drugs or alcohol influence us physically, what we see and hear affects our thoughts and emotions.

There is growing evidence that our warnings to civil leaders a few years ago that overturning the moral laws upon which this country was built would increase crimes of sex and violence were fully warranted. In the name of free speech and freedom of the press, we have polluted the minds of our young with pornography, until crime and sexual assaults are now commonplace.

And it's not only those who hold to traditional morality who worry about the spread of pornography. Feminists demonstrating in New York recently highlighted their concern that the widespread use of pornography is a threat to them, for women become the tragic victims of rape, assaults, and even murder.

Sociologist Marvin Wolfgang has stated that the portrayal of violence tends to encourage physical aggression. Of course it does! Whatever you see or hear influences your mind, which in turn affects your feelings and your emotional center. Feelings are aroused as much by what you see and hear as by who and what you are. If you want the right feelings, then see and hear the right things, so you can generate the right thoughts.

Thousands of minors have been taken into custody for crimes that never would have been committed were it not for pornography. I once visited a sixteen-year-old in juvenile hall just after he had committed a sex crime that startled everyone who knew him. In his room we found a drawer nearly filled with pornographic filth. It was easy to understand how this lad brought disgrace upon his family and shame to himself. At a time when he was beginning to experience sexual passions, he misused his eyes to fan his desires until his emotions ignited a fire that raged beyond control. He will probably be haunted by that evil action the rest of his life.

That boy, however, was not abnormal. He simply responded naturally to an abnormal stimulus. Pornography is abnormal! Our youth seem obsessed with sex because depraved adults are providing them with the pornographic fuel with which they burn up their lives.

It's true that not all visual filth—whether from the Internet, television, R-rated movies, music videos, or books—results in crimes of violence. But my counseling experience indicates that at the least it reduces the beautiful expression of love in marriage to a soulless activity of sexual passion. In fact, pornography is one of the leading causes of our skyrocketing divorce rate.

Another form of pornography should be mentioned as well, namely, pornographic music. As Cal Thomas says, "the new generation needed music and other forms of entertainment that would reflect its increasingly nihilistic worldview."[3] And they got it! Take, for instance, gangster rapper Eminem. Culture critic Gene Edward Veith states, "The biggest hardcore rapper—and the meanest, most violent, most lawless of them all—is the white Eminem."[4] His recording called *The Marshall Mathers LP* was the number one selling CD in America with more than 7 million sold.

What breaks my heart is the way Eminem gleefully raps about brutally sodomizing his mother (in "Kill You") with words too pornographic to reprint here. In "Amityville," he arranges to have his sister gang raped. He raps, "My little sister's birthday/She'll remember me/For a gift I had ten of my boys/take her virginity." As if these deplorable ideas weren't evil enough, he portrays two men performing oral sex on a third partner. Even sex with a dead animal is mentioned on the album.

As youth culture specialist Bob DeMoss told me, "Keep in mind that there are only approximately 29 million teens in America. Mathematically speaking, one-in-four young people own a copy of this socially irresponsible recording."[5]

According to Thomas, the three major social problems today are the consequences of sex outside of marriage (venereal diseases, out-of-wedlock children, abortion), drug abuse, and violent crime. Not incidentally, he points out that the three major themes of hard-rock music are "sex, drugs, and violence."[6]

Pornography, of course, is not the only phenomenon that influences the emotions. But it does graphically illustrate that what you see and hear greatly influences how you think, and how you think influences your feelings.

Whenever you recognize illicit feelings bubbling up inside you, here is a healthy rule of thumb to follow: Examine what you have been seeing and hearing, and ponder how your mind has been thinking. Feelings are *not* spontaneous. To control them, you must first control your mind.

The Will

The third characteristic of the brain is the will, which makes human beings unique from all other living creatures. No one knows where the will is located, but we suspect it resides in the brain, because it so depends on the mind and emotions. Many dying people have displayed a strong will long after most other bodily functions have ceased, but when the brain ceases to function, the will vanishes.

Like the heart and mind, the will is influenced by a person's inherited temperament, which explains why some people are weak-willed while others are strong-willed. The will is also influenced by parental training, education, and life experiences; by what a person reads, sees, and hears; and by the way in which he or she thinks and feels.

Someone has said that whenever the emotions and the will are in conflict, the emotions win. That is often true, particularly if a person's thoughts are permitted to inflame the feelings for a sufficient period of time. A friend of mine is an alcoholic, but for six years he had not touched a drop. One hot day an urgent thought flashed on the screen of his imagination: *An ice-cold glass of beer would sure taste good right now.* His conscious mind retorted, *Don't do it! You're an alcoholic.* Because the man's imagination visualized the beer in three-dimensional color, however, he convinced himself that after six years he had learned to control his problem. Within two hours he visited a bar, downed one drink, then another—and you can imagine the rest.

The importance of the will should never be underestimated. A man's life and eternal condition hang on it. If he chooses to rebel against God, his life will constantly be in turmoil. If, however, he surrenders control of his life to God, he will enjoy a life of fulfillment and oneness with both God and his fellowman.

Because parents play a significant role in training a child's will, we are alarmed at the current trend that emphasizes children's rights at the expense of parental rights. We believe it inhibits parents from administering loving discipline; in fact, many parents are already afraid of their children. Children raised in such homes will grow up without self-control and are in danger of becoming part of the "anti-values" generation that rebels against the laws of God and society. Such rebels provide ready fodder for the self-centered philosophy found in humanistic education, movies, books, and other media.

Good or Evil

Of the three interdependent areas of the human brain, the intellect is by far the most significant. It ultimately determines both our feelings and the strength and direction of our will. That is why we call this book *Mind Siege*. The principal question of life is this: Who will control your mind?

As far back as we can go in recorded history, we find that human beings have always been aware that life is a battle between good and evil. Thirty-five hundred years ago, evil was termed "the way of man" or "the way that seemed right to man." The good way has always been called "God's way." These two avenues of living are really philosophies of life dictating how a person lives.

The apostle Paul described the difference between the two when he wrote to the church in Corinth, Greece, where much of our *I*-dolatrous thinking originated:

> For Christ sent me not to baptize, but to preach the gospel: not with wisdom of words, lest the cross of Christ should be made of none effect. For the preaching of the cross is to them that perish foolishness; but unto us which are saved it is the power of God. For it is written, I will destroy the wisdom of the wise, and will bring to nothing the

understanding of the prudent. Where *is* the wise? where *is* the scribe? where *is* the disputer of this world? hath not God made foolish the wisdom of this world? For after that in the wisdom of God the world by wisdom knew not God, it pleased God by the foolishness of preaching to save them that believe. For the Jews require a sign, and the Greeks seek after wisdom: But we preach Christ crucified, unto the Jews a stumblingblock, and unto the Greeks foolishness; But unto them which are called, both Jews and Greeks, Christ the power of God, and the wisdom of God. Because the foolishness of God is wiser than men; and the weakness of God is stronger than men.

(1 CORINTHIANS 1:17–25, KJV)

In this passage Paul outlines two opposing lines of reasoning: man's wisdom and God's wisdom. Paul showed the Greeks—who in his day were the ultimate in intellectualism, science, art, literature, and philosophy—that man's wisdom was inherently wrong (Acts 17:16–34). He called it foolishness (or futility). By contrast, the wisdom of God is powerful—that is, it possesses the energy to produce godliness, contentment, fulfillment, and meaning, to which the wise aspire (1 Timothy 6:6). These benefits are not available through man's wisdom but only through God's. Man's wisdom continues to place him among the beasts, with no way of seeing the angelic, heavenly, spiritual realms.

Perhaps an example will help make the point. The fifty-year-old head of a university science department in San Diego accepted Christ through the faithful witness of his wife and family. Several months after his conversion, this longtime Ph.D. exclaimed, "I can hardly believe I could be so dumb for so long! I thought I knew something before I was converted, but the greatest period of learning in my life has taken place these past few months." The man was not dumb—just overly educated in man's wisdom to the exclusion of God's wisdom.

Millions today are in exactly the same predicament. In fact, the battle for the mind now raging is similar to the battle in Paul's day. Our generation speaks of humanism versus biblical truth, but it is the same battle between good and evil.

It's Everywhere

More people (including Christians) are adversely affected by secularist thinking than they realize. It is the dominant worldview or philosophy of life in the Western world, having captured education, government, law, medicine, psychology, sociology, the arts, business, television, publications, movies, and radio. Sometimes it seems omnipresent.

Its buzz words and catch phrases pop up everywhere. Consider the following list: "social" justice;[7] "hate" crimes;[8] living constitution; sensitivity training; globalism; global governance; global security; world citizenship; coming new world order; participatory democracy; Great Society; moral equivalence; celebrate diversity; democratic socialism; cultural imperialism; question authority; patriarchy; socialized medicine; universal healthcare; military-industrial-bureaucratic-technocratic complex; political correctness; progressive left; progressive constitutionalism; cultural Marxism; cultural hegemony; feminism; feminization of the military;[9] no-fault divorce; tolerance;[10] partial-birth abortion; free love; quality time; homophobic; phallocentric; sexism; animal rights; gay rights; queer theory; matriarchal theory; critical theory; facilitators; progressive education; women's studies; feminist math; gay studies; gay theology; green theology; critical-race theorists; eco-theology; deep ecology; speciesism; feminist theology; liberation theology; evolving morality; victimization; lesbian power; power to the people; socialism of the heart; redistribution of wealth; primates in the classroom; liberated art; trial marriages; domestic partnerships; OBE;[11] alternative lifestyle; "white male oligarchy"; Captain Condom; POC;[12] agents of change; vast right-wing conspiracy.

The list is endless.

Every pro-moral citizen of Western culture needs to understand and expose this *I*-dolatry for the religious, philosophical, moral, and scientific foolishness it represents. So to that exposé we now turn.

2

THE WISDOM OF GOD

The heavens declare the glory of God;
and the firmament shows His handiwork.
PSALM 19:1

My high school English teacher had an interesting way of shocking her lethargic class into attentiveness. She would pound on her desk, put her fist under her chin, and challenge her students to "strike the pose of *The Thinker*." She repeatedly called our attention to the bronze statue of a Greek athlete sitting in front of the Detroit Public Library. With muscles bulging, he remained forever deeply engrossed in thought.

That thinker—and all like him—could summon every ounce of psychic energy at his disposal and still never come to the truth. In fact, today man is further from the answers to the questions that for centuries have stumped theologians, philosophers, and sages than he was in the days of Greece. Any philosophy or theology text will show that the major questions of man have universally been

Who are we?
Where did we come from?
Where are we?
Why am I here?
What is wrong?
What is the solution?
Where are we going?
How can we get there?[1]

Recent surveys demonstrate that these questions continue to perplex the serious college student. Unfortunately, those who seek ultimate answers amid the writings of secularists are looking in the wrong place.

No Answers Among Men

The Friedrich Nietzsches and Michel Foucaults of the world do not have the answers. Nietzsche ended his life in a mental ward, and

Foucault ended his life in misery and disgrace. Before dying of AIDS, he gave the disease to all his "lovers" so they, too, could experience new pleasures beyond sex.[2] Here is Foucault's nihilism: "Every trace of ourselves that is shaped by others must be destroyed: our political, cultural, and sexual identities, our notions of right and wrong, sanity and madness, even what is true and false, all vanish."[3]

The wisdom of man cannot produce satisfactory replies to life's fundamental questions. Consequently, a populace educated on a diet of secularism is not prepared for life and certainly is not prepared to teach its children. Yet, as I write, books by Nietzsche and Foucault are the number one and two bestsellers at American college campus bookstores.

The apostle Paul warned the Greek thinkers of his day that God has made foolish the wisdom of this world. In fact, Paul says the wisdom of this world does not lead to knowing God (1 Corinthians 1:20–21). Without God the thinkers of the world can never grasp the secrets of life, origins, and destiny. As Paul explained, these things come only by revelation (the wisdom of God). No wonder the thinkers of his day failed to know God; they had not accepted Moses and the prophets. And today nothing has changed! Even though God has given a sufficient revelation of Himself and the mysteries of life (as recorded in the sixty-six books of the Bible), the wisdom of man has largely rejected it.

The Bible, which contains that portion of God's wisdom that He has chosen to share with mankind, not only produces a solid base for a morally sane society but gives us clear answers to the enduring questions of life. These revealed answers cannot be naturally deduced. They are from above and not from below. Consider the following basics, which we shall briefly survey.

True Wisdom

1. God

The Bible presents God as the uncaused Fundamental Cause of all things, infinite in wisdom, all powerful, holy in character, yet lovingly interested in every detail of human life.

Just because we find it difficult to conceive of a God so powerful that He could create more universes than we can count—yet is interested in each facet of our lives—does not negate that truth. The problem is that a finite and limited mind can conceive only a limited God. A God infinite in wisdom and strength is beyond man's finite ability to discover by natural means—hence the importance of God's revelation.

2. Creation

"How did life get here?" The answer to this question appears in the first chapters of divine revelation, Genesis 1 and 2. The text makes it clear that the formation of our physical universe and of mankind were not the result of a lengthy, natural, random process but a purposeful, creative act of God. In fact, Jesus said that from the beginning of creation "God 'made them male and female'" (Mark 10:6).

While accepting the creation of man by the direct act of God has always been a matter of faith in the revelation of God, the footprints and fingerprints of such a creation are everywhere to behold. The heavens display the wisdom, power, and glory of God (Psalm 19:1). Of course, the person who disbelieves in a supernatural God will find it impossible to believe in creation. Yet today there are many men of science who have sifted through the evidence and offered scientific documentation for the validity of creationism.

One of our colleagues, Dr. Henry M. Morris, is known as "Mr. Creation." This scientist, an educator for more than fifty years (thirteen as head of Virginia Tech's civil engineering department, the third largest in America) and the holder of a doctorate in hydrology from the University of Minnesota, is a prolific writer.

In 1970 he founded the Institute for Creation Research, which currently employs many well-known creation scientists. Dr. Morris also served for several years as president of the Creation Research Society. Voting membership in this society is limited to men and women who hold graduate degrees in science and who have signed a statement of their belief in creation.[4] No longer can it be said that all men of science and education reject the concept of creation!

According to Dr. Morris, "There has been a dramatic resurgence of creationism during the past quarter century, largely spearheaded by Bible-believing scientists. Considering that evolutionary scientists led the world to capitulate to evolutionism, it seems appropriate that creationist scientists attempt to win it back, by refuting the so-called scientific arguments that won it over in the first place."[5] The facts of science do not *prove* creation to be true (only the Word of the Creator can do that), but they do advance creationism as a much more scientific model of origins than evolutionism.[6]

"A Chinese paleontologist," writes Phillip E. Johnson, "lectures around the world saying that recent fossil finds in his country are inconsistent with the Darwinian theory of evolution. His reason: The major animal groups appear abruptly in the rocks over a relatively short time, rather than evolving gradually from a common ancestor as Darwin's theory predicts. When this conclusion upsets American scientists, he wryly comments: 'In China we can criticize Darwin but not the government. In America you can criticize the government but not Darwin.'"[7]

3. Civil Morality

The biblical base for morality is popularly referred to as the Judeo-Christian ethic. That is, the foundational writings of Jews and Christians provide the basic standards of morality upon which this country was founded. These precepts are absolute and not subject to revision or deletion by any earthly potentate or Supreme Court. To reject them always leads to personal and social chaos.

The Judeo-Christian ethic insists, for example, that it is always morally wrong to rape a child; it is always morally right to love one another; it is always morally right to be kind to the mentally ill; it is always morally wrong to murder.

In their powerful work *Relativism*, Francis J. Beckwith and Gregory Koukl list seven compelling reasons why relativism, the belief that there are no moral absolutes, is bankrupt: (a) Relativists cannot accuse others of wrongdoing; (b) Relativists cannot complain about the problem of evil; (c) Relativists cannot place blame or accept praise; (d) Relativists cannot make charges of unfairness or injustice; (e)

Relativists cannot improve their morality; (f) Relativists cannot hold meaningful moral discussions; and (g) Relativists can't promote the obligation of tolerance.[8]

If relativism were true, this would be a world "in which nothing is wrong—nothing is considered evil or good, nothing worthy of praise or blame. It would be a world in which justice and fairness are meaningless concepts, in which there would be no accountability, no possibility of moral improvement, no moral discourse. And it would be a world in which there is no tolerance."[9]

Author Erik von Kuehnelt-Leddihn agrees and argues that there is no such thing as purely empirical, "natural" morality. "Nature?" he asks. "Dog eats dog. The Auca Indians in the east of Ecuador, if their baby cries too much, dig a hole in the ground, put the baby in it, trample on it and declare, 'The next baby will cry less.'"[10]

Christians and Jews can agree on a basic civil-moral code of ethics because it is well defined in the Bible (Exodus 20; Romans 13). The New Testament proposes no new civil standards but rather addresses itself to a higher Christian code of ethics, voluntarily obeyed by individual believers. Because the Christian code is more exacting than the Old Testament civil-moral standard, Christians should automatically comply with the moral code of their land.[11]

Biblical morals are based on six of the Ten Commandments that refer to man's relationship to his fellowman. Consider:

- Thou shalt not steal;

- Thou shalt not bear false witness;

- Thou shalt not commit murder;

- Thou shalt not commit adultery;

- Thou shalt not covet thy neighbor's possessions;

- Honor thy father and mother.

This simple code of civil morality has insured the morally sane and safe society that almost all freedom-loving citizens desire. Government should be responsible to maintain a legal climate conducive to this kind of moral behavior. Educators should share the responsibility to maintain such a climate. Yet, as Charles Colson says, "In our public schools it has become nearly impossible to teach traditional precepts of right and wrong—which has led to disastrous consequences."[12]

4. Servants of God

"Why are we here?" The biblically instructed individual finds this an easy question to answer. Our chief purpose is to glorify God by obeying Him and serving our fellowman (see Revelation 4:11; Romans 6:11–13; 12:1–2; 1 Corinthians 6:19–20). Nowhere does Scripture instruct us to "do your own thing." We have a solemn responsibility to serve God, for He made us, died for us, and provided us His wisdom by which to live.

The happiest, most fulfilled, and most contented people in our land are those who obey God. Unlike our autonomous, self-centered, self-actualized friends, believers know who they are and how they should live. By contrast, on college campuses across the land, brilliant young people, studying with learned, experienced teachers, are facing what they call an identity crisis. Despite enormous libraries, unlimited access to the World Wide Web, sophisticated computers, and the finest information technology available, today's collegians are bewildered by the who and why of human existence. One fundamental law of teaching states, "You cannot impart what you do not possess." Contemporary secularist professors, curricula molders, and textbook writers do not themselves know the answers to these questions.

No Christian should ever suffer from this kind of an identity crisis! First, by the very fact of creation, you are created in the image of God (Genesis 1:26). Although this image has been marred by the Fall, it still is your inheritance. Second, if you have received Jesus Christ as your Savior and Lord (Acts 16:31), it is clear who you are: You are a child of God and a servant of God. You are an heir of God and a joint heir with Jesus Christ (Romans 8:17). The why has likewise been revealed: Your purpose on earth is to serve Him. "For to me, to live is Christ, and to die is gain" (Philippians 1:21).

This concept largely explains why Christians have always been the great humanitarians of the world.[13] With love and dedication they have built orphanages, hospitals, universities, and schools. They have championed literacy, abolitionism, modern science, adoption, homes for unwed mothers, benevolence, charity, justice, art, music, and the elevation of women, to name but a few.

Seldom have we heard of secularists championing such humanitarian projects with their own money. Their method is to infiltrate and take over such ministries, getting them financed with taxpayer money, while they infuse them with leftist principles. They call this "progress." Frankly, if the morally degenerate path we have traveled during the past half-century is progress, we owe Sodom and Gomorrah an apology.

As a counselor, I can testify that the increased breakdown of the home, alcoholism, suicide, homosexuality, and drug addiction—the guilt for which lays primarily at the door of humanist educators and their disciples—hardly indicates that secularist philosophy produces happiness.

Jesus Christ said, "Blessed [or happy] are those who hear the word of God and keep it" (Luke 11:28). Millions of happily married couples within the pro-moral majority of our nation's population testify that our Savior's promise is still valid.

5. Compassionate Worldview

The worldview termed "the wisdom of God" is twofold: temporal and eternal.

The temporal view in the Old Testament challenged the Jews to be God's torchbearers. Since the good news about God is not known innately through man's wisdom, God instructed the Jews to communicate this message to the lost Gentiles. My coauthor, David Noebel, has spelled out the details of a biblical worldview based on the creative order of the Old Testament.[14] He points out that all the major ingredients of a worldview—theology, philosophy, ethics, biology, psychology, sociology, etc.—are found in the first few chapters of Genesis.

New Testament Christians have been given a similar commission as "ambassadors for Christ" (2 Corinthians 5:20) to a lost, morally dark world. The Bible looks upon the world as a spiritual field of people ripe unto harvest (see Matthew 13:1–23). For that reason, almost sixty thousand American Christians are serving in foreign countries as missionaries, preaching the gospel of Jesus Christ, tending the sick, ministering to the poor, and educating the ignorant. David has also developed a biblical Christian worldview based on the redemptive order, in which Jesus Christ is the foundation stone of theology, philosophy, ethics, biology, psychology, sociology, law, economics, politics, and history.[15]

The second part of a biblical worldview is the promise of eternal life, an age of peace, righteousness, justice, and a new earth that some believers refer to as "heaven" (see Isaiah 65–66; Revelation 20–22). While not all Christians agree about the specific nature of the next life, all recognize that one exists. Both Old and New Testaments repeatedly refer to a life after death. The Bible is unquestionably a book of hope beyond earthly existence. It has spoken to the hearts and minds of millions of earth travelers over the centuries.

The Scriptures Speak

No better summary of a biblical worldview can be presented than the words of the Bible itself.[16] Here, then, is a collection of texts critical to forming a God-honoring worldview:

In the beginning God created the heavens and the earth. (Genesis 1:1)

God created man in His *own* image . . . male and female. (Genesis 1:27)

Therefore shall a man leave his father and his mother, and shall cleave unto his wife: and they shall be one flesh. (Genesis 2:24, KJV)

Blessed are they that hear the word of God, and keep it. (Luke 11:28, KJV)

Do you not know that your body is the temple of the Holy Spirit *who* is in you . . . and you are not your own? For you were bought at a price; therefore glorify God in your body and in your spirit, which are God's. (1 Corinthians 6:19–20)

The night is far spent, the day is at hand. Therefore let us cast off the works of darkness, and let us put on the armor of light. Let us walk properly, as in the day, not in revelry and drunkenness, not in lewdness and lust, not in strife and envy. But put on the Lord Jesus Christ, and make no provision for the flesh, to *fulfill its* lusts. (Romans 13:12–14)

Do not be deceived, God is not mocked; for whatever a man sows, that he will also reap. For he who sows to his flesh will of the flesh reap corruption, but he who sows to the Spirit will of the Spirit reap everlasting life. (Galatians 6:7–8)

For God so loved the world that He gave His only begotten Son, that whoever believes in Him should not perish but have everlasting life. For God did not send His Son into the world to condemn the world, but that the world through Him might be saved. (John 3:16–17)

In My Father's house are many dwelling places; if it were not so, I would have told you; for I go to prepare a place for you. If I go and prepare a place for you, I will come again and receive you to Myself, that where I am, there you may be also. (John 14:2–3, NASB)

3

THE WISDOM OF MAN

Professing to be wise, they became fools,
and changed the glory of the incorruptible God
into an image made like corruptible man.
ROMANS 1:22–23

Humanism is the world's oldest religion. It rests its case on the side of the serpent in the Garden of Eden who said to Eve, "You will not surely die. For God knows that in the day you eat of it your eyes will be opened, and you will be like God, knowing good and evil" (Genesis 3:4–5).[1]

All secularists are certainly "like God" in that they believe their knowledge is far superior to that of the Lord of the Bible. Or as Alvin Plantinga notes, some refuse to feel at home in any world they haven't created.[2] And they certainly use concepts of good and evil—except their understanding of good and evil is not God's version but the serpent's! What God calls good, the secularists call evil; what God calls evil, the secularists call good.[3] From a secularist point of view, for example, belief in the very existence of God is not good. On the other hand, believing that man can save himself is considered good. Believing that the God of the universe would love the human race and provide for human salvation through Jesus Christ is considered evil.

Secularists describe their ideas using words that mean one thing to parents with traditional moral values and another thing to students. So clever has been this semantic deception that millions have been duped.

For example, in the *Humanist Manifesto 2000*, Paul Kurtz parades his atheism under the title of "scientific naturalism." Such terminology is bound to fool many parents who think their son or daughter is learning only science. In reality, "scientific naturalism" is merely another term for atheism.

So is it possible for the non-college-trained person to understand this man-centered dogma? Yes! Once its ambiguous terms are simplified, any individual can not only understand it but meaningfully reject it. To do so requires knowledge of the five basic tenets of humanism: atheism, evolution, amorality, human autonomy, and globalism.[4]

First, we shall examine their major tenets individually, through the statements of their leading authorities. In chapter 6, we shall inspect them within the official humanist Bibles—*Humanist Manifesto I* (1933), *Humanist Manifesto II* (1973), and *Humanist Manifesto 2000* (1999). And in chapter 7, we shall demonstrate their unscientific basis.

The Five Basic Tenets of Humanism

The leading authorities of Secular Humanism may be pictured as the starting lineup of a baseball team: pitching is John Dewey;[5] catching is Isaac Asimov; first base is Paul Kurtz; second base is Corliss Lamont;[6] third base is Bertrand Russell; shortstop is Julian Huxley; left fielder is Richard Dawkins; center fielder is Margaret Sanger;[7] right fielder is Carl Rogers; manager is "Christianity is for losers" Ted Turner;[8] designated hitter is Mary Calderone; utility players include the hundreds listed in the back of *Humanist Manifesto I* and *II,* including Eugenia C. Scott, Alfred Kinsey, Abraham Maslow, Erich Fromm, Rollo May, and Betty Friedan.

In the grandstands sit the sponsoring or sustaining organizations, such as the American Humanist Association; the American Ethical Society; the American Ethical Union; Fellowship of Religious Humanists; Society for Humanistic Judaism; Humanist Society of Friends; the Center for Inquiry Institute; the American Civil Liberties Union;[9] the Emergency Civil Liberties Union;[10] the National Academy of Sciences; the National Center for Science Education, Inc.; National Association of Biology Teachers; National Organization of Women; Planned Parenthood; SIECUS; the National Education Association (and all state affiliates);[11] the major television networks, high-profile newspapers, and news magazines; the U.S. State Department; the Department of Education; Ford Foundation; Rockefeller Foundation; Turner Foundation; Carnegie Foundation; Samuel Rubin Foundation;[12] W. Alton Jones Foundation; Ploughshares Foundation; Merck Foundation; Playboy Foundation;[13] Hewlett Foundation; John D. and Catherine T. MacArthur Foundation (and scores more);[14] the League for Industrial Democracy; the United Nations; UNESCO; the World

Federalist Association; the Fabian Society of Great Britain; the Frankfurt School; the left wing of the Democratic Party; the Democratic Socialists of America; Harvard University; Yale University; University of Minnesota; University of California (Berkeley); and two thousand other colleges and universities.

1. Atheism

The foundation stone of all humanistic thought is atheism, the belief that there is no God. Descartes, the famous French philosopher who tried to project his mind into the universe, finally concluded with the well-known epithet, "I think, therefore I am." This deification of man launched the worship of man's wisdom. "With this ['I think, therefore I am'] Descartes unleashed the revolutionary idea that the human mind, not God, is the source of certainty; human activity is the fixed point around which everything else revolves."[15]

Descartes's humanistic rationalism was extended by the French skeptics, primarily Voltaire and Rousseau. It was further developed by German rationalists such as Georg Hegel, Ludwig Feuerbach, and Friedrich Nietzsche until they reached the verdict "God is dead." The modern existentialist maintains that the idea of God is self-contradictory.

In this way, the very God who gave us a mind by which to reason and believe true thoughts now finds that mind used to deny His very existence. Romans 1:18–25 speaks to this issue, for even when men knew God, they glorified Him not as God but became vain in their thinking and imaginations and ended up worshiping the cosmos or its parts.

In his definitive book *The Philosophy of Humanism*, Dr. Corliss Lamont makes the following statements that establish this religion's atheistic base:[16]

First, Humanism believes in a naturalistic metaphysics or attitude toward the universe that considers all forms of the supernatural as myth; and that regards Nature as the totality of being and as a constantly changing system of matter and energy which exists independently of any mind or consciousness.[17]

Humanism believes that Nature itself constitutes the sum total of reality, that matter-energy and not mind is the foundation stuff of the universe, and that supernatural entities simply do not exist. This nonreality of the supernatural means, on the human level, that men do not possess supernatural and immortal souls; and, on the level of the universe as a whole, that our cosmos does not possess a supernatural and eternal God.[18]

For Humanism the central concern is always the happiness of man in this existence, not in some fanciful never-never land [heaven] beyond the grave; a happiness worthwhile as an end in itself and not subordinate to or dependent on a Supreme Deity [God], an invisible King [Jesus Christ] ruling over the earth and the infinite cosmos.[19]

The originator of the useful word agnostic was Thomas H. Huxley,[20] noted English biologist and popularizer of the Darwinian theory. Since agnostics are doubtful about the supernatural [God and heaven] they tend to be Humanists in practice.[21]

Other major humanist spokespersons have also declared their atheism. According to Paul Kurtz, "Humanism cannot in any fair sense of the word apply to one who still believes in God as the source and creator of the universe."[22] Similarly, Bertrand Russell admitted that he believed in God until he was eighteen years of age. At that point he became convinced that the whole idea of God was derived from the ancient Oriental despotisms and concluded, "I am not a Christian. . . . I do not believe in God and in immortality; and I do not think that Christ was the best and wisest of men, although I grant Him a very high degree of moral goodness."[23]

For most of man's history, the existence of God seemed logical for anyone who saw His creative handiwork. For that reason, the ancients rarely mention atheism. As education expanded throughout Europe, however, atheism increased. Recent surveys reveal that the more educated a person becomes (especially in the social sciences and humanities), the more likely he is to be an atheist.

Yet it was the well-educated Francis Bacon who said, "a little philosophy inclineth man's mind to atheism; but depth in philosophy bringeth men's minds about to religion."[24] It would appear that our educational elite are serving pablum to our students instead of "depth in philosophy."

2. Evolution

Because humanists reject belief in God, they must explain man's existence independently of God. For this they resurrect one of the oldest religious beliefs of all time: the theory of evolution, which can be traced back to Babylon two thousand years before Christ.[25]

The theory of evolution, although ancient and certainly prescientific, was catapulted into world prominence by the publication of Charles Darwin's *On the Origin of Species by Means of Natural Selection or The Preservation of Favoured Races in the Struggle for Life*. Darwinism, as it came to be known, swept through the Western academic community like wildfire. Today it is the foundation upon which all Secular Humanist education rests.

Psychology, the most influential discipline of modern education, totally depends on the theory of evolution, as do such fields as sociology, anthropology, political science, biology, and geology. The theory of evolution exerts a drastic influence on art, music, and literature. Humanists are committed evolutionists. Corliss Lamont explains it:

Biology has conclusively shown that man and all other forms of life were the result, not of a supernatural act of creation by God, but of an infinitely long process of evolution probably stretching over at least two billion years. In that gradual evolutionary advance which started with the lowly amoebae and those even simpler things marking the transition from inanimate matter to life, body was prior and basic. With its increasing complexity, there came about an accompanying development and integration of animal behavior and control, culminating in the species man and in the phenomenon called mind. Mind in short, appeared at the present apex of the evolutionary process and not at the beginning.[26]

Like all humanists, Lamont believed that man is an animal, for he notes, "Man, like the higher primates from which he is descended, is a gregarious creature."[27] He boasts, "Biologically speaking, the animal, man, has been an enormous success."[28]

Sir Julian Huxley, one of the founders of the prestigious American Humanist Association and past president of the British Humanist Association, defined humanism in these words:

> I use the word "humanist" to mean someone who believes that man is just as much a natural phenomenon as an animal or plant; that his body, mind and soul were not supernaturally created but are products of evolution, and that he is not under the control or guidance of any supernatural being or beings, but has to rely on himself and his own powers.[29]

Many other statements could be cited to substantiate the humanists' obsessive belief in evolution.[30] This unscientific theory is a major part of official humanist doctrine.

Some informed educators admit that Darwinism is the most powerful influence in education today—even though *not one* of Darwin's theories can be proved 140 years after they were first proposed. Even Thomas Huxley, one of the leading exponents of evolution, had to admit, "Evolution was not an established theory but a tentative hypothesis, an extremely valuable and even probable hypothesis, but a hypothesis none the less."[31] Dr. D'Arcy Thompson concedes:

> In the study of evolution and in our attempts to trace the descent of the animal kingdom, our score years' study of *The Origin of Species*, has had an unlooked for and disappointing result. It . . . has not taught us how birds descended from the reptiles, mammals from other quadrupeds, quadrupeds from fishes, nor vertebrates from invertebrate stock. The invertebrates themselves involve the selfsame difficulties, so that we do not know the origins of the echinoderms, of the mollusks, of the coelenterates, nor one group of protozoa from another. . . . This failure to solve the cardinal problems of evolutionary biology is a very curious thing.[32]

That all scientists do not accept the theory of evolution becomes clear in Homer Duncan's book, with the following statement by a well-known biologist from the Smithsonian institute:

> There is no evidence which would show man developing step by step from lower forms of life. There is nothing to show that man was in any way connected with monkeys. . . . He appeared SUDDENLY and in substantially the same form as he is today. . . . There are no such things as missing links. . . . So far as concerns the major groups of animals, the creationists appear to have the best of the argument. There is NOT THE SLIGHTEST EVIDENCE THAT ANY ONE OF THE MAJOR GROUPS AROSE FROM ANY OTHER. Each is a special animal complex, related more or less closely to all the rest, and appearing therefore as a special and distinct creation.[33]

Despite its obvious weaknesses, secularists hold zealously to Darwinism because their disbelief in God requires it. The controversy now raging in the public schools over the prospect of teaching creation alongside evolution springs from the fear that if the theory of evolution is discredited, the entire humanist worldview would collapse like a house of cards.

Let me give you an illustration. An engineer in San Diego attended church regularly with his wife, though he was an atheist. Finally he invited me into his home. "I have three questions," he declared. "If you can satisfactorily answer them, I will become a Christian."

Providentially, I had been led to study those very questions just the week before. So for two hours I presented him with the logical, Bible-based answers he needed. When we finished, I asked, "Does that answer all your questions?"

"Yes," he replied, "I didn't realize there were such answers."

"Are you now ready to accept Christ?" I asked.

"Let's not be too hasty," he answered. "I do not want to rush into anything!"

Not until ten years later did his own daughter finally lead him to receive the Savior. Today he cannot believe he was so blind for so long.

It is impossible to overestimate the influence that evolution has exercised upon our society.[34] Former congressman John Conlan and attorney John Whitehead recognized this when they stated, "Evolution has altered the course of history by shifting the base of moral absolutes from traditional theism to Secular Humanism."[35]

3. Amorality

The doctrine of evolution has led naturally to the destruction of the moral foundation upon which this country was built. If you believe that man is an animal, you will expect him to live like one. Consequently, almost every law required to maintain a Bible-based, morally sane society—such as those involving marriage and divorce or sexual matters such as pornography and homosexuality—has been struck down so that man may follow his animal instincts and appetites. Such was predicted in *The Humanist* magazine more than thirty-five years ago: "Darwin's discovery of the principle of evolution sounded the death knell of religious and moral values. It removed the ground from under the feet of traditional religion."[36]

This country's leading secularist educators, lawmakers, and judges have consistently liberalized our statutes. They are committed to doing away with every vestige of the responsible, moral behavior that distinguishes man from animals. Why? Because man is an evolving animal, and his children are nothing but primates in the classroom!

This overt hostility toward Christianity is nowhere more apparent than in the successful attempt over the last five decades to destroy almost all biblical, moral standards. As one leading sexologist (as they like to call themselves) said, with her finger pointed toward the sky, "There is no one up there telling you what is right and wrong." In other words, without an eternal lawgiver, there is no moral order and no moral absolutes!

"The only thing that is absolute is there is nothing absolute!" With these words a philosophy professor begins his course of study. Yet no one has come forward to prove there are no absolutes. Secularists simply keep on repeating this maxim, vainly hoping that believing it will make it so.

This philosophy has opened the door to situation ethics, permissiveness, free love, sexually active youth, and a flock of code words for adultery, fornication, perversion, and abomination—all of which are simply sin. Students from junior high to college—the target of amoral teachings for the past five decades—have been encouraged toward gross immorality. One high-school principal admitted to me that 20 percent of his senior class has either had, or is a carrier of, a venereal disease.

Dr. Albert Ellis, long an advocate of situation ethics, has declared, "What are the main principles of humanistic ethics, from which the principles of sexual ethics can be logically derived? No one seems to know for sure, since variant and absolutistic ethical ideals do not seem to be achievable; nor are they particularly human." When a doctor of philosophy stands before students or sex education teachers and states that moral or ethical issues are not "human," it is only natural that he will discard such precepts as "Thou shalt not commit adultery."

In fact, Paul Kurtz does that very thing. Says Kurtz, "Short of harming others or compelling them to do likewise, individuals should be permitted to express their sexual proclivities and pursue their lifestyles as they desire."[37] When I debated Kurtz before seven hundred educators, he admitted that he would not discourage young people from practicing premarital sex.

Consider this advice on sexual experimentation by former SIECUS president Dr. Mary Calderone:

On sexual experimentation: The adolescent years are, among other things, for learning how to integrate sex usefully and creatively in daily living. Therefore, we must accept that adolescent sexual experimentation is not just inevitable but actually necessary for normal development.

On premarital sex: I advocate discussion of it, so that young people know they have choices beginning with masturbation, of course, and petting to climax and mutual orgasm before moving on to intercourse.

On extramarital sex: An extramarital affair that's really solid might have very good results.

On Sexology magazine: Sexology magazine is no more pornographic than the Bible.

There is no greater evidence of this obsession with sexual license than the fact that the leaders of the sexual revolution of the '70s were overwhelmingly humanists.[38] The sex-education authors, publishers, and SIECUS board members who proclaim homosexuality as an optional lifestyle are humanists. Indeed, the homosexual movement in America is a creation of the humanists.[39] It was designed to destroy Christian morality, just as sex education in the schools was so designed.[40]

Many do not realize that most of the leaders of the feminist movement, which presents itself as the preserver of sexual rights of women and children, are humanists. Many are Marxists as well. Gloria Steinem, for example, is a proud member of the Democratic Socialists of America. Margaret Sanger was a radical leftist, who edited a publication titled *The Rebel Woman* and spent her time partying with the Fabian Socialists of Great Britain. Madalyn Murray O'Hair was a bitter anti-American who tried to emigrate to the former Soviet Union, while Betty Friedan was a radical leftist who nearly succeeded in joining the Communist Party.[41] She also won the Humanist of the Year award and put her name on *Humanist Manifesto II*.

But the feminist agenda does not truly produce a better kind of society, as Cal Thomas explains:

Helen Gurley Brown, the female Hugh Hefner, who has sold women the same lies in her *Cosmopolitan* magazine that Hefner has been selling men in *Playboy,* offers some advice in her latest book, *The Late Show: A Semiwild but Practical Survival Plan for Women over 50.* Brown suggests that older women check out the husbands of other women as potential sexual partners. "Husbands are a source of supply [for sex]," she writes. Regarding the possibility that guilt feelings might arise from an adulterous relationship with another woman's husband, Brown says, "I never feel guilty about the wife, if she can't keep him at home. I'm espousing 'never let sex disappear no matter how old you are.' "[42]

Do not think for a moment that the secularists are satisfied, now that perversion is recognized as normal in some areas of our country. They will not stop until it is universally recognized. They are really after the young, who will be the key to controlling the next generation. That is why—in the name of health care, child's rights, child abuse, and the Year of the Child—secularists are pressuring political leaders to pass legislation that takes control of children away from their parents and gives it to the state. By the state, of course, they mean bureaucrats and social-change agents who have been carefully trained in amoral philosophy. They will use the government's power to teach sexual activity, contraceptives, birth elimination, and permissiveness to children, whether parents want it or not! Of course, government-financed abortions will be provided for those who fail to follow instructions.

Corliss Lamont maintained that the truly moral person will be obliged to "discard the outmoded ethics of the past. . . . The merely good is the enemy of the better. The Humanist refuses to accept any Ten Commandments or other ethical precepts as immutable and universal laws never to be challenged or questioned. He bows down to no alleged Supreme moral authority either past or present."[43]

The humanist rejects "the puritanical prejudice against pleasure and desire that marks the Western tradition of morality. Men and women have profound wants and needs of an emotional and physical character, the fulfillment of which is an essential ingredient in the good life. Contempt for or suppression of normal desires might result in their discharge in surreptitious, coarse, or abnormal ways."[44]

Of course, Lamont failed to notice that control of normal desires might also develop character and self-discipline. But what is that to a committed humanist, who conceives of man not only as an animal but as an amoral animal?

4. Autonomous Man

Humanists view man as an autonomous, self-directed, godlike person with unlimited goodness and potential—if his environment is properly controlled to let his free spirit develop. One of the worst sins (according to humanists) is not the killing of innocent, unborn children or even the murder of preemies or children born with defects; it is inhibiting the freedom of another to express himself.

Humanism assumes that man is innately good and capable of solving his problems independently of any Supreme Being. This assumption has become one of its basic tenets.

Jean-Jacques Rousseau (1712–1778) is a most influential writer-philosopher for today's college youth. They study him vigorously, and most college philosophers are well versed in his thinking. Rousseau basically insisted that if man is good by nature, it follows that he stays like that as long as nothing foreign to him corrupts him.

Professors who eulogize this hero of the Enlightenment rarely tell their students that Rousseau was a moral degenerate. For sixteen years he lived outside the bonds of marriage with his mistress in Paris, who bore him five illegitimate sons—all of whom he abandoned in the Paris General Hospital.[45] Secularists may exalt that kind of autonomous, self-centered thinking as "self-actualization," but we cannot help wishing that someone would have preserved testimony from his five orphaned sons, the true victims of his selfishness.

To our detriment we often overlook Voltaire's comments on Rousseau's *Social Contract*. When Rousseau sent him a copy of his work, Voltaire wrote, "I have received your new book against the human race, and I thank you for it. Never was such cleverness used in the design of making us all stupid. One longs, in reading your book, to walk on all fours. But as I have lost that habit more than sixty years ago, I feel unhappily the impossibility of resuming it."[46]

History shows that autonomous thinking leads not to world betterment, or even human improvement, but to chaos. Rousseau's philosophy, for example, was a major factor in producing the French Revolution, which wreaked its havoc not only on royalty but also on the poor.

Today's philosophy of education is obsessed with self-actualization, self-image, self-love, self-sufficiency, self-esteem, self-satisfaction—self, self, self. This change from soul to self is noted in a recent *Wall Street Journal* article by Katherine A. Kersten. "Thirty years ago," she writes, "the psychologist and scholar Philip Rieff shed light on this question in his classic work, *The Triumph of the Therapeutic*. Traditional Christianity, Mr. Rieff observed, made great moral demands on believers. Its goal was salvation; consequently, it exhorted believers to 'die to self,' repent of sin, and cultivate virtue, self-discipline and humility. Today, however, wrote Mr. Rieff, 'psychological man' is rapidly shouldering Christian man aside as the dominant character type in our society. For psychological man—the offspring of Freud and his ilk—life centers not on the soul, but on the self. Psychological man rejects both the idea of sin and the need for salvation. He aspires to nothing higher than 'feeling good about himself.' Mr. Rieff summarizes it this way: 'Christian man was born to be saved; psychological man is born to be pleased.' The difference was established long ago, when 'I believe,' the cry of the ascetic, lost precedence to 'one feels,' the caveat of the therapeutic." [47]

Consider the following:

The watchword of Humanism is happiness for all humanity in this existence as contrasted with salvation for the individual soul in a future existence and the glorification of a supernatural Supreme Being. Humanism urges men to accept freely and joyously the great boon of life and to realize that life in its own right and for its own sake can be as beautiful and splendid as any dream of immortality.

Humanism asserts that man's own reason and efforts are man's best and, indeed, only hope; and that man's refusal to recognize this point is one of the chief causes of his failures throughout history. The Christian West has been confused and corrupted for almost 2,000 years by the idea so succinctly expressed by St. Augustine, "Cursed is anyone who places his hope in man." [49]

Starting from an atheistic base, autonomous man emphasizes feeling rather than responsibility. Try to reason with a marijuana user or drug addict or an alcoholic, and you'll soon see that feelings predominate. The fact that he is destroying himself does not dissuade him from doing what he pleases. Dr. Francis Schaeffer points out, "As the Christian consensus dies, there are not many sociological alternatives. One possibility is hedonism, in which every man does his own thing. Trying to build a society on hedonism leads to chaos."[50]

More self-centered people live in our country today than at any other time in history. Why? There are two basic reasons: the self-centered philosophy of humanism, and the humanistic ideas of psychology, which have taught permissiveness in child raising. Children raised without loving parental correction grow up to be self-centered and selfish, and their attempt to be independent or autonomous leads them to futility or chaos.

A television talk-show host once asked me what I thought was the primary cause of marital disharmony. My response: selfishness.

In fact, the root cause of all social disharmony is selfishness. An indulgent attitude toward self begets the childish "I want my way" syndrome, causing an individual to stalk through life in an undisciplined, insensitive, unbridled fashion. He will seek to get, rather than give; lust, rather than love; demand, rather than contribute. When those around him do the same, the outcome is predictable: dissension, hostility, and eventually open combat.

The truth is that man is a dependent creature—first dependent on God, then on his fellowman. His failure to recognize that fact cheats him, both in life and in the eternity to come.

5. Globalism

Humanists have a long-running romance with big government.[51] Over two decades ago Julian Huxley, director of UNESCO for ten years, put it very simply: "It is essential for UNESCO to adopt an evolutionary approach . . . the general philosophy of UNESCO should, it seems, be a scientific world humanism, global in extent and evolutionary in background. . . . Thus the struggle for existence that underlies natural selection is increasingly replaced by conscious selection, a struggle between ideas and values in consciousness."[52]

Humanists generally assume that government is good and that big government is better than little government. Their practical interpretation of democracy seems to be freedom only for the individual within a socialist government—controlled of course, by humanists.[53] "A truly Humanist civilization," says Lamont, "must be a world civilization."[54]

The facts of life have somehow escaped the secularists' attention. They overlook or reject the historical truth that freedom has always been enjoyed in inverse proportion to the size and power of government. Generally speaking, the less government, the more individual freedom.

Anyone familiar with humanist writers is struck by their consistent hostility toward Americanism, capitalism, and free enterprise.[55] At the same time they extol the virtues and benefits of socialism, without acknowledging its historical failures.[56] Lamont repeatedly called for general disarmament or collective security. He eulogized a government that did away with "business monopoly," for "until we do so there will be no lasting international peace."[57]

What he failed to point out is that this requires virtual economic control by government—in other words, socialism. Since he had neither the time nor the patience to socialize the world gradually, he urged that it be done quickly—and for Lamont that meant communism. He demonstrates that a very important connection exists between Secular Humanism and communism, which few care to discuss. Humanism and communism are related: Humanism is the mother, communism the daughter; humanism is the root, communism the branch. Many of the ideas and beliefs that make up the communist worldview are similar to or identical with the humanist worldview. Unfortunately for us, both have headed into the twenty-first century.

The humanists discovered early that the United Nations offered a tremendous springboard to a one-world government with a socialistic economic system.[58] Humanism's purpose is to supersede national boundaries by a worldwide organization possessing international sovereignty. Many believe the UN provides them such a vehicle, which is why so many American leaders in the legion UN organizations are committed humanists. Three leading members of the American Humanism Association, for example, have been directors-general of three prestigious UN organizations: Julian Huxley of UNESCO, Brock Chisholm of the World Health Organization, and Lord Boyd Orr of the UN Food and Agriculture Organization.

If humanists can control UNESCO, UNICEF, and the UN's World Health Organization, as well as its food and agriculture organization, they will be a long way toward implementing a one-world socialist government. So zealous are humanists for a one-world order that, according to Claire Chambers:

> Some of their leaders combined forces with leading advocates of population control and nationalized abortion, World Federalists, and others, in the formation of the American Movement for World Government. This group's full-page advertisement in the *New York Times* of July 27, 1971, called for a "world federal government to be open at all times to all nations without right of secession," with the power to curb overpopulation.[59]

Other essentials supported by the twenty-six signatories of the *Times* ad included a "civilian executive branch with the power to enforce world laws directly upon individuals" (which would automatically supersede the U.S. Constitution) and the "control of all weapons of mass destruction by the world government with the disarmament of all nations, under careful inspection, down to the level required for internal policing." When and how would all this happen? The ad declared, "a federal world government must be established at the earliest possible moment by basic transformation of the UN or other reasonable means."[60]

This document was not signed by a few socialistic eccentrics but by the *Who's Who* of humanism. All committed humanists are one-worlders first and Americans second. Hear Corliss Lamont:

> All individuals of all countries are together fellow citizens of our one world and fellow members of our one human family. The Americans, the Russians, the English, the Indians, the Chinese, the Germans, the Africans, and the rest are all part of the same perplexed, proud, and aspiring human race.

. . . The Humanist viewpoint, surmounting all national and sectional provincialisms, provides a concrete opportunity for overcoming the age-long cleavage between East and West. Even those who cling to some form of supernaturalism can unite with Humanists, as they did during World War II, on a program of democracy and progress that reaches to the farthest corners of the earth. Humanism is a supranational, panhuman philosophy of universal relevance; it is the philosophic counterpart of world patriotism.[61]

If that is not clear enough, consider another statement by the same author:

The principle around which the United Nations and the International Court of Justice are organized is that the scope of national sovereignty must be curtailed and that nations must be willing to accept, as against what they conceive to be their own self-interest, the democratically arrived at decisions of the world community.[62]

Guided by this philosophy, our politicians have turned the most powerful country in the world into a global policeman under United Nations command—proving that they are more interested in world government, world citizenship, and world socialism than in America.

As you read this, remember the new pledge of allegiance being taught to America's third-grade children:

I pledge allegiance to the world
To care for earth, sea and air
To honor every living thing [except the unborn]
With peace and justice everywhere.

You'll quickly notice that a few important words are missing from our present pledge of allegiance, words such as "one nation under God." But then, humanists don't accept nation or God. And their favorite line is "Of course, we Americans will have to give up some of our sovereignty."[63]

No humanist is qualified to hold any governmental office in America—United States senator, congressman, cabinet member, State Department employee, Department of Defense employee, or any other position that requires him to think in the best interest of America. He is a socialist one-worlder first, an American second. Such politicians can be counted on to vote for increasing United States appropriations to the UN, placing American properties under UN control, placing American citizens under World Court jurisdiction, and placing U.S. armed forces under UN command. We forget so soon that every tax increase is a move toward bigger government and more humanist-trained bureaucrats dedicated to dragging us, kicking and screaming, into a New World Order.

Humanism's Hostility to Christianity

The spirit of tolerance so often extolled in humanist teachings does not extend to Christianity. Humanists look upon the church and its doctrinal absolutes as the greatest enemy of mankind. More than an enemy, the church is a deadly threat to humanism, for it is the only group that can save the Western world from humanism's control.

Christianity and humanism are 180 degrees in opposition to each other with regard to the promise of life after death. I just finished a book on that subject, so I can appreciate the humanist's frustration. Bible-taught Christians approach death with peace and confidence, whereas humanists usually fear and loathe this ultimate meeting with God. Humanism is a tragic philosophy to live by and a disastrous philosophy to die by. Consider Corliss Lamont and William James on immortality:

> The issue of mortality versus immortality is crucial in the argument of Humanism against supernaturalism. For if men realize that their careers are limited to this world, that this earthly existence is all that they will ever have, then they are already more than halfway on the path toward becoming functioning Humanists, no matter what their general attitude toward the universe and no matter what they think about a Deity. In my opinion, the history of philosophy and religion

demonstrates that in the West, at least, the idea of immortality has on the whole played a more important part than the idea of God. William James asserts unqualifiedly that "the popular touchstone for all philosophies is the question, 'What is their bearing on a future life?'" If this is true, then James is also correct in observing that for most men God has been primarily the guarantor of survival beyond the grave.

Christianity in particular, with its central emphasis on the resurrection and eternal life, came into being first and foremost as a death-conquering religion.[64]

The humanist's faith in man and his inherent goodness stands in marked contrast to the Christian position on the Fall. Man lost Paradise of his own volition, and he lacks the power and authority to reclaim it. Yet another humanist, John Galsworthy, dares to claim, "Humanism is the creed of those who believe that in the circle of enwrapping mystery, man's fates are in their own hands—a faith that for modern man is becoming the only possible faith."[65]

It Comes Down to This

Humanism is obsessed with merging Western democracies, the remnants of communism, and Third World dictatorships into a one-world, socialist state, where Plato's dream of "three classes of people" would be fulfilled:

- the elite ruling class;
- the omnipresent military;
- the masses, among whom no differences between sexes exist: men and women doing the same work and children being wards of the state.

Of course, humanists will be the elite ruling class!

Fortunately, we do not believe that this Orwellian nightmare is inevitable. If Christ's church becomes sufficiently aroused to the fact that humanism is winning the battle for the mind, she will awaken millions of pro-moral pro-Americans—and together they will vote their amoral, one-world humanist overlords out of office and replace them with traditional, pro-moral leaders.

We must never forget that the ultimate in big government is world government.

PART TWO:
THE SITUATION

4

AMERICA'S CHRISTIAN HERITAGE

The general Principles, on which the Fathers achieved Independence, were the general Principles of Christianity.
JOHN ADAMS

At the risk of sounding provincial, we would point out that, had it not been for the Christian influence in America, our world already would have lost the battle for the mind and would doubtless be living under a totalitarian, one-world state.

Volumes have been written on the secret of America's greatness and whether the nation was founded upon a Christian base. We believe that America is great and free because of her Christian foundation—and we are not the only ones who so believe.

Christianity and Liberty Entwined

In his two-volume work *Democracy in America*, Alexis de Tocqueville admitted "there is no country in the world where the Christian religion retains a greater influence over the souls of men than in America; and there can be no greater proof of its utility, and of its conformity to human nature, than that its influence is most powerfully felt over the most enlightened and free nation of the earth."[1] Elsewhere he declared, "The Americans combine the notions of Christianity and of liberty so intimately in their minds, that it is impossible to make them conceive the one without the other."[2]

De Tocqueville was not the only Frenchman who penned such observations. In his 1833 work, *A Moral and Political Sketch of the United States*, Achille Murat said, "There is no country in which the people are so religious as in the United States; to the eyes of a foreigner they even appear to be too much so. The great number of religious societies existing in the United States is truly surprising: there are some of them to distribute the Bible; to distribute tracts; to encourage religious journals; to convert, civilize, educate the savages; to marry the preachers; to take care of their widows and orphans; to preach, extend, purify, preserve, reform the faith; to build chapels, endow congregations, support seminaries; catechize and convert sailors, Negroes, and loose women."[3]

From the time of the Mayflower Compact ("having undertaken for the glory of God and advancement of the Christian faith") through Plymouth Plantation ("for the propagation and advance of the gospel of the kingdom of Christ") and on to Virginia's first charter ("propagating of the Christian religion"), Fundamental Orders of Connecticut ("purity of the Gospel of our Lord Jesus"), and the New England Confederation ("advance the cause of the gospel"), America's founding years were steeped in Christ and Christianity.

This country was founded on a basic consensus of Christian principles. While we do not claim that every Founding Father was an evangelical Christian (Thomas Jefferson and John Adams were Unitarians),[4] even John Adams admitted that the American army was "educated in the general Principles of Christianity; and the general Principles of English and American Liberty." He then said, "the general Principles, on which the Fathers achieved Independence, were the general Principles of Christianity."[5]

While secularists are doing everything in their power to degrade and distort America's Founding Fathers[6] and principles, we think Gary DeMar is much closer to the truth when he says, "A study of America's past will show that a majority of Americans shared a common faith and a common ethic. America's earliest founders were self-professing Christians and their founding documents expressed a belief in a Christian worldview."[7]

Rabbi Daniel Lapin certainly has it right when he says, "My extensive readings have left me without a doubt that this nation was founded by Christians, and was meant to be based on broad Christian principles. Religion was the bedrock upon which the nation stood, and without it these amazing men and women saw no future for the country they had established."[8] Elsewhere he says, "Christianity has been responsible, among other things, for the founding of America, the greatest civilization the world has ever known, and for making America great."[9]

The Work of David Barton

David Barton has done extensive research in this area in recent years. His conclusion: Of the approximately 250 Founding Fathers, about 95 percent would qualify as Bible-believing Christians. Fifty-two of the fifty-six signers of the United States Constitution would be so classified.

Barton establishes his case by noting (a) the education of the Founding Fathers; (b) their individual comments; and (c) the subsequent legal opinions and other historical data that reflect their character and thinking.

1. A Christian Education

Most of the Founding Fathers were graduates of Harvard, Yale, Princeton, Dartmouth, or Columbia, all of which in those days expressed Christian leanings and were considered Christian institutions of higher education.

Harvard's rules for learning included the following: "Let every student be plainly instructed and earnestly pressed to consider well [that] the main end of his life and studies is to know God and Jesus Christ which is eternal life (John 17:3) and therefore to lay Christ in the bottom as the only foundation of all sound knowledge and learning."[10] Harvard produced such men as John Adams, John Hancock, Elbridge Gerry, John Pickering, William Williams, Rufus King, William Hooper, William Ellery, Samuel Adams, and Robert Treat Paine.

Yale University instructed its students "to obtain the clearest conception of Divine things and to lead you to a saving knowledge of God in his Son Jesus Christ."[11] Yale produced such men as Oliver Wolcott, William Livingston, Lyman Hall, Lewis Morris, Jared Ingersoll, Phillip Livingston, and William Samuel Johnson.

Princeton University instructed her students "to attend worship in the college hall morning and evening at the hours appointed and behave with gravity and reverence during the whole service. Every student shall attend public worship on the Sabbath."[12] Princeton produced such men as John Witherspoon, James Madison, Richard Stockton, Benjamin

Rush, Gunning Bedford, and Jonathan Dayton. Indeed, 33 percent of the Founding Fathers were graduates of Princeton.

Dartmouth College was founded "for the education and instruction of youths in reading, writing and all parts of learning which shall appear necessary and expedient for civilizing and Christianizing the children."[13]

Columbia University (called King's College) accepted no student "unless he shall be able to render into English . . . the Gospels from the Greek. It is also expected that all students attend public worship on Sundays."[14]

Barton uses the following words to conclude his look at the various universities that provided America with her Founding Fathers: "Perhaps George Washington, 'The Father of the Country,' provided the most succinct description of America's educational philosophy when chiefs from the Delaware Indian tribe brought him three Indian youths to be trained in American schools. Washington first assured the chiefs that 'Congress . . . will look upon them as their own children.' And then he commended the chiefs for their decision, telling them that 'you do well to wish to learn our arts and ways of life, and above all, the religion of Jesus Christ. These will make you a greater and happier people than you are. Congress will do every thing they can to assist you in this wise intention.'"[15]

2. *The Comments of Christians*

Barton's extensive quotations about Christianity from the Founding Fathers fill chapter 6 of his book. For our purposes, only a few quotations are necessary.

William Samuel Johnson says, "I am endeavoring to attend to my own duty only as a Christian . . . let us take care that our Christianity, though put to the test . . . be not shaken, and that our love for things really good wax not cold."[16]

Robert Treat Paine says, "I desire to bless and praise the name of God most high for appointing me my birth in a land of Gospel light where the glorious tidings of a Savior and of pardon and salvation through Him have been continually sounding in mine ears."[17]

Dr. Benjamin Rush was not only a signer of the Declaration of

Independence but also a founder of the Philadelphia Bible Society. He said, "The Gospel of Jesus Christ prescribes the wisest rules for just conduct in every situation of life. Happy they are who obey them in all situations."[18] On his tombstone was recorded: "Father of American Psychiatry, Signer of the Declaration of Independence, Heroic Physician, Teacher, Humanitarian, Physician General of the Continental Army, Physician to the Pennsylvania Hospital, Professor of Physic, University of Pennsylvania."

Among scores of others we cite but one more, Charles Carrol: "On the mercy of my Redeemer I rely for salvation and on his merits; not on the works I have done in obedience to his precepts."[19]

Christian testimonies like these can be cited from the vast majority of our Founding Fathers! No wonder, then, that a House Judiciary Committee affirmed that "Christianity was the religion of the founders of the republic, and they expected it to remain the religion of their descendants."[20]

The truth about these Christian men and their beliefs has been suppressed. Our modern-day histories treat us to the least religious of the fathers, such as Thomas Paine, who trashed Christianity in *The Age of Reason*. What our students are never told is that, in turn, nearly every one of our founders trashed Paine and his work. Benjamin Franklin, John Adams, Samuel Adams, Benjamin Rush, Charles Carroll, John Witherspoon, John Quincy Adams, Patrick Henry, and Zephaniah Swift—all rejected Paine's work. In fact, as Barton notes, Paine's ideas were rejected "even by the least religious Founders."[21]

3. Christian Legal Opinions

Barton's historical data and citations of court decisions are impressive. They contain pages of documentation, which state, for example, that America is "a Christian nation" (an 1892 U.S. Supreme Court decision). Barton also quotes from a 1931 case in which Justice George Sutherland reviewed the aforementioned 1892 decision and reiterated that Americans are a "Christian people." Even liberal Justice William O. Douglas in 1952 affirmed the obvious: "we are a religious people and our institutions presuppose a Supreme Being."

Yet for our purposes, let's conclude Barton's case with his look at Noah and Daniel Webster. Said Noah Webster, "Our citizens should early understand that the genuine source of correct republican principles is the Bible, particularly the New Testament, or the Christian religion." And Daniel Webster stated a truth too often overlooked today: "The Christian religion—its general principles—must ever be regarded among us as the foundation of civil society."[23]

What About the Jews?

So where does that leave other religions? Says John Adams, "I will insist that the Hebrews have done more to civilize men than any other nation. They preserve and propagate to all mankind the doctrine of a supreme, intelligent, wise, almighty Sovereign of the Universe, which I believe to be the great essential principle of all morality, and consequently of all civilization."[24]

John Witherspoon said, "To the Jews were first committed the care of the sacred Writings. . . . Yet was the providence of God particularly manifest in their preservation and purity. The Jews were so faithful in their important trust."[25]

And Elias Boudinot, president of Congress in 1782–83, served as president of the "Society for Ameliorating the State of the Jews" and made personal provision to bring persecuted Jews to America where they could find safety.[26]

Barton's conclusion: "Today, we might accurately describe the 'general principles of Christianity' as the 'Judeo-Christian Ethic' since the Founders showed great attachment to the Hebrews."[27]

It is this very reasoning that Rabbi Lapin cites in his drive to defend American Christian conservatives. "I desperately want my children," says the rabbi, "to have the option of living peacefully and productively in the United States of America. I am certain this depends upon America regaining its Christian-oriented moral compass."[28]

Lapin concludes, "In defending Christianity in America, I am not suggesting that Jews ought to embrace the Christian faith. . . . But I am suggesting, at the very least, that Jews should stop speaking and acting as if Christian America is their enemy. I feel that all Americans who love freedom, whether or not they are religious, should be reassured, not frightened, by the reawakening of earnest Christianity throughout the land. I shall try to establish that Jews as well as other minorities have the most to fear from a post-Christian America."

Our Bible-Based Form of Government

There can be no doubt that America was founded on the biblical principles taught in the Old and New Testaments.[29]

Dr. Francis Schaeffer was certainly correct in seeing the theological, moral, and philosophical thought of early America as "the Christian consensus." Most colonists were Englishmen, and almost all were Europeans, who brought to the New World a Reformation mind-set. Some men, it is true, introduced the errors of Voltaire, Rousseau, and others, but these did not predominate. Therefore, our government was based on a respect and reverence for God and the realization that man was His special creation.

Such expressions as "divine Providence" and "nature and nature's God" appear in the Declaration of Independence as the source of man's inalienable rights. By contrast, secularism contends that man and the state are the sources from which human rights originate—as in the French Revolution—and if push came to shove, most present-day secularists would not be able to sign or defend the Declaration of Independence.

In addition, the last six commandments of the Decalogue, dealing with man's treatment of his fellow man, along with the civil laws of the Old Testament, formed the basis for our laws and the U.S. Constitution. As Dr. Schaeffer pointed out, while a government based on biblical principles, particularly shaped through Reformation thinking, was not perfect, it "gave society the opportunity for tremendous freedom, but without chaos."[30]

Our unique checks-and-balances system of government would never have been conceived through secularism. It was borrowed directly from Scripture (Isaiah 33:22) and is based on the premise that human nature is fallen, not inherently good, and that power must be distributed or freedom will perish.

"The Founders," says William F. Buckley, "had no such categorical illusions about the causes of human strife. James Madison cherished the prospect of a favorable balance in human performance, but a balance it would always be. 'As there is a degree of depravity in mankind which requires a certain degree of circumspection and distrust, so there are other qualities in human nature which justify a certain portion of esteem and confidence.'"[31]

Today's secularists ridicule the Puritan's God, Bible, work ethic, free enterprise, private ownership of land, and capitalism—even though these concepts, which emanated from biblical teaching,[32] have produced the greatest good for the largest number of people in history. We discard them at our national peril.

Our Bible-Based School System

Until a few years ago, America led the way in providing its citizens with the greatest educational system in the world. We were the first nation to ensure compulsory education, enabling even the poorest of children to learn to read and write. Our nation's amazing industrialization and mechanization were due largely to the high degree of education attained by the common people.

The New England colonies and Pennsylvania (under Governor William Penn) originated the idea that every household should seek to educate its children. We must not forget the motivation of godly Pilgrims and Puritans who lived during the great age of biblical translation, making it possible for the common people to read God's Word for themselves. That was a monumental time in English history. The New World settlers yearned not only for religious freedom but carried a burning desire that their children be able to read the Bible for themselves.

Among the early settlers, of course, were ministers of the gospel who founded churches in the hearts of the new communities. Because the minister was one of the few highly educated people in the community, and because he had to work to supplement his small salary (usually by farming), townsmen often engaged him as the teacher of their young. In exchange, settlers did his farming. The term "one-room schoolhouse" is more than a cliché in American history; that one-room building not only accommodated all the grades, first through sixth or eighth, Monday through Friday, but it housed the church and its activities on Sundays.

It would be impossible to overestimate the profound moral influence of the churches on the young and on education during the seventeenth and eighteenth centuries. First graders did not learn to read by sounding out "See Jane run" or "Jump, Spot, jump." Instead, the man of God would normally start them out with "In the beginning, God created the heavens and the earth." The *McGuffey Reader*—often ridiculed by today's secularist educators, who are doing such a disastrous job of teaching Johnny to read—would tell the first grader, "God made the world and all things in it." The text was filled with references to God, obedience, morality, and character building. Such moral character training is essential to the maintenance of a morally sane and safe society. Moral goodness has to be taught clearly and consistently to our young because mankind is not good by nature. Man is marred by sin—body, soul, spirit, mind, and conscience.

As the young nation matured and its cities grew, the ministry began to demand all of the pastor's time. Schoolteachers were trained to take the minister's place in the classroom, but even they reflected biblical thought.

In 1636, Harvard College was founded by Rev. Thomas Shepherd and John Harvard, the latter contributing the land and his own private library. On the gateposts even today appears an inscription that explains the reason for the school's foundation: to maintain "A Literate Clergy." John Harvard recognized that only a handful of ministers from England would be willing to migrate to this new and rough land, so he was burdened to start a Christian college in America.

For the first 100 years of American history, every college begun in the country was founded by a church, denomination, or religious group. Or put another way, of the first 150 colleges in America, 150 were started by Christians. American education and Christianity went together like hand in glove. American education was never intended to be godless.

For over 250 years, Harvard, Princeton, and Yale were the primary teacher-training centers in America. Although each had a different denominational origin, they shared a common goal: to prepare ministers and missionaries to preach the Word of God. Educating teachers for the growing schools was a natural outgrowth of that vision. Teachers trained in these schools understandably reflected the biblical moral values of their respective colleges. Consequently, public education, though never intended to be a source of evangelism, was highly flavored with biblical morals and formulated the greatest mass-character-building program in the history of the world.

But if that is true, someone may wonder, *then how did the world's greatest educational system, based solidly on biblical principles, get taken over by secularists?* We answer, "Very gradually!"

It is to that sad story that we now turn our attention.

5

SECULARIZING AMERICA

America, which once promoted God and biblical values, now opposes them, and Russia, which once opposed God and biblical values, now welcomes and promotes them.
CAL THOMAS

During the last 200 years, man's wisdom—*I*-dolatry—has capti-
vated the thinking of the Western world. After conquering Europe's
colleges and universities, it spread to America, where it has developed
a stranglehold on all state-supported public education.[1]

Recognizing the strategic nature of both education and the communications field, secularists gradually moved in until they virtually controlled both. Today almost every major magazine, newspaper, television
network, secular book publisher, and movie producer is a committed secularist, surrounding himself or herself with editors and newscasters who
seldom permit anything to be presented that contradicts their viewpoint.

Today's wave of crime, violence, pornography, promiscuity, venereal diseases,[2] no-fault divorce, guilt-free sex education, out-of-wedlock
births, abortion, homosexuality, bisexuality, AIDS, self-obsession, shat-
tered dreams, and broken hearts can be laid right at the door of Secular
Humanism. "The nation we live in today," says Bill Bennett, "is more
violent and vulgar, coarse and cynical, rude and remorseless, deviant
and depressed, than the one we once inhabited."[3]

Just how bad is it?

Bennett's *Index of Leading Cultural Indicators: American Society at
the End of the Twentieth Century* found, among other things:

- violent crime up 467 percent in forty years;

- the number of state and federal prisoners up 463 percent in
  forty years;

- out-of-wedlock births up 461 percent in forty years;

- the number of children living in single-parent households up
  threefold;

- out-of-wedlock births account for 32 percent of all births nationally—the highest rate in Washington, D.C., at 64 percent, and the lowest in Utah, at 17 percent;

- 26 percent of all pregnancies are aborted;

- gonorrhea infection rates of 150 per 100,000 persons;

- television is turned on seven hours and twelve minutes per day in the average household.[4]

Another study on the family conducted by Rutgers University reports, "Key social indicators suggest a substantial weakening of the institution of marriage. Americans have become less likely to marry. When they do marry, their marriages are less happy. And married couples face a high likelihood of divorce. Over the past four decades, marriage has declined as the first living together experience for couples and as a status of parenthood. Unmarried cohabitation and unwed births have grown enormously, and so has the percentage of children who grow up in fragile families."[5]

The Rutgers study also found that 54.6 percent of girls and 62 percent of guys felt cohabitation was a good idea and that 50 percent of teens believe that out-of-wedlock childbearing is now a "worthwhile lifestyle."

What is worse, Sandy Burchsted maintains that in one hundred years Americans will marry at least "four times and have extramarital affairs with no public censure." She says this will be looked upon as "a conscious, evolutionary process."[6]

What irony! "America, which once promoted God and biblical values, now opposes them, and Russia, which once opposed God and biblical values, now welcomes and promotes them."[7]

How did we get to this tragic point? How did America, founded on biblical principles, succumb to the disease of Secular Humanism? It's a long, gradual, painful story.

The Roots of Humanism

The origins of humanism can be traced to the distant past. The Greeks were the first to systematically lay out a philosophy of humanism.

Their version was based on two misconceptions by Protagoras in the fifth century B.C: Man is the measure of all things, and contradictory statements are equally true. These concepts have been amplified through the years by scores of atheists, until today a well-defined system of thought exists that contradicts almost every basic concept of biblical revelation.

The philosophy of the Greeks declined with the Roman occupation of their homeland. But the Romans quickly adopted the philosophy, art, architecture, and social customs of Greece, merged them with their own, and propagated Hellenistic culture throughout the Roman world. They diligently preserved the writings of the Greeks, despite the spread of Christianity during the early centuries after Christ.

Nevertheless, Christianity became so effective in influencing the thought of Western man that, from the death of Christ until the twelfth century, man-centered thinking is seldom found. Most of Europe was dominated by Catholic thought.

Interestingly enough, however, one of the most important thinkers to lay the foundation for modern humanism was a dedicated Dominican (later sainted) named Thomas Aquinas (1225–1274). Notes Francis A. Schaeffer:

> He was the outstanding theologian of his day and his thinking still dominates in some circles of the Roman Catholic Church. Aquinas held that man had revolted against God and thus was fallen, but Aquinas had a incomplete view of the Fall. He thought that the Fall did not affect man as a whole, but only in part. In his view the will was fallen or corrupted but the intellect was not affected. Thus people could rely on their own human wisdom, and this meant that people were free to mix the teachings of the Bible with the teachings of non-Christian philosophers.[8]

> Among the Greek philosophers, Thomas Aquinas relied especially on one of the greatest, Aristotle (384–322 b.c.). . . . Aquinas managed to have Aristotle accepted, so the ancient non-Christian philosophy was reenthroned.[9]

Western man's romance with human wisdom reignited in the medieval period with Aquinas. It is an irony of history that a man sainted by his church was the one responsible for reviving an almost dead philosophy, which has become the most dangerous religion in the world.

By giving human wisdom equal weight with biblical revelation, Aquinas opened the door for free-thinking educators to implant ever more of the wisdom of man, even as they discarded the wisdom of God. Eventually man's wisdom became "truth" and God's wisdom became "error."

Upon the foundation laid by Aquinas—considered by many humanists the most influential thinker in history—additional building blocks of man's wisdom were added to "Thus saith the Lord." Gradually the focus of education shifted from God to man, "the measure of all things." It was a short step to total autonomy and independence from God. This freed man from moral absolutes and permitted him to *be* God, to act as the judge of his own behavior.

When Florence, Italy, became the cultural headquarters of the Renaissance, art soon reflected this glorification of mankind. Even today, a giant replica of Michelangelo's magnificent *David* stands nude, overlooking the beautiful city. This contradicts the wisdom of God, for early in the book of Genesis, the Creator gave man animal skins to hide his nakedness. The Renaissance obsession with nude art forms was the forerunner of the modern demand for pornography in the name of freedom.[10] Both resulted in a self-destructive lowering of moral standards.

French Skepticism and Modern Humanism

Two long-dead men continue to wield great influence upon the ideals, morals, and philosophy of today's college students. The French skeptics Voltaire and Rousseau both were trained in Jesuit colleges, yet both rejected anything supernatural and adopted an ethically amoral code.

Voltaire's skepticism is a classic example of the danger of providing a child with the wrong kind of teacher. When his parents saw their son was obviously endowed with a superior mind, they hired a tutor, "a dissolute abbé who taught him skepticism along with his prayers."[11] It is no wonder that he rejected Christianity and became an agnostic, for his skepticism had taken root long before he entered college.

Schaeffer summarizes the role of Enlightened Humanism in the following way:

In June 1789, the first phase of the liberal bourgeois plan of the French Revolution was at its height. Here the members of the national Assembly swore to establish a constitution. Their base, consciously, was purely a humanistic theory of rights. On August 26, 1789, they issued the Declaration of the Rights of Man. It sounded fine, but it had nothing to rest upon. In the Declaration of the Rights of Man what was called "the Supreme Being" equaled "the sovereignty of the nation"—that is, the general will of the people. Not only was there a contrast to England's Bloodless Revolution, but a sharp contrast with what resulted in the United States from the Declaration of Independence which was made thirteen years earlier. One had the reformation base [i.e., importance of the Bible and God's wisdom regarding the fall of mankind], the other did not.

It took two years for the National Constituent Assembly to draft a constitution (1789–1791). Within a year it was a dead letter. By that time what is often known as the Second French Revolution was in motion, leading to a bloodbath that ended with the revolutionary leaders themselves being killed.

To make their outlook clear, the French changed the calendar and called 1792 the "year one" and destroyed many of the things of the past, even suggesting the destruction of the cathedral at Chartres. They proclaimed the goddess of Reason in Notre-Dame Cathedral in Paris and other churches in France, including Chartres. In Paris, the goddess was personified by an actress, Demoiselle Candeille, carried shoulder-high into the cathedral by men dressed in Roman costumes.

Like the humanists of the Renaissance, the men of the Enlightenment pushed aside the Christian base and heritage and looked back to the old pre-Christian times. In Voltaire's home in Ferney the picture he hung (in such a way on the wall at the foot of his bed that it was the first thing he saw every day) was a painting of the goddess Diana with a small new crescent moon on her head and a very large one under her feet. She is reaching down to help men.

How quickly all the humanists ideals came to grief! In September 1792 began the massacre in which some 1,300 prisoners were killed. Before it was all over, the government and its agents killed 40,000 people, many of them peasants. Maximilian Robespierre (1758–1794), the revolutionary leader, was himself executed in July 1794. This destruction came not from outside the system; it was produced by the system. As in the later Russian Revolution, the revolutionaries on their humanist base had only two options—anarchy or repression.[12]

Humanism's Incurable Optimism

In view of the total failure of the Enlightenment to produce reason, freedom, and progress through the French and Russian revolutions— and in light of the chaos, suffering, slaughter, and totalitarian repression they instituted—one might hope that deep thinkers would become suspicious that, just perhaps, man without God and divine law cannot be trusted. But those lessons were lost (and continue to be lost) on the humanist mind. In point of fact, the slaughter of the twentieth century makes the bloodletting of the French Revolution a Sunday School picnic—except, of course, for the forty thousand who lost their heads.

Instead of recognizing that the elimination of moral absolutes always produces chaos, followed by repression, Enlightenment thinkers decided they had acted in haste. As a result, they established a two-pronged siege on man's mind: books and education. Ironically, they utilized the most significant invention of the fifteenth century—the printing press, first used to publish the Bible in 1451. This amazing machine, coupled with new translations of Scripture, contributed greatly to the Reformation in northern Europe and England by enabling the common man to read God's revelation in his own language. In addition, Calvin, Luther, and other reformers, all of them prolific writers, likewise used the printed page to explain God's wisdom to the people.

Enlightenment humanists knew that a siege on man's mind would be won or lost largely through reading and education, so they, too, began to communicate their worldview through art, fiction, plays, poetry, and teaching. Voltaire alone produced eighty-three volumes of books, pamphlets, and plays. Because some of the northern European kings forbade the distribution of certain Enlightenment writings, their noxious spread was somewhat checked until the eighteenth and nineteenth centuries.

The colleges and universities of Europe, supported by taxes seized from the working man, became the ideal source of transmission for "enlightened" humanism. Universal education was unknown, and thus only bright young people, the sons of politicians or the rich, could gain a higher education. Man-centered literature gradually took over most of the colleges and universities on the continent, preaching with missionary zeal its prejudices of "No God, No Masters—no absolutes—but self-sufficient and self-indulgent man."

Many parents abhorred what they saw taking place among their sons and daughters. "Are not thousands of children," said Frederic Bastiat, "cast each year into its current, where they lose their faith and moral principles, the feeling of human dignity, the love of freedom and the knowledge of their rights and their duties? Do they not emerge completely imbued with the false ideas of paganism, with its false ethics, its false virtues, as well as its vices and its deep contempt for mankind?"[13] While Bastiat's lament sounds thoroughly modern, he actually penned his complaint more than a century and a half ago in an article titled "Academic Degrees and Socialism."

As technology advanced, government increased, and almost every country in Europe began to multiply its number of state officials.[14] Where did these bureaucrats receive their education? In colleges and universities committed to a man-centered worldview.

A Deadly Import

So powerfully did existentialist thought permeate European education and government before the turn of the century that the continent soon crossed what Schaeffer called "the line of despair." While England saved

Europe from Napoleon in the first quarter of the nineteenth century, by the twentieth century, she had so lost her biblical, Reformation base of thought that she needed the assistance of America to defeat Germany's Kaiser Wilhelm and Adolf Hitler—both of whom would have imposed totalitarianism upon Europe. Sir Winston Churchill himself admitted that World War II was a struggle over Christian civilization.

Schaeffer thought that, because of her stronger biblical base of thought, America did not cross "the line of despair" until the 1930s. Since then, humanism has run rampant in our public educational system[15] and has swallowed up official government thinking, the media, and virtually every area of communication except church-related ministries.

In 1920, approximately one government employee existed for every 100 citizens; today, closer to one American in six works for the local, state, or federal government. The establishment of big government and its level upon level of regulations has so eroded liberty that many experts fear we are well on our way to losing our traditional freedoms. For example, small business "is being gradually choked by hostile regulations, mandatory procedures, and punitive taxation. Foremost is the suspension of the right to enter into contract with employees freely. The federal government has become a kind of 'super' labor union. A battery of commissars enforces edicts prescribing who must be employed, as well as the terms of the employment."[16]

And it's worse in the educational arena. Today, American public education is plain anti-God. "No institution," says Rabbi Dennis Prager, "is so devoid of reference to God and Judeo-Christian religion as the university."[17] With God expelled from the schools, it was a short step to rejecting the view that man was created by God and thus responsible for obeying His moral absolutes. The chaos of today's public education system is in direct proportion to its obsession with humanism and especially its teaching of naturalistic science, the Darwinian theory of evolution, and moral relativism. Humanism ultimately destroys everything it touches, despite its promises of utopia.

Consider the predictions of Dr. Horace Mann, who probably did more to corrupt the American school system than any other person. In 1850, he convinced America that state-funded, secular education would solve the problems of crime and poverty in 100 years. Clearly it did no such thing—even though we spend billions of dollars each year promoting the religion of Secular Humanism in our public schools.[18]

This process of decay did not begin with Mann, however, although we tend to trace the collapse back to him. Mann was vigorously opposed by ministers of his day, who foresaw the shift from a biblical to a secular base for education, but their resistance gradually was overcome.

The Slide of American Education

During the latter part of the nineteenth century, many of our bright young educators went to Europe to pursue their graduate degrees. They enrolled at the Sorbonne in France, Bonn University in Germany, Edinburgh University in Scotland, Oxford University in England, and many other breeding grounds for humanism. In time, these professors returned with their doctorates in hand, bringing with them skepticism, atheism, collectivism, statism, socialism, evolutionism, rationalism, and existentialism.[19]

John Dewey, the most influential educator of the twentieth century, did more for the secularist takeover of American education than anyone else.[20] The leader of the liberal, progressive movement in education, Dewey was an atheist, an evolutionist, a socialist, a board member of the American Humanist Association, and president of the League for Industrial Democracy, the American arm of the British Fabian Society.[21] Dewey signed the 1933 *Humanist Manifesto*.

Dewey undergirded his experimental and pragmatic theories of education by claiming that truth is relative, that absolutes are not admissible, and that evolutionary theory is valid. "There is no God and there is no soul,"[22] he affirmed. Dewey believed that a fixed constitution hindered man's social evolution, which in turn was based on man's biological evolution.

Dewey viewed traditional education with alarm. When he observed fixed standards and rules of conduct, the moral training that naturally flowed from these standards, and the sense of conformity that guided so many institutions, he rejected traditionalism and proposed the following:

- expression and cultivation of individuality (as opposed to imposition from above);

- free activity (as opposed to external discipline);

- learning through experience (as opposed to texts and teachers);

- acquiring skills as a means of attaining ends that have direct vital appeal (as opposed to drill);

- making the most of the opportunities of this present life (as opposed to preparation for a more or less remote future);

- acquaintance with a changing world (as opposed to static aims and materials).[23]

In his book *A Common Faith*, Dewey summarized his own religion. He claimed that religion is basically an attempt to adjust to the difficulties of life and should therefore be freed from the outmoded ideas of ancient faiths, such as Christianity. Since the world changes through time, so must religion. And science must be the guide for any modern faith, for it alone is the gateway to reliable knowledge.[24] Attempting to apply evolution, socialism, and secular science to education, Dewey succeeded in stripping from American education its final vestiges of the Christian message and purpose.

Back in the days when moral principles and character building were taught along with the basics, the schoolhouse was not a hazardous place to work. But federal aid to education, which started in earnest in 1957, began the secularist domination of our schools. Since then, philosophical control of our schools has largely passed from local communities to the federal government.

The situation got worse in 1979, when the federal government established a Department of Education with a $3 billion budget. Because America's educational system has been subverted and overrun by humanism,[25] and because humanism is a legally declared religion,[26] government is now in the process of establishing the religion of Secular Humanism and giving its high priest a position in the president's cabinet.

Today, the federal education budget runs to tens of billions of dollars a year. The mischief humanist educrats can accomplish with these billions of *your* tax dollars is beyond imagination. And education has grown progressively worse during the years of increasing federal budgets and federal control of education!

In her book *The Change Agents*, Barbara Morris points out that the individuals we used to call schoolteachers are now social "change agents." Their goal is to modify the morals of our nation's schoolchildren. They are more interested in moral modification (which they call "values clarification") than they are in academic standards and good learning.

Our Lord warned that it would be better for a man to hang a millstone around his neck and jump into the sea than to destroy the minds of children who believe in Him. America's public education is purposely designed to eradicate Jesus from the scene and replace Him with the likes of John Dewey, Sigmund Freud, Wilhelm Wundt, Friedrich Nietzsche, Karl Marx, Charles Darwin, and many more.

Educational programs such as Goals 2000 and Outcome Based Education amount to the nationalizing of American education.[27] In order to procure federal aid, schools have to accept federally approved policies that feature secularist thinking—regardless of community moral standards.

Today our schools have become war zones. But even as we count the dead, no one dares look at the secular curriculum. Everything is on the table for discussion—except humanism.

As Cal Thomas put it: "The humanist left knows the only way it can create substantial numbers of new ideological and social robots eager to follow in their failed footsteps is to imprison substantial numbers of children in government schools where they are force-fed liberal ideology and lied to about sex, about history, and about a whole lot of other things at taxpayers' expense."[28]

The situation, if not so serious, would be laughable. A first grader in a Medford, New Jersey, public school is censored for reading a Bible story about Jacob and Esau, in spite of the fact that the story does not mention God. The teacher refused to let it be read in class "because of its religious content."[29]

A federal judge, at the urging of the American Civil Liberties Union, forced schools in eastern Kentucky to remove the Ten Commandments, the Mayflower Compact, the Declaration of Independence ("All men are endowed by their Creator"), the preamble to the constitution of Kentucky ("grateful to Almighty God"), the national motto ("In God We Trust"), President Ronald Reagan's 1983 "Year of the Bible," and President Lincoln's statement regarding the Bible being God's best gift to man. The judge said such displays were a violation of the First Amendment.[30]

According to British historian Paul Johnson, Jesus' teaching remains of peculiar relevance today, for his "central theme is that God, not man, is the final authority. God has rights. Human beings have duties; we deny God his rights at our peril."[31] But then, we cannot tell American students such a simple message in the classroom. It is unconstitutional. Instead we accent their rights while downplaying their duties and responsibilities.

As long as biblical thought prevailed in the public school system, no real need existed to put on a drive to get moralists elected to government office, for the majority of our lawmakers reflected the morals of the people. But all that has changed. Humanism has surreptitiously commandeered our once-great school system. It has ingeniously conceived a plan to introduce an inordinate number of secularists into government, where they continually pass laws that favor the advancement of their deadly doctrine. In the words of Cal Thomas,

> They and the value system they forced on America have given us condoms in the schools, not self-control and virtue; "recreational" drugs, not a "high" that comes from honor, duty, and character; no-fault divorce, not commitment and a determination to work things out no matter how one feels; prenuptial agreements and a nuclear strike on the family; AIDS and low-quality television that increasingly focuses on the region between waist and the thigh, rarely visiting the things of the mind and spirit.[32]

The Challenge Ahead

The next hundred years will be a time of destiny for America.

The new century will become either increasingly secular or Christian.

It will certainly be a century of exciting challenges for all those committed to Christian aims, absolutes, and biblical principles.

Rush Limbaugh has it absolutely right: "Americans are growing weary of supporting a public-education system which bans God, encourages licentiousness, decries Western civilization, indicts American tradition, promotes cultural disharmony, and serves as a breeding ground to indoctrinate new little liberals."

We have some momentous decisions to make.

Will we go back to the Christ of the Bible?

Or will we go on to atheism, statism, socialism, chaos, and despair?

Part Three:
THE TRUTH

6

THE HUMANIST BIBLE

No deity will save us; we must save ourselves.
PAUL KURTZ

What the Bible is to Christians, the *Humanist Manifesto* is to humanists. It represents the official position of the humanist movement, and each of its various incarnations have been accepted as the current primer on humanist ideas, beliefs, values, and goals. The manifestos show how confident humanists are in their ultimate triumph.[1]

These amazing documents blueprint a long sought takeover of the world. *Humanist Manifesto I* was compiled in 1933 by thirty-four secularists in the United States.[2] Many of its signers were leaders in education, government, and the Unitarian clergy. *Humanist Manifesto II*, a 1973 update of the original work, proclaims itself a "positive declaration for times of uncertainty."[3] Literally hundreds of humanists put their names to this *Manifesto*, including such luminaries as Isaac Asimov, Paul Blanshard, Francis Crick, Edd Doerr, Paul Edwards, Herbert Feigl, Antony Flew, Alan F. Guttmacher, Sidney Hook, Lester A. Kirkendall, Paul Kurtz, Corliss Lamont, Lester Mondale, P. H. Nowell-Smith, John Herman Randall, Andre D. Sakharov, Roy Wood Sellars, B. F. Skinner, Bertram D. Wolfe, Joseph Fletcher, Betty Friedan, Sir Julian Huxley, and A. Philip Randolph.

The *Humanist Manifesto 2000: A Call for a New Planetary Humanism* (subtitled "A Plan for Peace, Dignity, and Freedom in the Global Human Family") was printed in the fall 1999 edition of *Free Inquiry* and was written by Paul Kurtz, editor of the magazine. This version was endorsed by such humanists as Richard Dawkins, Sir Arthur C. Clarke, E. O. Wilson, Steve Allen, Paul D. Boyer, Sir Harold W. Kroto, Richard Leakey, Alan Cranston, and Jens C. Skou.

One sees an interesting progression from *Humanist Manifesto I* to *Humanist Manifesto II* and on to *Humanist Manifesto 2000*. Religious Humanism characterized the 1933 document, Secular Humanism the 1973 document, and Planetary Humanism the most recent version.

Nothing of substance, however, has changed. All promote atheism, naturalism, evolution, moral relativism, and world government.

1. Atheism

Kurtz is a bit more careful in *Manifesto 2000* than were his predecessors and so uses the term "scientific naturalism" to veil his atheism. But their meanings are identical. Religious Humanists regard the universe as self-existing and not created.[4]

> We find insufficient evidence for belief in the existence of a supernatural; it is either meaningless or irrelevant to the question of the survival and fulfillment of the human race. As nontheists, we begin with humans not God, nature not deity. Nature may indeed be broader and deeper than we now know; any new discoveries, however, will but enlarge our knowledge of the natural.[5]

> But we can discover no divine purpose or providence for the human species. While there is much that we do not know, humans are responsible for what we are or will become. No deity will save us; we must save ourselves.[6]

> The unique message of humanism on the current world scene is its commitment to scientific naturalism. Most worldviews accepted today are spiritual, mystical, or theological in character. Scientific naturalism enables human beings to construct a coherent worldview disentangled from metaphysics or theology and based on the sciences. . . . Scientific naturalists hold a form of nonreductive materialism.[7]

2. Evolution

> Humanism believes that man is part of nature and that he has emerged as the result of a continuous process.[8]

> Holding an organic view of life, humanists find that the traditional dualism of mind and body must be rejected.[9]

Humanism recognizes that man's religious culture and civilization, as clearly depicted by anthropology and history, are the product of a gradual development due to his interaction with his natural environment and with his social heritage. The individual born into a particular culture is largely molded to that culture.[10]

Science affirms that the human species is an emergence from natural evolutionary forces. As far as we know, the total personality is a function of the biological organism transacting in a social and cultural context. There is no credible evidence that life survives the death of the body. We continue to exist in our progeny and in the way that our lives have influenced others in our culture.[11]

The scientific theory of evolution, however, provides a more parsimonious account of human origins and is based upon evidence drawn from a wide range of sciences. We decry the efforts of a few scientists, often heralded by the mass media, to impose transcendental interpretations upon natural phenomena.[12]

Kurtz wants no competition from any scientist who might see design or purpose in nature, for he knows that design and purpose spell hard times for atheism. Nearly every week the newspapers or magazines carry some type of story supporting evolution—but let one article dare to suggest that design may be present, and Kurtz protests. What hypocrisy!

3. Amorality

We affirm that moral values derive their source from human experience [not from God]. Ethics is autonomous and situational [could change at any time depending on the circumstances], needing no theological or ideological sanction. Ethics stems from human need and interest. To deny this distorts the whole basis of life.[13]

In the area of sexuality, we believe that intolerant attitudes, often cultivated by orthodox religions [namely Christianity] and puritanical cultures [Western civilization], unduly repress sexual conduct [homosexuality, bisexuality, transgender, transsexual, etc.]. The right to birth control, abortion, and divorce[14] should be recognized. While we do not approve of exploitive, denigrating forms of sexual expression, neither do we wish to prohibit, by law or social sanction, sexual behavior between consenting adults. The many varieties of sexual exploration should not in themselves be considered "evil." Without countenancing mindless permissiveness or unbridled promiscuity, a civilized society should be a tolerant one. Short of harming others or compelling them to do likewise, individuals should be permitted to express their sexual proclivities and pursue their life-styles as they desire. We wish to cultivate the development of a responsible attitude toward sexuality, in which humans are not exploited as sexual objects, and in which intimacy, sensitivity, respect, and honesty in interpersonal relations are encouraged. Moral education for children and adults is an important way of developing awareness and sexual maturity.[15]

Humanists have called for liberation from repressive puritanical codes [homosexuality, transgendered, transsexual, premarital intercourse, extramarital intercourse with the consent of both partners, bisexuality, genital association].[16]

This amoral worldview is officially endorsed by our government and by the public educational system. For over seventy-five years, judges, legislators, governors, mayors, and presidents have introduced legislation based on this destructive philosophy.

4. *Autonomous, Self-Centered Man*

Human life has meaning because we create and develop our futures. Happiness and the creative realization of human needs and desires, individually and in shared enjoyment, are continuous themes of humanism. We strive for the good life, here and now. The goal is to pursue life's enrichment despite debasing forces of vulgarization, commercialization, bureaucratization, and dehumanization.[17]

Reason and intelligence are the most effective instruments that humankind possesses. There is no substitute: Neither faith nor passion suffices in itself. The controlled use of scientific methods, which have transformed the natural and social sciences since the Renaissance, must be extended further in the solution of human problems.[18]

To enhance freedom and dignity the individual must experience a full range of civil liberties in all societies. This includes freedom of speech and the press, political democracy, legal right of opposition to government policies, fair judicial process, religious liberty, freedom of association, and artistic, scientific and cultural freedom. It also includes a recognition of an individual's right to die with dignity, euthanasia, and the right to suicide. We oppose the increasing invasion of privacy, by whatever means, in both totalitarian and democratic societies. We would safeguard, extend, and implement the principles of human freedom evolved from the *Magna Carta* to the *Bill of Rights*, the *Bill of Rights of Man*, and the *Universal Declaration of Human Rights*.[19]

The preciousness and dignity of the individual person is a central humanist value [except, of course, for the unborn who may be slaughtered at will]. Individuals should be encouraged to realize their own creative talents and desires. We reject all religious, ideological, or moral codes that denigrate the individual, suppress freedom, dull intellect, dehumanize personality. We believe in maximum individual autonomy consonant with social responsibility. Although science can account for the causes of behavior, the possibilities of individual freedom or choice exist in human life and should be increased.[20]

Women should have the right to control their own bodies. This includes reproductive freedom, voluntary contraception, and abortion. The opportunity for appropriate sexual education should be made available from an early age. This should include responsible sexual behavior, family planning, and contraceptive techniques. We need to develop a new human identity—membership in the planetary community.[21]

The purpose of life for the humanist contrasts sharply with that of the Christian. "Religious humanism considers the complete realization of human personality to be the end of man's life and seeks its development and fulfillment in the here and now. This is the explanation of the humanist's social passion."[22]

These writers fail to point out that in order to grant such unbridled freedom, we must remove all restraints. As we have seen, total liberty—or, as they call it, "democracy"—leads to anarchy.

5. Socialistic One-World Government

Although humanists claim to prize individual freedom and loathe external restraints, for some reason they clamor for a mandatory, international oneness of all people and seem willing, even eager, to sacrifice national benefits for international unity.

We stand in disbelief at their naive determination to discard the freedoms guaranteed by American legal documents (particularly the Bill of Rights) in order to place all of us under the rule of international laws and judicial processes. Even in our own country, when we "let Big Brother do it," we complain about red tape, lack of personal concern, higher prices, and large-scale bungling. If a national bureaucracy can grow so awkward, imagine how inept a global bureaucracy would be! Yet hear the humanists' glowing resolution:

> We deplore the division of humankind on nationalistic grounds. We have reached a turning point in human history where the best option is to transcend the limits of national sovereignty and to move toward the building of a world community in which all sectors of the human family can participate. Thus we look to the development of a system of world law and a world order based upon transnational federal government. This would appreciate cultural pluralism and diversity. It would not exclude pride in national origins and accomplishments nor the handling of regional problems on a regional basis. Human progress, however, can no longer be achieved by focusing on one section of the world, Western or Eastern, developed or underdeveloped. For the first time in human history, no part of humankind can be iso-

lated from any other. Each person's future is in some way linked to all. We thus reaffirm a commitment to the building of world community, at the same time recognizing that this commits us to some hard choices.[23]

The problems of economic growth and development can no longer be resolved by one nation alone; they are worldwide in scope. It is the moral obligation of the developed nations to provide—through an international authority that safeguards human rights—massive techni- cal, agricultural, medical, and economic assistance, including birth control techniques, to the developing portions of the globe. World poverty must cease. Hence extreme disproportions in wealth, income, and economic growth should be reduced on a worldwide basis.[24]

The world needs at some point in the future to establish an effective World Parliament—and elected to it based on population—which rep- resents the people, not their governments. The idea of a World Parliament is similar to the evolution of the European Parliament, still in its infancy. The detailed formal structure can only be worked out by a charter review convention that we recommend should be convened to examine thoroughly options for strengthening the UN and/or sup- plementing it with a parliamentary system. . . . We recommend an international system of taxation. . . . This would not be a voluntary contribution but an actual tax [to fund UNESCO, UNICEF, the World Health Organization].[25]

All Christians deplore world poverty. But even if it could be eliminated by world socialism (which it cannot, because socialism stultifies pro- duction[26]), the price would be too great, for it would come at the expense of control by atheistic, amoral humanists.

"One worldism" is lauded by the humanist's egalitarian pose:

The principle of moral equality must be furthered through elimination of all discrimination based upon race, religion, sex, age, or national origin. This means equality of opportunity and recognition of talent and merit. Individuals should be encouraged to contribute to their own betterment. If unable, then society should provide means to satisfy their basic economic, health, and cultural needs, including, wherever resources make possible, a minimum guaranteed annual income.[27]

Continuous, guaranteed welfare relief is the worst human disincentive ever conceived by government. No other system has been devised that has a more stultifying impact on creativity and human initiative.

The humanist's intellectual ideal of peace also impels him to declare:

> This world community must renounce the resort to violence and force as a method of solving international disputes. We believe in the peaceful adjudication of differences by international courts and by the development of the arts of negotiation and compromise. War is obsolete. So is the use of nuclear, biological, and chemical weapons. It is a planetary imperative to reduce the level of military expenditures and turn these savings to peaceful and people-oriented uses.[28]

The problem with such idealism is that it misunderstands the basic nature of man. Humanists consider man inherently good, whereas the Bible pictures humanity as fallen, sinful, and untrustworthy. Humanists naively envision a utopian, secular, worldwide millennium, when all countries renounce war and revel in peace, prosperity, and brotherhood.

If humanists understood history, they would know that such a utopia never has existed and never will exist. Men and women must experience a change in nature before they can live together as brothers and sisters in a world of peace. The dictators of the world prove that ruthless man will always trample the rights of the weak.

Humanistic myopia cannot get this one principle in focus: A one-world, socialist government must select a supreme governor to make final decisions, and such a person must be human. History shows that such leaders invariably turn out to be Stalins, Hitlers, and Maos—rigid, ruthless, iron-fisted dictators who have accounted for the deaths of millions of their own countrymen. No sensible person could imagine that such an international ruler would treat in a humane way the people he rules. Perhaps humanists should check into the UN's role in the genocide in Rwanda, where 800,000 human beings were butchered. UN forces actually handed over the people they were supposed to defend to the government that murdered them.

Humanism's Hostility toward the Bible

The *Humanist Manifesto* also is quite clear in its denunciation of traditional religious beliefs:

> The time has come for widespread recognition of the radical changes in religious beliefs throughout the modern world. The time is past for mere revision of traditional attitudes [Christianity]. Science and economic change have disrupted the old beliefs. Religions the world over are under the necessity of coming to terms with new conditions created by a vastly increased knowledge and experience.[29]

> We believe, however, that traditional dogmatic or authoritarian religions that place revelation, God, ritual, or creed above human needs and experience do a disservice to the human species.[30]

> As in 1933, humanists still believe that rational theism, especially faith in the prayer-hearing God, assumed to love and care for persons, to hear and understand their prayers, and be able to do something about them, is an unproved and outmoded faith. Salvationism, based on mere affirmation, still appears as harmful, diverting people with false hopes of heaven hereafter. Reasonable minds look to other means for survival.[31]

> Promises of immortal salvation or fear of eternal damnation are both illusory and harmful. They distract humans from present concerns, from self-actualization, and from rectifying social injustices. Modern science discredits such historic concepts as the "ghost in the machine" and the "separable soul."[32]

Today man's larger understanding of the universe, his scientific achievements, and his deeper appreciation of brotherhood have created a situation which requires a new statement of the means and purposes of religion. Such vital, fearless, and frank religion capable of furnishing adequate social goals and personal satisfactions may appear to many people as a complete break with the past. While this age does owe a vast debt to traditional religions, it is none the less obvious that any religion that can hope to be a synthesizing and dynamic force for today must be shaped for the needs of this age. To establish such a religion is a major necessity of the present.[33]

Humanism's Goals

Where does humanism want our world to end up? What are its ultimate goals? We don't have to wonder.

The next century can be and should be the humanistic century. Dramatic scientific, technological, and ever accelerating social and political changes crowd our awareness. We have virtually conquered the planet, explored the moon, overcome the natural limits of travel and communication; we stand at the dawn of a new age, ready to move farther into space and perhaps inhabit other planets.[34]

Religious humanism maintains that all associations and institutions exist for the fulfillment of human life. The intelligent evaluations, transformation, control, and direction of such associations and institutions with a view to the enhancement of human life is the purpose and program of humanism. Certainly, religious institutions, their ritualistic forms, ecclesiastical methods, and communal activities must be reconstituted as rapidly as experience allows in order to function effectively in the modern world.[35]

According to such texts, humanists want to control the lives and destinies of the world's peoples, and they intend to accomplish their goals in the twenty-first century.

Consistent Doctrines

The tenets of humanism described in the three *Humanist Manifesto* are not the weird ideas of a few obscure individuals unworthy of our consideration. They are the religious beliefs of some of the most influential people in America. Educators lead the list, many of whom head the universities and college departments that mold the thinking of our children's teachers.

Since its initial publication in 1933, *The Humanist Manifesto* has been widely recognized as the Bible of the Secular Humanists. Its dogma has consistently been taught to our youth,[36] and its supporters have used their influence to implement its objectives and ideals.

But when it comes to choosing a Bible, do yourself a favor and forget about the manifestos. The only salvation they offer is from life itself.

7

HUMANISM IS UNSCIENTIFIC

This belief [in God and Creation] formed the bedrock on which science rose.
STANLEY L. JAKI, scientist

I now believe that the balance of reasonable considerations tells heavily in favor of the religious, even of the Christian view of the world.
C. E. M. JOAD, philosopher

As we have seen, humanism is known by a variety of titles: Secular Humanism, Rationalistic Humanism, Religious Humanism, Ethical Humanism, Evolutionary Humanism, Enlightened Humanism, and Planetary Humanism. But the favorite term used by the humanists themselves for their religious faith is Scientific Humanism. The title appears repeatedly in their journals, books, and advertisements.

Ironically, humanism is completely unscientific! As we shall see, not one humanist doctrine stands up to scientific investigation. It is all a zealously defended fraud, funded by U.S. taxpayers.

Humanism's Five Unscientific Tenets

No matter what our students may hear in the classroom, not one of humanism's five basic tenets can be proved scientifically.

1. Atheism

If a man came to town saying, "No one, plus nothing, times blind chance, equals everything," we would say he was crazy and overdue for retirement. Why? Because he would expect us to believe that effects can be achieved without causes and that design emerges without a designer.

But if that same man came to town displaying a Ph.D. in philosophy or anthropology from the University of Oklahoma or an Ed.D. from the University of Massachusetts (Amherst) and proclaimed, "Educated people do not believe in God. Instead, they believe that this magnificent universe began with an accidental explosion, and life emerged spontaneously and then evolved over three and one-half billion years. We, like our animal brothers and insect sisters, are the products of chance and accident," he is acclaimed a great thinker and hired to chair the department at the state university.

In fact, neither the Christian nor the humanist can scientifically prove the existence or nonexistence of God. The inductive method is useless in such an endeavor. The universe is so vast and so complex that it literally staggers the mind. God must of necessity be superior to His creation. He must be not only greater than man but greater than all of His creation—the earth, the other planets, and the universe. He obviously is not discernable with the human eye, for then any controversy related to His existence would cease. It is impossible to prove empirically whether God exists. The nonexistence of God is just as scientifically unprovable as the existence of God.

Still, we can look around us and see evidence in one direction or another. We do not have to verify things directly with our five senses to conclude they are real. Have you ever seen gravity, electricity, or love? Yet they exist, and their reality is provable by what they do. When we see light emanating from a bulb, we know that electricity is coursing through the element, although we have not observed its essential form. When a mother declares that she loves her baby, we cannot see her love. But when she throws her body in front of an onrushing truck to save the life of her child, we know by what she does that she loves.

So it is with God. We do not see Him, but we observe His works everywhere (Romans 1:20). The 120 trillion brain connections in your head loudly proclaim a Designer. The capillaries in your body—which, if laid end to end, would wrap five times around the earth—carry blood, nutrition, and oxygen to your entire body. Because we must accept either creation or evolution by faith, it seems more logical to believe that a Designer planned and created the human body. So it is with mountains, streams, rivers, stars, and everything in this world; they are effects that demand an adequate cause.

Cambridge University physicist John Polkinghorne said, "When you realize that the laws of nature must be incredibly finely tuned to produce the universe we see, that conspires to plant the idea that the universe did not just happen, but that there must be a purpose behind it."[1]

The 1964 Nobel Prize winner in physics, Charles Townes, goes further: "Many have a feeling that somehow intelligence must have been involved in the laws of the universe."[2] Townes, who teaches at the

University of California at Berkeley, admits, "As a religious person, I strongly sense the presence and actions of a creative being far beyond myself and yet always personal and close by."[3]

When a famous evolutionist sees design in nature, then humanists need to take a second look. Evolutionist Paul Amos Moody acknowledges that the more he studies science, the more he is impressed that this world and universe have "a definite design—and a design suggests a designer." Moody says the evidences for design are everywhere, from the starry heavens to the electrons swirling in orbit around the atomic nuclei. What happens when we seek the natural laws that lie behind such design? "There we find the Creator," says Moody.[4]

Little wonder that Henry Margenau noted, "If you take the top notch scientists, you find very few atheists among them."[5] Most of the signatories of the *Humanist Manifestos* are not from the "hard" sciences but from the social sciences and humanities. Paul Kurtz and Corliss Lamont, for example, are philosophers, not scientists. Margaret Sanger and Betty Friedan were radical feminists, not scientists.

Consider also the Bible, the most amazing book in the world. Written over a period of sixteen hundred years by more than forty people, it has a supernatural consistency about it. No other book has been so loved, so hated, so vilified, or so widely and devoutly used as the Bible. From beginning to end, it declares a persistent message: There is a God; He is the uncaused or Fundamental Cause of all things; and He loves us very much. More than nineteen hundred years ago this book was completed. Its pages contain many signs of the supernatural, including hundreds of prophecies that were fulfilled in history. Archeology has confirmed its incredible historical accuracy.[6] To those who have studied it carefully, it bears all the signs of what it claims— divine authorship.

Humanists can muster no scientific proof for God's nonexistence to counterbalance the many evidences of His existence. They certainly cannot offer a single illustration to prove that anything complex has ever come into existence without a designer. The truth is, atheism is a theological and philosophical notion, not a scientific fact. And it is not only bad science but totally *un*scientific.[7]

2. *Evolution*

The biggest hoax of the nineteenth and twentieth centuries is that evolution is a scientific fact. Certainly it is a widely accepted theory of man's origin and development, advanced chiefly by those who reject belief in God, but theories are not scientific fact. The hypothesis that traces man's lineage back to spontaneous generation (life from nonlife, man from ooze and amoebas) has never been sustained. Spontaneous generation has not been scientifically proved, and there is mounting evidence to the contrary.[8] A growing number of nontheistic scientists admit to a startling lack of evidence to support the theory of evolution.[9]

Because the universe came into being before any human was around to witness the event, it is impossible to verify what happened except by the witness of God. In fact, the best evidence for evolution should appear in fossils embedded in rocks, but so many questions arise in this study (paleontology) that even many evolutionary paleontologists put little stock in the fossil record. Basing one's belief in evolution on the shaky ground of paleontology can scarcely be considered scientific.

"The more one studies paleontology," says L. T. More, "the more certain one becomes that evolution is based on faith alone; exactly the same sort of faith which is necessary to have when one encounters the great mysteries of religion. . . . The only alternative is the doctrine of special creation, which may be true, but is irrational."[10]

Dr. David Raup, curator of geology at the Field Museum of Natural History in Chicago, stated that the "250,000 species of plants and animals recorded and deposited in museums throughout the world did not support the gradual unfolding hoped for by Darwin."[11]

Dr. Robert A. Millikan, a physicist and Nobel Prize winner, stated in a speech before the American Chemical Society, "The pathetic thing about it is that many scientists are trying to prove the doctrine of evolution, which no science can do."

Karl Popper, in his autobiography, *Unended Quest*, goes further than Millikan: "I have come to the conclusion that Darwinism is not a testable scientific theory, but a metaphysical research programme—a possible framework for testable scientific theories."[12]

My first experience with evolution probably best illustrates why so many accept as fact such an unscientific theory. In my junior-high biology textbook, I saw with my own eyes a picture of the missing link. As a matter of fact, I saw four of them: photographs of the Java man, the Piltdown man, *Pithecanthropus erectus,* and Peking man. These photos of manlike creatures really shook my faith in the Bible, thus fulfilling the intentions of their humanist inventors.

Subsequent research disclosed that all four of those "missing links" were frauds—nothing more than one or two bones or teeth of humans or animals. From a few bones, scientists or educators made plaster-of-Paris models, photographed them, and put them in our science textbooks.[13] It is no wonder that so many Americans believe that man descended from monkeys, even though not one scientific fact can prove such a fantastic claim.

Two other "proofs" of evolution have since been tossed in the cosmic wastepaper basket: England's peppered moth and Archaeoraptor. Both had been used for many years to brainwash naive school children with the theory of evolution. Now it turns out that both were fakes.

British scientist Cyril Clarke spent twenty-five years investigating the peppered moth and found that H. B. Kettlewell, who once boasted that had Darwin known about these moths "he would have witnessed the consummation and confirmation of his life's work," was dishonest in his presentation of the facts. When humans glue dead moths to trees so birds can eat them, one gets the feeling that the theory is crumbling. The moths that were filmed being eaten by birds were actually bred in the laboratory and placed on tree trunks by Kettlewell. University of Chicago evolutionary biologist, Jerry Coyne, agrees that the peppered moth story, which was "the prize horse in our stable," has to be thrown out.[14]

Chinese paleontologist Xu Xing contends that Archaeoraptor, long used by evolutionists as "proof" that birds evolved from dinosaurs, is a combination of two fossils: one of the body and head of a birdlike creature and the other of the tail of a dinosaur. Xing says he has found another fossil, in a private collection in China, that contains the mirror image of the supposed tail of the Archaeoraptor. *National Geographic* magazine published a note in its March 2000 issue saying that CT scans of the fossil appear to confirm Xing's observations and "revealed anomalies in the fossil's reconstruction."[15] The magazine said details "will be published as soon as the studies are completed."

Translation: We have been lied to again!

Evolutionists want us to believe that a great miracle (spontaneous generation) happened three and one-half billion years ago and that life, contrary to any observable scientific evidence, developed into higher and higher forms until man resulted. This is the supposedly scientific theory that causes humanists to insist man will continue to get better and better.

George Wald acknowledged the bizarre nature of this belief and yet wrote, "One has only to contemplate the magnitude of this task [getting life from nonlife] to concede that the spontaneous generation of a living organism is impossible. Yet here we are—as a result, I believe, of spontaneous generation."[16]

Spontaneous generation is not the conclusion of science but of belief. Wald further admitted that spontaneous generation is a miracle: "Time is in fact the hero of the plot. The time with which we have to deal is of the order of two billion years. What we regard as impossible on the basis of human experiences is meaningless here. Given so much time the 'impossible' becomes possible, the possible probable, and the probable virtually certain. One has only to wait: Time itself performs miracles."[17]

Evolutionists want us to believe that something happened several billion years ago—a biological accident, which man in his most technologically advanced laboratories cannot reproduce today. The process of evolution *demands* a miracle—in fact, several miracles. Dr. Richard Bliss, former professor of biology and science education at Christian Heritage College, has asserted, "The miracles required to make evolution feasible are far greater in number and far harder to believe than the miracle of creation."[18]

Now, if it takes a miracle either way, doesn't it seem more reasonable to believe that those miracles were performed by a Miracle Worker with infinite intelligence? After all, nearly everyone acknowledges that the atom, life,[19] and the whole universe reveal infinite design.

"Everywhere we look," says physicist Paul Davies, "from the far-flung galaxies to the deepest recesses of the atom, we encounter regularity and intricate organization . . . . Moreover, the behavior of physical systems is not haphazard, but lawful and systematic."[20]

The theory of evolution is a philosophy based on faith, not hard scientific fact. "It is," says Phillip Johnson, "sustained largely by a propaganda campaign that relies on all the usual tricks of rhetorical persuasion: hidden assumptions, question-begging statements of what is at issue, terms that are vaguely defined and change their meaning in midargument, attacks on straw men, selective citation of evidence, and so on. The theory is also protected by its cultural importance. It is the officially sanctioned creation story of modern society, and publicly funded educational authorities spare no effort to persuade people to believe in it."[21]

Nancy Pearcey makes the same point when she says, "Darwinism has become our culture's official creation myth, protected by a priesthood as dogmatic as any religious curia."[22] She notes that biology professor Kevin Haley was fired from his teaching position for exposing "students to flaws in evolutionary theory."[23] Little wonder Pearcey subtitles her article "Defenders of Darwinism Resort to Suppressing Data and Teaching Outright Falsehoods."

By contrast, real science is a method of investigation based on the study of cold, hard facts. Therefore, evolution is unscientific!

3. Amorality

During our lifetime the "new morality" has overturned centuries of moral values and created a virtually new lifestyle for millions of people, particularly for those under thirty. That is not to say that preceding generations were moral purists. I spent two years in the Air Force, including one year in Germany, so I know better! But back then, an adulterer or fornicator was labeled *immoral*. Today's generation is *amoral*—without a conscience and denying a Bible-based morality.

In past generations only animals, prostitutes, and moral degenerates could "sleep around," "bed hop," or practice "free love" without feeling guilty about it. But the new morality, spawned in the minds of

God-rejecting secularists, is presented as science. Because it appeals to the baser appetites of mankind while giving him clinical or academic approval to practice his sinful urges, it silences his conscience.

A human being whose conscience has been killed is amoral. Consequently, he is capable of performing like the animal he considers himself to be. It is no trouble for him to be inhumane if inhumanity is thought to be an evolutionary advance. Does that sound like an exaggeration? If so, you have forgotten that the doctors and psychiatrists[24] of the Third Reich advocated and practiced euthanasia (the killing of those considered unfit to live) before Hitler made it state policy.[25] The Nazis could easily practice genocide against the Jews because by 1940 they had already made a practice of eliminating the weak, old, and unwanted.

Not a modern enough illustration for you? Then consider abortion. Nothing shows the amoral influence of humanism like the 1973 decision of the United States Supreme Court to legalize abortion. How could the majority of that august body come to such a low estimation of human life? How could they decide that the unborn is a nonperson? How could any group of humane individuals decide that the answer to a terrible social problem was to slaughter the most innocent and defenseless?

Humanist medical opinion led these judges to make their decision. As Dr. C. Everett Koop noted, "I find it hard to understand why biologists have no trouble recognizing life in worms, frogs, rats, and rabbits, but medical doctors have a difficult time determining when life begins in the highest form of life—human beings." The truth is, these so-called men of science have no problem determining when life begins; they know. But they have a low view of life itself, for they have been taught that life is an accident.

Since 1973, tens of millions of abortions have been performed in America—and that number increases by nearly four thousand each day. At this rate we will soon have to apologize to Adolf Hitler and Joseph Stalin. Margaret Sanger and her Planned Parenthood supporters have already shed more blood than Hitler, and they are fast approaching Stalin. And remember—all this bloodletting is done under the guise of science and eugenics, or, in Sanger's case, to get rid of what she considered the "weeds" of society.

Those who favor abortion-on-demand are not necessarily humanists, but they certainly have been influenced by the view that man is merely an evolving animal. The Bible, by contrast, sets a premium on human life; that is why God gave His only Son for mankind. Jesus told us that human life was worth more than the whole world (Matthew 16:26). Therefore, anyone who favors abortion opposes a biblical view of life and instead favors the views of humanism.

The big lie is that sexual promiscuity or any form of amorality leads to happiness. While it is true that self-gratification may lead to immediate pleasure, invariably it sacrifices the permanent (morals and health) on the altar of the immediate (pleasure and disease). Greece, Rome, and eighteenth-century France were sexually free, but they destroyed their own culture by their sin. Ask the 56 million Americans who are infected with a sexually transmitted disease if that disease brings them pleasure or fun.[26] Individually as well as nationally, fleshly self-indulgence breeds misery and death.

The Bible teaches, "Happy is he that *hears* the word of God and *keeps* it" (see Luke 11:28). A survey I once conducted of thirty-four hundred Christian married people revealed the highest sexual-satisfaction level of any survey to date. It also showed that those who were virgins at the time of marriage registered a higher satisfaction level than those who were not.

And the response to my book *The Unhappy Gays* surprised even me. My counseling of homosexuals had convinced me that they were anything but gay, enduring more loneliness and heartache than "straight" men and women and sustaining a higher incidence of suicide. I expected to get quite a bit of hate mail—and I did receive some—but to my surprise, homosexuals themselves responded favorably by ten to one. One man, the superintendent of a fourteen-thousand-acre park in one of the nation's largest cities, read the book and told an associate of mine that the people in his park naturally congregate into four groups: Hispanics, blacks, Caucasians, and homosexuals. He also said that through the years the only area from which he had to haul out the bodies of suicide victims was the homosexual section.

Only the blind deny that perversion leads to wretchedness.

One need not be a scientist to deduce that homosexuality does not produce happiness. It is really a shame that humanists cannot be forced to take the responsibility for their faulty teaching that homosexuality is "gay" or "just as good as straight." This simply is not true—and it is not scientific! "Homosexuality is not hereditary, according to a new study that casts doubt on the work of a National Cancer Institute researcher who claimed to have discovered a 'gay gene,'" said a recent story in the *Washington Times*. "These results do not support an X-linked gene underlying male homosexuality," lead author, Dr. George Rice, a neurologist at the University of Western Ontario, said of the study published in the journal *Science*.[27]

And with the latest findings on the human genome, the "gay gene" theory is further compromised. Says Jennifer Kabbany, "The human genome finally has been sequenced, and with that, one theory seems to have fallen from favor—that of the 'gay gene.' Ideas about the origins of sexual preferences are reverting to the argument that homosexuality is a decision rather than an inherited trait."[28]

If you wish to see a snapshot of where humanism takes a country, look no further than Holland, and especially Amsterdam. The place is now called "Sodom among the tulips."[29] Amsterdam is the sex and drugs capital of Europe; worldwide, it's second only to Bangkok. Hear how Don Feder describes the situation: "Running along the canals in Amsterdam's old city is an area roughly a mile in length crammed with porn shops, live-sex shows, bikini-clad hookers behind glass doors, and coffee houses selling pot, hash, and psychedelic mushrooms."[30]

Feder makes the following telling observation: "The Netherlands has the lowest church attendance in Europe, itself the most secular continent. Many of Amsterdam's beautiful churches have been turned into museums; others are municipal offices."[31] He also rightly notes that "if America were ruled by a triumvirate of Larry Flynt, the Mayflower Madam, and the late Dr. Timothy Leary, it would look pretty much like Amsterdam today."

Amsterdam, of course, isn't the only place where the amorality of humanism has taken a terrible toll. Sweden has its own sad story to tell. Back in the early '60s, Sweden was presented as the ideal society—humanist, sexually liberated, and socialist. A number of our sex-education courses were modeled after theirs. Current reports reveal that Sweden has the highest suicide rate in the world. Venereal disease and drunkenness are rampant, and the people have lost all hope for change.

A recent television documentary presented an interview with several Swedish youth, none of whom expressed any interest in getting married, having children, or securing a job; none had any hope for the future. On the other end of the spectrum, the despair of the elderly was appalling. Interviews with both young and old made clear the common dread of growing old. Senior citizens acknowledged an endless struggle between another meaningless, boring day of life and the legal right to commit suicide.

We need not look to other countries, however, to refute the unscientific claim of humanism that amorality leads to happiness. All we have to do is ask the young men who are impotent due to venereal disease or the promiscuous girls who underwent hysterectomies to save their lives. Or consider the report from Ohio State University that indicated a *higher* divorce rate among couples who had lived together for at least three years before marriage than among those who had not.

The silence of sex educators on the dangers of venereal disease is not only unscientific but borders on the criminal. Dr. Rhoda L. Lorand, a practicing New York City psychotherapist with prestigious academic qualifications, has written an indictment of modern sex educators for their silence on the growing problem of cancer of the cervix among sexually promiscuous girls. In a paper titled "The Betrayal of Youth," she quoted prominent medical research, pointing out the little-known fact that, at the same time the government was advocating contraceptives (without parental consent) for children aged ten to fourteen, doctors were discovering teenage promiscuity can increase a girl's vulnerability to cancer by as much as *five times*.[32] Dr. Lorand stated:

One does not have to be a religious fanatic to recognize nature's message; the vulnerable immature reproductive system of the pubescent and adolescent girls is at risk of being prematurely damaged by prematurely engaging in the adult sexual activity of coitus.

Moreover, multiple partners do not appear to be part of nature's design for the human species, as research on males confirms. Promiscuous boys and men risk becoming cancer-carriers, giving cervical cancer to women. In 1966, Dr. Clyde E. Martin presented these findings in a paper entitled "Marital and Coital Factors in Cervical Cancer" at the annual meeting of the American Public Health Association. Dr. Martin's research revealed that women whose husbands were involved in extramarital coitus showed a much higher incidence of cervical cancer than those whose husbands were faithful.[33]

Dr. Irving I. Kessler of Johns Hopkins found that "extramarital sexual practice by either the woman or her spouse is also associated with cervical cancer risk."[34] The process is not as yet understood, but it is clear that promiscuity is the central factor. Venereal disease—for this generation a rapidly escalating menace—is a consequence of humanist propaganda.

Dr. Lorand added another interesting comment: "Other investigators have discovered that the disease is almost non-existent in nuns, whereas there is a high rate of cervical cancer in prostitutes."[35]

Evidently, morality is good for your heath, whereas amorality can shorten your life span. AIDS reduces the average life expectancy by almost 50 percent. Twenty-year-old active homosexuals are finding it difficult to live past the age of forty. While humanist philosophers may be silent on the implications of amoral behavior, scientists should not be so taciturn. They should mount a serious campaign to warn teenagers that promiscuity leads to cancer, that abortion may well lead to cancer, and that homosexual activity leads to an early death.

Scientists should certainly look at the Best Friends/Diamond Girls program, a curriculum-based program for girls in the fifth to eighth grades that teaches self-respect and self-restraint, and compare its results with those of humanist programs. Out of a recent study of 2,631 Diamond Girls:

- 59 percent were asked out on a date;

- 3 percent had sexual intercourse;

- less than 1 percent became pregnant;

- 77 percent say they plan to delay sex until after high school and 75 percent until marriage;

- 14 percent were offered illegal drugs, while 3 percent used them;

- 22 percent drank beer, liquor, or wine coolers, and 11 percent smoked cigarettes.[36]

For the Diamond Girls who completed the program (offered in ninety public schools in twenty-six cities), 100 percent graduated from high school.

A program like this should be in every school in every district in America. But it will not be. Why not? Because the program emphasizes "the joys of the preteen and teen-age years free of the complications of sexual activity."[37] Such a goal runs counter to the humanist idea of sexual freedom. It appears to resemble the biblical Christian moral code, and because that code is religious, it is prohibited in the classroom.

The truth is, amorality does not provide a happy, fulfilling life. Its hallmarks are disease, discouragement, and death. To claim otherwise is unscientific.

4. AUTONOMOUS MAN

All notions about man being autonomous, self-actualized, and capable of solving his personal problems are based on the unscientific principle that man is basically good by nature.

As every Christian knows, that is contrary to biblical teaching: "there is none good" (Mark 10:18, KJV). "All have sinned, and come short of the glory of God" (Romans 3:23, KJV). "The heart is deceitful . . . and desperately wicked" (Jeremiah 17:9). Jesus began one of His commentaries, "You then, being evil" (Matthew 7:11). The Bible consistently assumes the sinfulness of man is due to the Fall. Humanists, however, categorize the Fall as myth and insist that man is evolving godlike goodness.

Unfortunately for the humanist, the "goodness of man" cannot stand up to scientific scrutiny. As G. K. Chesterton observed, the Christian doctrine of the Fall is one doctrine that can be proved scientifically. The front pages of any newspaper proclaim man's inhumanity to man. If man is inherently good, then he ought to reflect that goodness by the way he lives. We should have abundant empirical evidence of man's goodness.

Some humanists are beginning to realize that history is against their theory. Fredrick E. Edwards, director of the California chapter of the American Humanist Association, said in a published interview in the *San Diego Evening Tribune*: "Humanists no longer have the extravagant faith they had in the 17th and 18th century Age of Enlightenment in man's ability to create a perfect world. I think cold, hard reality has thrown cold water on some of those naive illusions. We may be finding that our powers are limited and that we're not such perfectly wonderful creatures after all."[38]

The best way to judge the quality of human nature is to examine what it does when it is free and unrestrained—and history proves that unrestrained man has a natural penchant for criminality and inhumanity. In fact, the humanists are having a terrible time explaining Thornhill and Palmer's *A Natural History of Rape*. This work explains that rape is merely natural selection at work. "In short," says Nancy Pearcey, "Darwinism and its unpalatable moral implications are a package deal; protest, and you invite a return to the theistic worldview."[39]

It is impossible to read an 850-page work such as *The Black Book of Communism: Crimes, Terror, Repression* and come away with the idea that man is basically good. Highly educated Marxist V. I. Lenin wrote out instructions to hang "at least 100 kulaks, publish their names, seize all their grain, do all this so that for miles around people see it all, understand it, tremble, and tell themselves that we are killing the bloodthirsty kulaks and that we will continue to do so."[40]

"The First World War," says Carroll Quigley, "was a catastrophe of such magnitude that, even today, the imagination has some difficulty grasping it. In the year 1916, in two battles (Verdun and the Somme) casualties of over 1,700,000 were suffered by both sides. . . . Later, on an 11-mile front at Passchendaele, the British fired 4,250,000 shells in a preliminary barrage, and lost 400,000 men in the ensuing infantry assault. . . . On all fronts in the whole war almost 13,000,000 men in the various armed forces died from wounds and disease."[41]

Quigley's analysis of such slaughter drove him to the following conclusion: "To a people who believed in the innate goodness of man, in inevitable [evolutionary] progress, in the community of interests, and in evil as merely the absence of good, the First World War, with its millions of persons dead and its billions of dollars wasted, was a blow so terrible as to be beyond human ability to comprehend. As a matter of fact, no real success was achieved in comprehending it."[42]

Man tends to selfishness or egoism, not goodness, but the humanists refuse to acknowledge that. One would think the reports now coming out of the former Soviet Union, Cambodia, South Vietnam, North Korea, Cuba, China, Uganda, Rwanda, and Kosovo, and the dozens of wars being conducted nearly every week would convince the humanists. But just as they refused to heed the testimony of Dr. Tom Dooley (written into the *Congressional Record*) regarding unbelievably barbaric Communist Chinese and North Korean tortures, they refuse to concede that unrestrained man is notoriously inhumane.

If man is, in fact, innately good, humanists should be able to scientifically prove it. We are still awaiting such proof. This article of humanistic faith, like the others, is unscientific.

5. Global Socialism

Socialism has proven to be a classic failure in every country or region in which it has been tried (Russia, China, Eastern Europe, Africa, Cuba, and the welfare state in the United States). Socialism demotivates individuals and causes them to underproduce, plunging millions into a second-rate, despairing way of life.

It is well known that during the era of the Soviet Union, peasants grew better and bigger crops on their tiny, privately owned gardens than were produced in the great, government-owned-and-controlled cooperatives.

State socialism has proved to be so demotivating that even the Chinese communists have started to experiment with some free-enterprise policies in an attempt to increase their productivity. The only people still enamored by socialism are American humanists, who have never lived under it.

One conservative economist, educated in the late 1960s and early 1970s, surprised me when I asked how he had escaped the clutches of the socialist, one-world view. "I didn't," he replied. "I used to be a social liberal, but five years ago I took a three-week trip to the Soviet Union. That opened my eyes."

Perhaps all Ph.D.'s need to visit Cuba for three weeks, hoping for such a cure. Unfortunately, that trip would not improve the tunnel vision of many humanists, who doggedly preserve their unscientific obsession with world socialism. They willfully forget that the socialistic revolutions of the twentieth century alone resulted in the murder of between 170 and 360 *million* human beings.[43] Hear the cry of the men, women, and children who were "shot, beaten, tortured, knifed, burned, starved, frozen, crushed, or worked to death; buried alive, drowned, hung, bombed, or killed in any other of the myriad ways governments have inflicted death on unarmed, helpless citizens and foreigners."[44]

Africa today has twenty-seven dictators, most of them ruthless and inhumane, although not as excessive as Idi Amin and Jomo Kenyatta. The latter, remember, served as a professor at Columbia University, teaching thousands of educators, who in turn educate the teachers of our children.

Here is a simple test to prove that socialism has failed to provide the freedom, liberty, and prosperity that its proponents have predicted for two hundred years: How many human beings are clamoring to gain citizenship in communist countries? How many people in Miami, Florida, are throwing inner tubes into the Atlantic Ocean and heading for Cuba?

Rarely does anyone set out for countries that repress the people and that implement elaborate "Big Brother" security systems to keep people from escaping. If the so-called worker's paradise is such a paradise, why does it not open its borders and let its people choose whether to stay or leave?

Humanist-inspired socialism is a scientific failure, as is the total humanist worldview—including every one of its basic articles of faith.

Darwinian Brainwashing

But if this is true—if humanism is really completely unscientific—then why do so many intelligent educators endorse it completely? We think the answer is that they've been brainwashed.

"Darwinian medicine is revolutionizing the way physicians combat public-health problems," shouted a paid advertisement in the December 9, 1999, edition of the *Oklahoma Daily*. The ad was signed by 124 scientists and historians of science from the University of Oklahoma.

How could 124 of Oklahoma's finest be so deceived about a theory that has placed millions of human beings in the grave and will place millions more there in the new century? We believe they have been brainwashed by the Darwinian philosophy of John Dewey, the father of so-called progressive education, and his legion of followers.[45] The 124 Oklahoma scientists who signed a petition to the governor of Oklahoma protesting the softening of Darwinian teaching in the classroom illustrates just how effective Dewey has been.

Long before the 55 million children in our American school system are old enough to understand or examine humanism for themselves, already they are convinced it is scientific. After all, their teachers told them Darwinian evolution is scientific; that the philosophy of naturalism is scientific; that moral relativism is based on Einstein's theory of relativity; that "scientific socialism" is based on the social sciences; that society and law are evolving along with the human animal and hence are scientific; that all left wing, environmental, collectivistic, statist policies are firmly based on the physical and social sciences and not on the myth of religion; and finally, that everything related to the Bible is prescientific gibberish. If you were served such an educational smorgasbord, we bet you would believe that humanism is scientific, too.

The truly amazing thing is that 87 percent of the American people, according to a 1991 Gallup poll, believe in some kind of creation by the God of the universe. They certainly did not learn *that* in public school!

Honest educators must answer one question: Is it education or brainwashing to teach young people that something unscientific is really scientific? Until educators in the public school system awaken to the fraud they are perpetrating, humanists will continue to dominate them and force them to disseminate unsupported and unscientific dogma.

8

HUMANISM IS A RELIGION

Here are all the elements for a religious faith that shall not be confined to sect, class, or race. Such a faith has always been implicitly the common faith of mankind. It remains to make it explicit and militant.

JOHN DEWEY

Even though humanists through the decades have freely admitted the religious nature of their faith, many people are still under the delusion that it is philosophy, an expression of science, or an academic theory, and thus worthy of dissemination in tax-supported educational institutions. Under the guise of science, humanism has been granted a reputable position in American society.

The truth is, humanism is unmistakably and demonstrably a religion. One need merely visit the second edition of *A World Religions Reader* to note the prominence given to Secular Humanism as one of the world's religions. Indeed, in a list of the world's religions—Hinduism, Buddhism, Shintoism, Judaism, Christianity, Islam, and Sikhism, Secular Humanism is at the top.[1] We hope the following facts will motivate you to expose it and oppose it vigorously in your city, state, and nation.

Humanists Call It a Religion

Roy Wood Sellars, author of the 1933 *Humanist Manifesto* and a former president of the New York chapter of the American Humanist Association, wrote a book as far back as 1918 titled *The Next Step in Religion.* In it he said, "The coming phase of religion will reflect man's power over nature and his moral courage in the face of the facts and possibilities of life. It will be a religion of action and passion, a social religion, a religion of goals and prospects. It will be a free man's religion, a religion for an adult and aspiring democracy."[2]

Sellars was never reticent about calling humanism a religion. In fact, ten years later he wrote another book, *Religion Coming of Age,* and stated rather matter-of-factly, "The present book is an attempt to show the import of this recent development for religion. Its keynote is the union of humanism and naturalism. The spiritual must be natural-ized and humanized; but it is equally true that the scientific view of the world requires deepening and illumination. Moreover, human and social evolution must be taken seriously and fitted into the scheme of things. . . . A religion founded on realities is a religion coming of age."[3]

To remove all doubt as to whether Sellars was placing Religious Humanism on the same level as the Christian religion, we quote: "Now I am convinced that the humanistic religion into which Christianity will gradually be transformed will correct this mistake."[4]

A few years later another humanist, Charles Francis Potter, wrote *Humanism: A New Religion*. In that work Potter said, "So Humanism is not simply another denomination of Protestant Christianity; it is not a creed; nor is it a cult. It is a new type of religion altogether."[5] This is the same Potter who admitted founding the first humanist church in New York City and in 1933 attached his name, along with that of John Dewey, to the *Humanist Manifesto*. He is also the one who admitted, "Education is the most powerful ally of Humanism, and every American public school is a school of Humanism. What can the theistic Sunday Schools, meeting for an hour once a week, and teaching only a fraction of the chil-dren, do to stem the tide of a five-day program of humanistic teaching?"[6]

The same year the *Humanist Manifesto I* emerged, Potter wrote *Humanizing Religion*. In that work he said, "When eleven eminent pro-fessors of philosophy, theology, economics, medicine, and sociology, and twenty-three other leaders in editorial, literary, educational, and reli-gious fields come out publicly over their own signatures and confess to belief in a new religion called Humanism, and state fifteen theses [doc-trines] upon which they all agree, then something of more than ordi-nary importance in religious circles has occurred."[7]

One year later John Dewey called for a new religion. He titled his work *A Common Faith* and frankly stated, "Here are all the elements for a religious faith that shall not be confined to sect, class, or race. Such a faith has always been implicitly the common faith of mankind. It remains to make it explicit and militant."[8] The 1933, 1973, and 2000 *Humanist Manifestos* have all made humanism explicit. The NEA has made it militant and the basis of public education.[9]

Tolbert H. McCarroll, executive director of *The Humanist* magazine, the official organ of the American Humanist Association, wrote an article titled "Religions of the Future." In it he envisioned four major religions and predicted that the one designated as "private humanism" would be the "largest religious body of the future."[10]

Lloyd Morain, former president of the American Humanist Association, stated, "Down through the ages men have been seeking a universal religion or way of life. . . . Humanism . . . shows promise of becoming a great world faith. Humanists are content with fixing their attention on this life and on this earth. Theirs is a religion without a god, divine revelation, or sacred scriptures. Yet theirs is a faith rich in feeling and understanding. . . . We may now note several facts about this rapidly growing philosophy and religion."[11] Incidentally, Morain titled chapter one "The Fourth Faith" (Protestantism, Catholicism, and Judaism being the other three). Clearly, with humanism we are talking the language of religion.

Another humanist leader, Edwin H. Wilson, admitted, "Many well-known thinkers have given voice to the hope of Religious Humanism that a comprehensive world religion will develop through the creative processes of our times. Roy Wood Sellars in 1928 held humanism to be the next step in religion. John Dewey, in his book, *A Common Faith*, believed that we have all the materials available for such a faith. Sir Julian Huxley predicts that the next great religion of the world will be some form of humanism."[12]

Elsewhere Wilson said, "The popular notion that religion is identical and exclusively concerned with God, immortality, and revelation is denied in the writings of Curtis Reese, J. A. C. F. Auer, E. E. Ames, H. N. Wieman, Alfred Loisy, Julian Huxley, A. E. Haydon, and many others."[13]

Wilson's reference to Curtis Reese is obviously to Reese's series of humanist sermons. In 1926 Reese edited a series titled *Humanism*, which contained the sermon "Humanizing Religion."[14] A year later he edited another series, *Humanist Sermons*. In 1931 he wrote *Humanist Religion*, in which he said, "Today, as never before, Humanism is making itself felt in religious circles."[15]

Henry Nelson Wieman, a signatory of *Humanist Manifesto I*, wrote a textbook (along with Bernard Eugene Meland) titled *American Philosophies of Religion*. Not surprising, humanism was included in the work. "As a theory of religion," state the authors, "religious humanism may be said to be the culmination of the gradual shift in theological and philosophical thinking from the God-ward to the man-ward side of religious thought."[16]

Harvard University Press got involved when it published Herbert Wallace Schneider's *Religion in 20th Century America*. Again, humanism was included as a religion. Says Schneider, "Intellectually humanism has not yet achieved an orthodoxy of its own, though humanist creeds are being circulated, and a 'fourth faith' is in the making."[17]

But leave it to the lawyers to make a great case for humanism as a religion. ACLU lawyer Leo Pfeffer, Humanist of the Year for 1988, presents the case. "In this arena [college arena], it is not Protestantism, Catholicism, or Judaism which will emerge the victor," he wrote, "but Secular Humanism, a cultural force which in many respects is stronger in the United States than any of the major religious groups or any alliance among them."[18] Pfeffer places humanism squarely among the religions of the world.

And so did Julian Huxley, former president of the British Humanist Association and a signatory of *Humanist Manifesto II*. In his 1957 book, *Religion Without Revelation*, Huxley stated, "Twentieth-century man needs a new organ for dealing with destiny, a new system of beliefs . . . in other words, a new religion."[19]

Huxley reached this conclusion, according to Norman L. Geisler, while browsing through a library in Colorado Springs, Colorado. Says Geisler, "Huxley came across some essays by Lord Morley in which he found these words: 'The next great task of science will be to create a religion for humanity.' Huxley was challenged by this vision. He wrote, 'I was fired by sharing his conviction that science would of necessity play an essential part in framing any religion of the future worthy of the name.'"[20] Huxley called his religion "Evolutionary Humanism," the *de facto* faith of America's public schools.

The first official humanist organization in America was the Society for Ethical Culture, founded in 1879 by Felix Adler, a former rabbi and professor at Columbia University. Thirty additional societies were soon formed, and in 1889, Dr. Adler formed a national federation of these societies. In 1896, the Ethical Movement, or Religious or Secular Humanist Movement, as it later came to be known, went international.[21]

The religious nature of this original humanist organization becomes evident in the following statement appearing in the publication *Ethical Culture Today*: "Ethical Culture is listed as a religion in the Census of Religious Bodies published by the Federal Government, and in various religious publications and general reference works. Federal tax exemption rulings have been issued to the American Ethical Societies."[22]

By the late seventies James K. Uphoff offered a broad definition of religion that "envisions religion as any faith or set of values to which an individual gives ultimate loyalty. . . . Ethical Culture, Secularism, Humanism, Scientism . . . illustrate this concept of religion."[23]

The religious nature of humanism is apparent even in a letter which appeared in a recent newspaper column of Abby Van Buren: "I am a Humanist minister from the Humanist Society of Friends whose celebrants, ministers, chaplains, counselors and pastors are all Secular Humanists. You can find us throughout the United States and Canada. For details, your readers can call the American Humanist Association toll-free number: (800) 743-6646, or e-mail them at humanism@juno.com. I have performed nonreligious weddings, funerals and naming ceremonies since 1963, when I first obtained my license from the state of Ohio to solemnize marriages. My state license is identical to that of any other clergy."[24]

The *Dallas Morning News* printed an article on the North Texas Church of Freethought and referred to it as "the nation's largest atheist congregation."[25] According to the article, "the church offers atheists, humanists and other 'free thinkers' many of the same things that theistic places of worship provide."[26]

Humanism is indeed a religion and has been since its inception.

Humanist Bibles Call It a Religion

Nine times the *Humanist Manifesto I* plainly calls the beliefs it espouses a religion. For instance: "Humanism is a philosophical, religious and moral point of view as old as human civilization itself."[27]

Discarding traditional religion as having lost its significance and being "powerless to solve the problems of human living in the twentieth century," *Manifesto I* calls for "a break with the past" and the establishment of a "vital, fearless, and frank religion capable of furnishing adequate goals and personal satisfactions." Naturally, that religion is humanism. The *Manifesto* then lays out fifteen tenets of its religion, concluding with the words, "So stand the theses of Religious Humanism."

Manifesto II makes it clear that man serves as his own God: "as nontheists we begin with humans not God, nature not deity." Calling traditional religions an obstacle to human progress, this manifesto, which rejects the revelation of God in the Scriptures, speaks with an authority that comes either from an all-knowing deity or an all-consuming ego—and that is what humanism really is: human ego gone mad. So the work bluntly states, "No Deity will save us; we must save ourselves."

In a *Free Inquiry* editorial speaking to the question "Is Secular Humanism a religion?" editor Paul Kurtz frankly admits, "The organized humanist movement in America is put in a quandary; for the Fellowship of Religious Humanists, the American Ethical Union, and the Society for Humanistic Judaism consider themselves to be religious. Even the American Humanist Association, which has both religious and nonreligious members and is often considered to be a 'naturalistic humanist' association, has a *religious* tax exemption."[28]

In a later editorial, Kurtz again mentioned that the American Humanist Association has a religious tax exemption. Said Kurtz, "The American Humanist Association still retains its religious exemption, despite an erroneous 1990 announcement that its tax status had changed; in any event AHA continues to emphasize that its Counselor program is religious and performs 'pastoral' and 'ministerial' duties."[29]

In 1993 the *Harvard University Gazette* openly admitted that humanism is indeed a religion. "When first year students voluntarily indicate their religious affiliations during registration each year, fewer than 200 check off humanism [as their religion],"[30] the paper said.

For the record, Harvard is not the only university admitting that humanism is a religion. The Student Directory of Auburn University for 1985–1986 includes a list of Auburn pastors and campus ministers. On page 11, "humanist" is mentioned, along with Baptists, Catholics, Episcopalians, Lutherans, Methodists, and Jews. The directory notes that Dr. Delos McKown was the humanist counselor on campus.[31] (McKown is still a senior editor of *Free Inquiry* magazine.) The University of Arizona's 1990–1991 Student Handbook lists humanists under "Religious Services," among such groups as Ambassadors for Christ, American Baptist Campus Ministry, Baha'i, Baptist Student Union, Campus Crusade for Christ, Hillel Foundation, Islamic Center, and The Navigators.[32]

Likewise, the University of Minnesota's 1995 listing of student organizations places atheists and humanists under "Religious," along with the Buddhist Association, Baptist Student Union, Campus Crusade for Christ, Christian Student Fellowship, etc. Since then, humanists have decided to list themselves instead in the "Political and Social Action" section of the university's student guidebook. Why? Everyone involved in the switch from "Religious" to "Political and Social Action" knows it was done to fool naive freshmen.

But ask yourself this: Why didn't the atheists and humanists list themselves under the "Scientific" section?

United States Supreme Court
Calls It a Religion

In 1961 humanism was officially recognized as a religion. Corliss Lamont describes the famous *Torcaso v. Watkins* case from the humanist perspective:

> The U.S. Supreme Court took official cognizance of Religious Humanism in the case of Roy R. Torcaso, a Humanist who was refused his

commission as a Notary Public under a Maryland law requiring all public officials in the state to profess belief in God. In delivering the unanimous opinion of the Court that this statute was unconstitutional under the First Amendment, Justice Hugo L. Black observed: "Among religions in this country which do not teach what is generally to be considered a belief in the existence of God are Buddhism, Taoism, Ethical Culture, Secular Humanism, and others."[33]

The *Texas Tech Law Review* states that "The Seeger decision defined religion as all sincere beliefs based upon a power or being or upon a faith, to which all else is subordinate or upon which all else is ultimately dependent." Thus, according to Seeger, religion "includes atheists, agnostics, as well as adherents to rational theism."

Such court decisions may account for Webster's dictionary definition of religion, which includes "any system of belief, practices, ethical values, etc., resembling, suggestive of, or likened to such a system [humanism as a religion]."

In the *Texas Tech Law Review*, attorney John W. Whitehead and former Congressman John Conlan published a lengthy article titled "The Establishment of Religion of Secular Humanism and Its First Amendment Implications." These lawyers cited several court decisions that have ruled or referred to humanism as a religion. For example, "One Federal Court in Reed v. Van Hoven has held that 'In light of the decided cases, the public schools, as between theistic and humanistic religions, must carefully avoid any program of indoctrination in ultimate values.'"[34] Obviously, this judge considered both theism and humanism to be religions.

Thomas Jefferson Called Unbelief a Religion

We tend to think that belief in God is a religion and therefore disbelief is not a religion. Actually, it is more accurate to say that one's view of God—whatever it might be—is a religious belief. Atheists believe in the religion of atheism.

Thomas Jefferson, writer of the Declaration of Independence, clearly understood this. During debate over the separation of church and state—which ultimately led to the First Amendment—he defined religion to include "all believers or unbelievers of the Bible." This principle applies equally to believers or unbelievers in God.

Therefore, according to Thomas Jefferson's thesis, if belief and its accompanying biblical moral values are expelled from our public schools, so also should be ejected humanist unbelief and its resultant amorality.

Humanism Is a Religious Worldview

All religious worldviews are based on teachings that relate to God, origins, man, values, and the future life. As we have seen, humanism has constructed a well-defined worldview:

- belief in no God;

- belief in matter as eternal;

- belief in spontaneous generation;

- belief in man as an evolving animal;

- belief in no moral absolutes;

- belief in humanist man as the final authority;

- belief in the innate goodness and malleability of man;

- belief in no soul or spirit;

- belief in new sexual rights and responsibilities;

- belief in no eternal law;

- belief in humanist rule (which they call "democracy");

- belief in a one-world socialistic government;

- belief in no judgment or afterlife.

The religious worldview of humanism is so well-defined[35] that if it were expelled from our public schools and its disciples were retired from government service through the ballot box, they would immediately declare themselves a religion and enjoy their tax-exempt religious status.

They cannot do so now because they receive billions of dollars annually to operate their vast network of churches, schools, colleges, and universities. Why should they collect donations to support the propagation of their religion when, through our taxes, we pay for everything?

Whitehead and Conlan describe the issue in these words:

> While Secular Humanism is nontheistic, it is religious because it directs itself toward religious beliefs and practices, that are in active opposition to traditional theism. Humanism is a doctrine centered solely on human interests or values. Therefore, humanism deifies Man collectively and individually, whereas theism worships God. Moreover, while humanism draws its values and absolutes from the finite reasoning of relativistic Man, theism has received its values and absolutes through the revelation of the infinite Deity or Creator. Both theism and humanism worship their own "god." The difference is the object of worship, not the act. Therefore, Secular Humanism is a religion whose doctrine worships Man as the source of all knowledge and truth, whereas theism worships God as the source of all knowledge and truth.[36]

Humanism Must Be Accepted by Faith

Christians have never denied that its followers accept its teachings by faith. This is not done blindly or irrationally but is the result of using our minds, wills, and hearts in response to the revelation God has provided in the Bible. Faith comes by hearing the Word of God and then basing our reasoning on it. That is what God meant when He said through the prophet, "Come now, and let us reason together, saith the LORD" (Isaiah 1:18, KJV).

The humanist religion is likewise accepted purely by faith. In fact, Corliss Lamont concludes his book with these words: "For his great achievements man, utilizing the resources and the laws of Nature, yet without Divine aid, can take full credit. Similarly, for his shortcomings he must take full responsibility. Humanism assigns to man nothing less than the task of being his own savior and redeemer."[37] That concept, like every other in humanism, is totally unprovable scientifically and thus must be accepted by faith.

It is true that Christianity is a religious belief based on faith. But then, so is Islam, Confucianism, and every other religion in the world, including Secular Humanism.

No one has made this point clearer than Irving Kristol: "Merely because it incorporates the word 'secular' in its self-identification does not mean that it cannot be seriously viewed as a competitive religion— though its adherents resent and resist any such ascription."[38] Again, "Secular humanism is more than science, because it proceeds to make all kinds of inferences about the human condition and human possibilities that are not, in any authentic sense, scientific. Those inferences are metaphysical and in the end theological. . . . It is secular humanism that is the orthodox metaphysical-theological basis of the two modern political philosophies, socialism and liberalism. The two are continuous across the secular humanist spectrum, with socialism being an atheistic, messianic extreme while liberalism is an agnostic, melioristic version."[39]

Kristol further warns us that at the root of moral chaos is the spiritual disarray brought about by humanism. "If there is one indisputable fact about the human condition," says Kristol, "it is that no community can survive if it is persuaded—or even if it suspects—that its members are leading meaningless lives in a meaningless universe."[40] Kristol concludes: "Secular humanism is brain dead even as its heart continues to pump energy into all of our institutions."

Humanism Is Rooted in Religion

Although humanism as a system began in Greece four centuries before Christ, the Greeks did not originate the religion's basic ideas. Such teachings can be traced to Confucius, Buddha, and even to Babylon, the vile source of all pagan religions. Even Lamont acknowledges the polytheistic origin of humanism.[41]

Because humanists themselves freely admit their teachings originated in pagan religions, we may conclude that humanism is a religion—particularly when we notice that it has maintained many of the concepts found in these religions. Humanism is as much a religion as Buddhism, Islam, or Christianity. In fact, there are really only two kinds of religion in the world, biblical and pagan:

BIBLICAL (Wisdom of God)	PAGAN (Wisdom of Man)
Judaism	Confucianism
Christianity	Buddhism
	Islam
	Babylonian Mysticism
	Humanism

One religion in particular, Unitarianism, has done more to advance the humanist cause in America than any other. Unitarianism broke from Christianity over the essential deity of Jesus Christ. Like humanists, Unitarians believe Jesus to be merely human.

Unitarianism gained prominence in Europe due to its liberal view of God, reducing Him to an impersonal Source of all things. It also taught the autonomy and self-sufficiency of man, who served as captain of his own fate.

Many Americans embraced Unitarianism during the eighteenth century, but it was not until 1825 that the Unitarians formally broke away from the Congregational Church and founded their own denomination. Many leading Unitarians today serve as leaders in the humanist movement, and some have belonged to the same Ethical Cultural Societies. Unitarians made up 25 percent of those who signed *Humanist Manifesto I*.[42] A sermon preached in 1925 by the Reverend John H. Dietrich also showed "how Unitarianism had naturally laid the basis for Humanism."[43]

By the twentieth century, higher criticism had so influenced Unitarianism that its members' deistic beliefs were hardly discernible from the humanist position. Unitarianism is largely and significantly humanistic, for it accepts four of the doctrines of humanism—evolution, amorality, autonomy, and a socialist one-world government. The only difference between them is that one embraces deism and the other atheism. In other words, a Unitarian Sunday school teacher can promote nearly all his religious beliefs in the public school by labeling them "education," "Secular Humanism," or "Scientific Humanism." Monday through Friday taxpayer dollars pay him to do so—the religious fraud of the century!

Humanism Is a Way of Life

Early Christians were often called "followers of The Way" because their religious beliefs caused them to live in a particular fashion. So it is with humanism.

One leading humanist, Lloyd Morain, past president of the American Humanist Association, claimed that humanism had doubled in each of the last few years. He then boasted that an increasing number of Protestants, Jews, and Catholics were beginning to follow this way of life.

The fact that humanism *is* a way of life—just like any other religion—provides further evidence that it should be classified as a religion.

Humanism Inspires Missionary Zeal

The late Dr. Mary Calderone, leading humanist and radical sex-education advocate, at seventy years of age continued to travel more than a hundred thousand miles a year to preach the humanist gospel. I can personally appreciate the toll such a schedule takes on a person, for I have traveled several times that amount annually for thirty years, conducting Family Life Seminars. Humanists make similar sacrifices because they have a missionary zeal to propagate their religion.

For years we could not understand why individuals with doctorates would spend their lives traveling the country, teaching permissive sex to anyone who would listen. It did not appear to make sense. But according to Dr. James M. Parsons, a Florida psychiatrist, "They are trying to create such an obsession with sex among our young people that they have no time or interest in spiritual pursuits."[44]

Secular Humanists devote themselves to years of sex-education instruction, not because sexual function is so complex—it is not—but because it takes years to undermine the traditional sexual ethic found in most American families. Their dedication can easily be explained when we understand that humanism is a religion and that its educational high priests are driven with a missionary zeal.

Listen to the zeal of their pronouncements: "The battle for humankind's future must be waged and won in the public school classroom by teachers who correctly perceive their role as the proselytizers of a new faith: a religion of humanity that recognizes and respects the spark of what theologians call divinity in every human being. These teachers must embody the same selfless dedication as the most rabid fundamentalist preachers, for they will be ministers of another sort, utilizing a classroom instead of a pulpit to convey humanist values in whatever subject they teach, regardless of the educational level—preschool day care or large state university. The classroom must and will become an arena of conflict between the old and the new—the rotting corpse of Christianity, together with all its adjacent evils and misery, and the new faith of humanism, resplendent in its promise of a world in which the never-realized Christian ideal of 'love thy neighbor' will finally be achieved."[45]

Until the American people realize that humanism is a religion, not simply a naive philosophy or modern educational theory, the humanists will continue their siege on the minds of our children. Once humanism is identified as the most dangerous religion in the world and expelled legally from our public schools, it will collapse under its own weight, for the American people—particularly parents—will never agree to subsidize the spiritual destruction of their children.

Revelation at the White House

The inability of many Christian leaders to understand the dangers of Religious, Secular, or Planetary Humanism can be best illustrated by an astonishing experience I had back in 1980. Twelve ministers—most of them prominent television and radio preachers—were invited to have breakfast with Jimmy Carter, president of the United States. For fifty minutes he answered six questions, mainly on family living, morals, and national defense, all of which had been submitted in advance. The final one was the most revealing.

"Mr. President," we asked, "in view of the fact that in your 1976 campaign you openly sought the evangelical Christian vote, why is it that in the first three years of your administration you have not appointed one visible Christian to your cabinet—a judgeship or other high-level position in your government?" He paused and then denied that this was the case. "I have several religious people in my administration," he explained. "Vice President Mondale is a very religious man and came from a very religious family. His father was a minister, his father before him was a minister, and his brother is a minister."

What the president said was true—but what he did not say is that Vice President Mondale was a self-acknowledged humanist, as attorneys Whitehead and Conlan point out:

> Vice-President Mondale, who has in the past been a contributor to *The Humanist*, was a major participant in the 5th Congress of the International Humanist and Ethical Union held at the Massachusetts Institute of Technology in August 1970. In his opening remarks, Mondale made the following comment:
>
> "Although I have never formally joined a humanist society, I am a member by inheritance. My preacher father was a humanist—in Minnesota they call them Farmer Laborites—and I grew up on a very rich diet of humanism from him. All of our family has been deeply influenced by this tradition including my brother Lester,[46] a Unitarian minister, Ethical Culture Leader, and Chairman of the Fellowship of Religious Humanists."[47]

That visit to the White House convinced me that this book was sorely needed. If a president of the United States does not understand that humanism and its grandfather, Unitarianism, are the unalterable foes of freedom and humanity, then someone needs to unmask this religion and expose its deadly dogmas and practices.

It took little more than a generation to reduce our nation to moral anarchy and degeneracy, to the point where we now are the laughing-stock of nations and the drug consumption capital of the world. America is #1 in all the wrong moral categories: teenage pregnancies, divorce, violent crimes.

But if Christians and other pro-moralists work together, we can return this nation to moral sanity in but a few years. If we do not, the soul destruction of 55 million young people will proceed apace.

9

HUMANISTS CONTROL AMERICA

The [secular] humanistic system of values has now become the predominant way of thinking in most of the power centers of society.
JAMES C. DOBSON

America is supposed to be the land of the free and the home of the brave, a place flowing with milk and honey. And in one sense, it really is.

America's citizens enjoy a life expectancy nearing eighty years. The nation's technology is unsurpassed. Her standard of living is the highest in the world. As one writer has put it: "Today, in many ways, even the poor have routine access to a quality of food, health care, consumer products, entertainment, communications, and transportation that even the Vanderbilts, the Carnegies, the Rockefellers and the 19th Century European princes, with all their combined wealth, could not have afforded."[1]

There is more to a nation and its culture, however, than the mere physical, material, external parts. There is also the soul, the immaterial and internal parts—the moral, the spiritual, the esprit de corps. It is one thing to invent and produce electric lights and build magnificent movie theaters; it is quite another to show moral, uplifting, socially redeeming films.

America's standard of living remains high, but her moral standard of living has plunged. All of us who love her should be very concerned. Only rarely can we turn on the television and find it unpolluted by amoral, pro-humanist thinking. We are not free to send our children to a public school and expect they'll be safe from violence, drugs, and anti-American, pro-one-world-government, proevolution, pro-homosexual, pro-abortion, and pro-condom teaching.

A free country, where the government is "of the people, by the people and for the people," should elect governmental leaders who respond to their pro-moral, pro-American constituency. Ours do not. For example, polls showed that 80 percent of the American people objected to the giveaway of the Panama Canal; yet our politicians handed it over anyway (and not one government official of note attended the official ceremony, including the president or vice president). Today, we are seriously wondering if we gave it to the Panamanian government or to the Communist Chinese.

Why do such political travesties occur? Because we are being ruled by a small but very influential cadre of committed humanists. These politicians are determined to turn America into an amoral, humanist country ripe for merger into a one-world, socialist state. Of course, they do not call it "humanist"; they call it "democracy." But they mean humanist in all its atheistic, amoral, one-world-government sense.

Rabbi Daniel Lapin comments on the tremendous influence of the anti-God worldview currently seducing America. Says Lapin:

> I suspect that most of our cultural institutions are now firmly in the hands of those who reject the Almighty. Those who run our entertainment and news media are consistently shown by polls to attend worship service far less, and to be less likely to have a religious affiliation, than the nation's population as a whole. Those who run our schools, universities, and courts are constantly implementing anti-God doctrines no matter how often they might invoke His name.[2]

Degeneracy by Design

Many years ago my mother, along with others of her generation, lamented the rapid decline of morality in America. She considered the natural descent of fallen, secular man an irreversible trend. No doubt she echoed the feeling of most active Christians of her time.

What her generation did not realize was that the majority of Americans were being led down the path of moral degeneracy by humanist social planners who dominated the nation's leadership.[3] A typical example is the widespread distribution of pornography. In my mother's youth, it was exceedingly difficult to purchase hard-core pornography. Today it comes through the mail (often whether one wants it or not) or is otherwise so accessible that any schoolchild can obtain it. Changes like this are largely the result of the work of organizations such as the American Civil Liberties Union. For over half a century, this pernicious group has busied itself by harassing our city councils, county boards of supervisors, legislators, courts, and ultimately the supreme courts of states and the nation, until it finally has destroyed the laws intended to protect innocent eyes from the filth of the printed page.

Or consider the world of art. In recent times we have witnessed artists placing a plastic figure of Jesus Christ into a vat of urine; placing condoms on a figure of Christ; even smearing the virgin Mary with elephant dung—all done under the guise of freedom of expression. But who seriously believes the humanists or their media friends would tolerate an artist placing a figure of Martin Luther King in a vat of urine, showing him all dressed up in a condom, or smearing pictures of Hillary Clinton, Gloria Steinem, or Betty Friedan with elephant dung?

Until enough morally minded Americans understand what has taken place in recent decades, humanists will continue to lead us toward the chaos of the French Revolution—a catastrophe that destroyed France and paved the way for the dictator Napoleon Bonaparte. This time the humanists hope to name their own dictator, who they believe will create—out of the ashes of our pro-moral republic—a humanist "utopia."

Although the left is determined to turn America into an amoral, socialist state similar to China or Cuba, it is not inevitable. We still have time to turn back the tide to traditional moral and spiritual values and to restore genuine individual freedom. But we must understand how the humanists have gained such mind control that 10 to 15 million of them can literally overpower a nation of more than 270 million people.

When the humanists first arrived in America, the obstacles confronting them seemed overwhelming. But rather than waste their resources, they concentrated on using four vehicles to penetrate the minds of our people. We have already considered education. Now let us turn our attention to the media, humanist organizations, and government.

The Media

While John Dewey and his fellow humanists took over education, their compatriots were busy working their way into the media, controlling not only how Johnny reads and sees but, to a large extent, *what* he reads and sees.

Space does not permit a detailed account of how newspapers from coast to coast were gradually purchased by powerful humanist interests. As radio emerged, it, too, was bought up by some of these same interests. Later, when television licenses became available, humanists flooded the field. Today, humanists control nearly all media by dominating a few wire services and a handful of major television networks. The exceptions would be Christian and independent radio, Christian television, and some cable programming.

Says Cal Thomas:

> The only "sin" left in America is the presumption that truth can be found, or worse, that you have found it. All questions remain open and unresolved except those that the elite have determined are closed [e.g., evolution] and which they themselves resolved. The television networks and most print journalists refuse to grant legitimacy to any other view [e.g., creationism] except the prevailing one. So they trash those views with which they disagree (if they condescend to consider them at all) and promote the views with which they agree, often unfairly and in an imbalanced manner, presenting fiction as truth and error as doctrinal purity.[4]

The Print Media

Even if a newspaper is privately owned, it depends on the wire services (e.g., Associated Press and Reuters) for its daily source of world and national news. This news is carefully edited before being sent out. No reporter can possibly report everything that is said or done. He must select the issues that *he* thinks are important. If he is a secularist, his outlook inevitably colors what he considers important. If one of his favored politicians says something detrimental to his public image, that statement can be edited out. If he misspells a word, it can be ignored. If, on the other hand, a politician representing traditional moral values or economics makes a misstatement that can put him in a bad light, you can be sure it will hit the front page of every paper in the country (think "potato").

This came to the fore in 1992 when then Vice President Dan Quayle provoked howls of derision from the left with his "Murphy Brown" speech. How dare he defend the traditional family, which every enlightened person knows is restrictive and "old fashioned"? Chuck Colson says Quayle was ridiculed and called "arrogant," "aggressive," and "offensive" because he argued for objective moral truths—not personal preferences. "This subtle distinction," says Colson, "is at the heart of the moral conflicts dividing our culture today."[5]

Reed Irvine, Joseph C. Goulden and Cliff Kincaid, in their timely and powerful indictment of the humanist press, insist that the news is slanted in at least six ways:

1. promotion of leftist agendas

2. acceptance of Chicken Little science scares

3. the promotion of odious leftist leaders

4. political partisanship

5. cynicism toward organized religion

6. pack journalism (all running in the same pack instead of pursuing stories that the majority decide no longer exist)[6]

An example of cover-up is the newspaper coverage given President John F. Kennedy. Kennedy's moral indiscretions were well known to Washington news reporters, but because secularists see nothing wrong with infidelity, they carefully sidestepped the truth. Indeed, *Today* co-host Katie Couric referred to the Kennedy administration as "those golden years." President Nixon, however, was relentlessly exposed by the newspapers—and rightfully so—for his wrongdoing.

And then there is the spectacle of William Jefferson Clinton. The press did everything in its power to make sure the most immoral president in American history remained in office. Indeed, to the press the "bad guys" were the House of Representative managers who dared question Clinton's moral and legal right to the highest office in the land. They were tarred and feathered with the Ku Klux Klan brush as "night riders minus the white sheets,"[7] while the *New York Times* tried to compare the congressional atmosphere to Nazi Germany. The interviews given night after night and the comments made day after day generally came from the left. It is amazing how fast the media can find one of their own to give a six-second snippet to exonerate one of their own.

The more recent flak taken by presidential candidate George W. Bush (over his mention of Jesus Christ in answer to a question about who most influenced him and whom he considered the greatest philosopher) more than proves the point.[8] The news media could not find enough words to condemn Bush for mentioning the person of Christ and using the *J* word. A few weeks earlier another presidential candidate said that Jimmy Carter and Mikhail Gorbachev were the greatest influences on his life, and no one in the media raised an eyebrow. Mention Jesus Christ, and angry voices rise in contempt; mention a former communist dictator, and the humanist media bow in worship.

The left has now decided to make Hillary Clinton its cause célèbre as it sees in her the ticket into the next century. She is portrayed as a masterful politician. *Time* magazine's Lance Morrow said of her: "I see a sort of Celtic mist forming around Hillary as a new archetype (somewhere between Eleanor and Evita, transcending both) at a moment when the civilization pivots, at last, decisively—perhaps for the first time since the advent of Christian patriarchy two millenniums ago—toward Woman."[9]

Marvin Olasky says that one of the tricks of some in the media is to identify their own preferred leftist positions with those "of the people" or with "wisdom" generally. That way, if you disagree with the liberal line, you can be identified as being against the people or just plain stupid.[10]

Another area of concern is the book-review section of newspapers. The *Los Angeles Times* Sunday Book Review is dominated by the left. David Horowitz noted that in the May 9, 1999, issue of the *Times*, "Three [nonfiction reviews] were of conservative books—all of which were attacked from the left. The fourth was a review of two books on Clinton, both written by leftists, both praised by reviewers from the left."[11]

This was the same *Los Angeles Times* that gave Marxist Eric Hobsbawm a 3000-word spread to celebrate the sesquicentennial of the publication of the *Communist Manifesto*. (An accurate tribute should have noted the 100 million human beings dead on the teachings of the *Manifesto*, but for some reason Hobsbawm didn't mention that side of Marx's genius.) To show "balance," the *Times* did ask Horowitz for a 125-word response.

The humanist wire services frequently show their bias in photographs. They rarely depict a liberal politician with his mouth open or in an uncomplimentary pose, but not so their counterparts on the right. For years they portrayed Mrs. Phyllis Schlafly—an attractive, articulate, conservative lawyer who opposed the Equal Rights Amendment—as a fanatic. We are happy to say that Mrs. Schlafly survived the ERA battles in excellent shape while the humanist left took a well-deserved beating. Her courageous stand against powerful odds (the President of the United States, most governors, the news media) should encourage all of us as we battle against the same forces. She was able to open an eye of the sleeping giant, and so must we.

Television: Mind Control

Television is the most powerful vehicle available for controlling the minds of a generation. Scientists tell us we remember 60 percent of what we see and only 10 percent of what we hear. Because television and movies combine these primary entries to the mind, they became principal targets for a humanist takeover.

The year-by-year degeneration of television programming proves that the major broadcast and cable networks are controlled predominantly by secularists. A medium that once featured family-oriented programming and observed discretionary moral standards now makes jokes about such things and instead promotes homosexuality, incest, wife swapping, and depravity. One network seems bent on being not only immoral in its programming but anti-Christian.

But as bad as television "entertainment" is, its news reporting is sometimes even more dangerous. More people get their current-events information through television news than from any other source. Most cities have a local affiliate of one of the major networks, so consequently the networks control the slant of the news. Of course, not everyone who controls network news is a committed humanist, but most of them are.

If you doubt that, then try to name a few nationally known commentators who are strong conservatives. Jot down the name of your favorite national television newsperson; then identify others you know. Likely you will find a few moderates, several liberals, and a few superliberals. But rarely a conservative. (National Public Radio is so far left that even some liberals cannot locate it on the dial.)

A truly free medium should equally represent both liberal and conservative points of view. But most of the news we get comes with a liberal slant. Why is this so, given the fact that those who call themselves liberal have never accounted for more than 32 percent of the population? If the majority of the population considers itself conservative, then why can we not have at least one conservative network?

Watch the commentaries after presidential debates or speeches. Conservative spokesmen—those who favor traditional moral values and free enterprise—are held up to ridicule and scorn by the reviewers, even as they subtly endorse or approve the liberal candidate's views. Slanted presentations help to explain why a nation that calls itself conservative consistently votes liberals and moderates into public office. Nevertheless, this kind of media electioneering is not always successful. Sometimes the media favorites are so superliberal that their radical, socialist views cannot be disguised, and thus they are defeated at the polls. But when an election is close, the media usually make the difference.

A simple rule of thumb goes like this: If a story can be slanted to the left of the political or religious spectrum, it will be. If an event involves abortion or homosexuality, the news will be slanted in a pro-abortion and pro-homosexual direction. If there is a clear contest between good and evil, the slant will be toward the evil. If there is a contest between beautiful art reflecting God's lovely creation and ugly art reflecting the darkness of the human psyche, the slant will be toward the ugly. If there is a dispute between two textbooks, with one saying something positive about Western civilization and the other vilifying it, the slant will be against Western civilization. If there is barely time to report only one event and the choice is between the Chinese dictator and some American conservative, you already know which report will get airtime.

And so it goes.

Talk Shows

A good deal of mindless chatter can be heard on talk shows, but to the discerning ear, an abundance of humanist propaganda also is presented. The overwhelming number of guests are amoral in their beliefs and personal lives. Occasionally a Christian or conservative is invited, but we would judge this amounts to only one out of thirty—in a population in which one out of five professes Christianity and a large majority believe in a society based on the moral principles of the Ten Commandments.

Admittedly, these shows are not generally filled with ideological propaganda. Yet the liberal slant is relentless. One spokeswoman asked to represent the American homemaker has commented, for instance, that "homemaking is a bore"—even though the speaker in question represented a feminist organization and had never married or had children. Of course, this was not pointed out; it might have spoiled her chance to promote her cause on national television.

We have seen so-called sexologists ("experts" on sex and marriage) offer very bad—and in some cases frighteningly harmful—advice on relational subjects, abetted by the talk-show host who fawns all over the alleged expert. By contrast, the person who holds a pro-moral position is often attacked or ridiculed. Conservatives are treated almost as a threat to the personal lifestyle of the host.

Humanists see television as a vehicle—first, to indoctrinate and, second, to make money. Shortly after learning that Norman Lear produced six of the most amoral "comedy" series on television, I had lunch with a Christian businessman, who told me how relieved he was to have sold his cable television stations. Guess who bought them? Norman Lear.

No wonder our Lord said, "The children of this world are . . . wiser than the children of light" (Luke 16:8, KJV).

Television is continually used to promote antimoral, anti-God books or causes. Very few Christian authors or recording artists are interviewed on television; in fact, it is so hard to penetrate the liberal wall that several big publishers of Christian books have stopped trying. Christians write good books and boast many articulate, interesting authors, but since these writers reject secularist beliefs, they get excluded from television. Christians may appear on a handful of local shows, but with the exception of Billy Graham or Amy Grant, few make it on the national scene. Former Green Bay Packer Reggie White did grab national attention but only because he was criticized for his stance on homosexuality.

Television can be a marvelous means of communication, depending on who controls it. Fortunately, a courageous few—Jerry Falwell, D. James Kennedy, Charles Stanley, the Radio Bible Class, Pat Robertson, and a few others—use it to communicate moral and Christian convictions. Without their voices, this valuable medium would be overwhelmingly in the hands of humanists or their sympathizers.

The Movie Industry

Volumes could be written on how Hollywood has devastated America's morals in the past half-century. Film moguls try to defend their exaltation of infidelity, homosexuality, violence, and corruption by suggesting they are "just supplying the public with what it wants." Nonsense! Some of the best-loved films and top moneymakers—such as *Toy Story* or *The Straight Story*—have been clean and family oriented.

For the most part, Hollywood shocks the sensibilities of pro-moral citizens.[12] Recently a successful wheat broker sat next to me on a plane headed for Kansas City. He was not an active churchman but did want his three teenage children to be raised with moral values. As we talked about the depraved movies coming out of Hollywood, he spoke of an incident that happened three weeks before. He had taken his family to a well-advertised film, only to be so disgusted with its moral filth that he and his family left merely ten minutes into the story.

Hollywood films amoral stories and plays not because they make good art but because they offer a tremendous vehicle for assaulting the minds of our citizens with humanistic propaganda. Once you understand the doctrines of humanism, you will find them subtly slipped into these stories—and sometimes obtrusively.

When was the last time you saw a film out of Hollywood that showed communism as a world aggressor and a mass murderer? Many films disclose the seamy side of America, but you rarely see an anticommunist film—and not because such movies would lack intrigue or drama. Eighty years and counting of communist terror should provide ample material to draw on—but only if you are willing to show atheism and socialism in a bad light. If the truth were told, we probably would all be shocked at the procommunist influence in Hollywood.[13] This situation is not hard to understand, for many of us remember back in the 1950s when ten Hollywood screenwriters were sent to jail as communists. We may not remember, however, that all but two of them were reemployed by Hollywood after serving time.

When you read a list of Hollywood notables endorsing homosexuality, promiscuity, foul language, abortion, legalized marijuana, unilateral disarmament, and everything else that is harmful to America, just remember that a humanist stands up for his beliefs. Says Michael Medved, "Hollywood no longer reflects—or even respects—the values of most American families."[14]

Fortunately, some Christians are beginning to get into the movie business and provide the public with an alternative. But it will be an uphill fight all the way, not because Christians and other pro-moral Americans lack talent but because, for the most part, humanists control the outlets.

For twenty years the city of Dallas has authorized its own movie-review committee: the Dallas Motion Picture Classification Board. Twenty-six unpaid people are appointed to rate films with minors in view, taking advantage of a United States Supreme Court ruling that upheld the right of communities to limit young people's exposure to certain books and films.

When board members were first empaneled, howls of "censorship!" rose from the West Coast, insisting that the twenty-six were not qualified to judge films. One Dallas board member's response was interesting:

"We may not be qualified to rate movies, but we're qualified to tell what we would like our children to see."[15]

Hollywood will never improve its morals unless community pressure forces it to do so. If every pastor and pro-moral parent in the country would write his city mayor and councilman, we could compel Hollywood to adopt some degree of moral sanity. That kind of moral activism has been sadly lacking.

Myriad Humanist Organizations

Humanists soon found that establishing a variety of organizations and societies would give them access to many special-interest groups throughout the nation.

One of their early organizations was the National Association for the Advancement of Colored People (founded in 1909–10), followed by the Chicago Urban League (1917), both formed by ethical societies.[16] Since then, scores of organizations have been spawned or assisted by these societies, such as Americans for Democratic Action (ADA); Women's International League for Peace and Freedom; the Fellowship of Reconciliation; American Union against Militarism; Church Socialist League; Federal Council of Churches; National Council of Churches; International League of Working Women; National Consumers League; League for Industrial Democracy; the American Ethical Union (AEU); the American Civil Liberties Union (ACLU); the Sex Information and Educational Council of the United States (SIECUS); and the National Organization of Women (NOW). Many of these organizations shared the same founders and/or directors.

Humanist leaders founded and continue to direct the United Nations, UNESCO, UNICEF, and the World Health Organization. Many of the patrons and leaders of the WHO were signers of the *Humanist Manifesto* and unsurprisingly champion abortion and other murderous population-control measures. We must not forget that both Dr. Francis Schaeffer and Dr. C. Everett Koop have warned us of the euthanasia movement—that is, the killing of the elderly. Look soon for a supposedly scientific endorsement for this horrific practice from the prestigious WHO.

The UN and its related organizations have supplied humanists with an ideal springboard from which to vault into government, both as elected politicians and as career diplomats and government bureaucrats. By getting their leaders appointed to UN commissions—easily arranged through their supporters in Washington—they have used the vast fortune paid to the UN by the United States to advance the cause of world humanism.[17]

Many citizens do not know that from the very beginning it was decided to exclude God from the UN, in order to avoid offending the communists. One need not have been a prophet in 1945 (when the UN was founded) to predict it would never meet its goals, for our Lord warned us, "Without Me, you can do nothing" (John 15:5).

Nevertheless, these leaders promised that the new organization would solve the problem of war and usher in world peace. Of course, the experiment failed miserably. We have suffered more wars, violent deaths, and international catastrophes during the past fifty years than in any comparable period in world history. The world has put billions of dollars at the disposal of these secularist world planners, who repay their supporters with dividends of futility.

The American Civil Liberties Union

The most effective humanist organization for destroying the laws, morals, and traditional rights of Americans has been the ACLU. Founded in 1920, it is the legal arm of the humanist movement, established and nurtured by the Ethical Culture Movement.

"Such organizations as the American Civil Liberties Union," says *The Great Deceit*, "are examples of . . . socialist fronts."[18] One of the founders of the ACLU—along with Felix Frankfurter, Morris Hillquit, Roger N. Baldwin, Scott Nearing, and Norman Thomas—was Dr. Harry F. Ward.[19] Ward was a professor of social ethics at Union Theological Seminary and for thirty years worked tirelessly to socialize the United Methodist Church. The well-known parallel between the social positions of the Methodist Church and the Communist Party can be attributed largely to Dr. Ward's three decades of indoctrinating the young minds of Methodism's finest ministerial candidates.

Other influential ACLU founders include William Z. Foster, formerly the head of the United States Communist Party; Dr. John C. Bennett, a president of Union Theological Seminary; humanists John Dewey, Clarence Darrow, Norman Thomas, Roger Baldwin, Corliss Lamont, and many others.

After ten years under the directorship of Roger Baldwin, the ACLU was probed in the early '30s by the United States House of Representatives special committee to investigate communist activities in the United States. On January 17, 1931, the committee report stated:

> The American Civil Liberties Union is closely affiliated with the communist movement in the United States, and fully 90 percent of its efforts are on behalf of communists who have come into conflict with the law. It claims to stand for free speech, free press, and free assembly, but it is quite apparent that the main function of the ACLU is to attempt to protect the communists in their advocacy of force and violence to overthrow the Government, replacing the American flag by a red flag and erecting a Soviet Government in place of the republican form of government guaranteed to each State by the Federal Constitution.[20]

According to the California state legislative committee that investigated un-American activities in 1943 and 1948, "The American Civil Liberties Union may be definitely classed as a Communist front or 'transmission belt' organization." A police undercover agent, David D. Gumaer, revealed in 1969 that "206 past leading members of the ACLU had a combined record of 1,754 officially cited Communist front affiliations." He continued: "The present ACLU Board consists of sixty-eight members, thirty-one of whom have succeeded in amassing a total of at least 355 Communist Front affiliations. That total does not include the citations of these individuals which appear in reports from the Senate Internal Security Subcommittee."[21]

Other activities of the ACLU will sound familiar to anyone conversant with the events of the past few decades:

- legal defense for those who have supported Fidel Castro;

- legal defense for the communist DuBois Clubs;

- dogged opposition to voluntary prayer and Bible reading in the public schools;

- antagonism toward laws which control subversive organizations;

- efforts to delete the words "under God" from the Pledge of Allegiance;

- opposition to state narcotics laws.

The ACLU, with its many chapters all over the country, has worked tirelessly against all laws forbidding pornography. Certain leaders got themselves appointed to a presidential commission that called for federally funded sex education (which now floods the schools with amoral SIECUS materials, including the erotic and sometimes pornographic *Sexology* magazine).

Score: humanism, 7; Christianity and moral sanity, 0.

The anti-Christian attitude of the ACLU is evident not only in its persistent attack on moral legislation but also in its efforts to compel our country to become totally secular.[22] Every Christmas its minions do battle with the religious symbols that remind our people of the virgin-born Son of God.

Because of the ACLU, prayer, Bible reading, the Ten Commandments, God, Bible study, released-time classes, Easter and Christmas celebrations have all been curtailed or eliminated. Even graduation speeches mentioning God or Christ are forbidden. Prayers before sporting events are out. Easter has been changed to "spring break," Christmas to "winter vacation." Christmas programs that feature Santa, Rudolph, and Scrooge are fine, but forget about the One whose entrance into the world we are celebrating.

We have watched ACLU lawyers eagerly come to the aid of anyone who has a conflict with morality, human rights, civil disobedience, or anything else that chips away at the foundation stones of biblical morality that undergird this country. Thankfully, over the last few years Christian lawyers such as Jay A. Sekulow have banded together to establish some Christian legal societies to combat the ACLU. All we can say is, Amen!

The American Humanist Association

The American Humanist Association was established in Illinois "as a nonprofit, tax-exempt organization conceived for educational and religious purposes." Additionally,

> the AHA is the command vessel for a flotilla of federated associations that are moored in strategic locations in the United States and Canada. Humanist House, the AHA's official headquarters in San Francisco, is a five-story mansion overlooking Golden Gate Bridge and the Pacific Ocean. This building was officially opened on December 10, 1967, Human Rights Day, with the raising of the United Nations flag.[23]

When I debated the treasurer of the American Humanist Association at its annual meeting in San Diego in 1994, this UCLA philosophy professor bragged that his greatest delight in the classroom is to reorient the minds of students "from fundamentalist families." In other words, on this university campus, where ministers of the gospel of Christ are not welcome, our tax dollars pay the salary of this humanist professor-minister to subvert the minds of our nation's twenty-year-old youths. Not a good investment!

The Council for Secular Humanism and Related Groups

Paul Kurtz heads another humanist organization, the Council for Secular Humanism. The official journal of this group is *Free Inquiry* magazine. Its main aim, of course, is to destroy biblical Christianity and replace it with Secular Humanism. It is assisted in this crusade by another organization called the Fellowship, an outreach to liberal Christian ministers:

> In 1963 a group of liberal Humanist clergymen founded the Fellowship (FRH) with the aim of drawing into the Humanist movement Protestant

ministers who regard Humanism as a religion. Located in Yellow Springs, Ohio, this Humanist faction is affiliated with the American Ethical Union, the American Humanist Association, the Unitarian-Universalist Association, and the International Humanist and Ethical Union.[24]

FRH publishes a quarterly journal, *Religious Humanism*, and a membership bulletin, *The Communicator*, in addition to sponsoring conferences with the above groups and another less-well known fraternal organization, the Society for Humanistic Judaism.[25] A branch of FRH's Humanist Center Library is located at Cocoa Beach, Florida. This library houses the archives of the humanist movement in America. FRH stands among those who voice the hope that a "comprehensive world religion will develop through the creative processes of our times."[26]

The National Council of Churches, a successor to the socialistic, pro-communist Federal Council of Churches and a leading voice of Religious Humanists in America, wants the nation to think it speaks for the Protestant community. *It does not.* Yet whenever the government or media wants to hear from the religious community, it turns to the NCC, which represents only the minority views of some liberal Protestants.

These organizations and scores more like them (the Alliance of Secular Humanist Societies lists dozens more in the fall 1999 issue of *Free Inquiry* magazine) exert a profound influence on education, government, and the media.

The Vehicle of Government

Never underestimate the importance of government. God did not! He established it and knew that if it fell into the wrong hands, it would be the most harmful organization ever conceived.

Hebrew history shows that government was either good or bad, depending on the moral convictions of the king. In fact, kings were judged on a moral standard ("he did right in the sight of the Lord" or "he did evil in the sight of the Lord"). As Scripture warned, when the righteous rule, the people rejoice. But when a wicked man rules, the people groan (Proverbs 29:2).

The power of government to influence and control the minds of its citizens has certainly not been lost on the humanists. Early on they saw the need to get their people into office or to identify those already in office who were vulnerable to pressure.

Today, all one needs to do is check the Web site of the Democratic Socialists of America (DSA) to find humanists in high office. Fifty-five members of Congress are currently listed on the DSA Web site. Some of the leading voices of the Democratic Party are on that list. And how a hard-core, procommunist humanist could head the House Armed Services Committee is nearly impossible to comprehend.[27] We are convinced that if the United States slips into world government any time soon, it will be a Republican who will pull us in and an evangelical religious leader who will second the motion.

The federal government consists of 537 elected officials—435 representatives, 100 senators, a president, and a vice president. Not all of those 537 individuals are humanists, of course, but as a group they have supported humanistic goals often enough to bring us to the threshold of a secular, amoral society ready to collapse.

Humanists do not mind voting for outsiders as long as they agree with a number of key secularist doctrines. Humanists will vote for and protect Bill Clinton, for example, because he is pro-abortion, pro-homosexual, and promiscuous. He supports placing American servicemen under UN command. He supports women in combat even though he avoided the draft. He loves to rule by executive order. He loves to bomb foreign countries despite the U.S. Constitution (a document which all leftists consider confining and reactionary). The humanist left loves Bill Clinton. The fact that he attends a liberal, humanist Methodist church and carries a large Bible does not disturb them at all.

Humanists also will vote for Al Gore because of his radical environmentalism,[28] his proevolutionary and pro-world-government stance in *Earth in the Balance*,[29] his pro-abortion and pro-homosexual planks. The fact that Gore claims to be a born-again Christian does not disturb them in the least. That is his private life; his public life is humanistic, and that is sufficient.

Some politicians, and only God knows how many, are truly evil. They sell their souls to the industrialists or big corporations who get them elected and then remain quiet when these behemoths seek to celebrate Christmas with a condom Christmas tree.[30] They sell out to the abortion industry. They sell out to the drug kingpins. They sell out to the gambling industry. They sell out to the Mafia. They sell out to the radical feminists.[31] They sell out to radical leftists and act as the transmission belt between the academy and the culture.[32] Consequently they vote whatever is in the best interest of their bosses. They also use their votes to incur debts on future issues that directly concern their bosses. (The average citizen has no idea how much vote trading goes on behind legislative doors.) Morality is a very low priority with such public officials. As an example, consider just one current issue on the political landscape.

If the humanists and their powerful homosexualist[33] friends succeed in forcing the pro-moral majority to accept homosexuality as normal behavior, two thousand years of Western culture and more than three hundred years of American history will go up in smoke. Once the homosexuals win their case, you can be sure that legalizing prostitution, drugs, gambling, and who knows what else is right behind. In fact, we will go on record and predict that if the homosexual juggernaut is not stopped, pederasty (man-boy sex) will be declared normal and legalized within twenty years.[34]

But perhaps it's even later than we think. Already the humanists are seeking to bring pro-homosexual education to the earliest grades. According to *Just the Facts About Sexual Orientation and Youth*, a twelve-page booklet produced by a group of school psychologists, counselors, educators, and doctors, "homosexuality is normal and not mentally unhealthy."[35] That booklet was mailed to all of the nation's public school districts by the Just the Facts Coalition. The coalition consists of the American Psychological Association, the American Academy of Pediatrics, and the Gay, Lesbian and Straight Education Network. The Coalition also included the American Federation of Teachers and the National Education Association. So as not to take any chances, the booklet cautions school officials that "endorsement or promotion" of religious ministries aimed at overcoming homosexuality "by officials or school employees of a public school district in a school-related context could raise constitutional problems."[36]

But you can bet the farm that gay activists will be working the schools!

The voting record of many current politicians shows them to be amoral humanists with strong socialistic convictions who, in the name of human rights, have deprived the country of the protection necessary to maintain a morally sane society. Such individuals can hardly be expected to enact pro-moral measures.

Nor should we look for help to the current Supreme Court. The humanist interpretation of law has been favored by the Supreme Court in many ways during the past century.

For example, says David Barton, "Oliver Wendell Holmes, Jr. (1841–1935), appointed to the Supreme Court in 1902, explained that original intent and precedent held little value: 'The justification of a law for us cannot be found in the fact that our [founding] fathers always have followed it. It must be found in some help which the law brings toward reaching a social end.'"[37]

Referring to Benjamin Cardozo (1870–1938), Barton says Cardozo "refused to be bound by any concept of transcendent laws or fixed rights and wrongs: 'If there is any law which is back of the sovereignty of the state, and superior thereto, it is not law in such a sense as to concern the judge or lawyers, however much it concerns the statesman or the moralist.'"[38] It was also Cardozo who said, "I take judge-made law as one of the existing realities of life."[39]

And then there is Charles Evans Hughes (1862–1948), who remarked, "We are under a Constitution, but the Constitution is what the judges say it is."[40]

Looking for True Patriots

How far we have strayed from our godly heritage! British historian Paul Johnson says that George Washington, in the light of the dreadful events which had occurred in Revolutionary France, "wished to dispel for good any notion that America was a secular state. It was a government of laws but it was also a government of morals. 'Of all the dispositions and habits which led to political prosperity,' he insisted, 'Religion and Morality are indispensable supports.' Anyone who tried to undermine these 'firmest props of the duties of Men and Citizens' was the very opposite of a patriot."[41]

It's time to put the props of religion and morality back where they belong. It's time to remember that America was founded as a nation of both laws and morals. And it's time to see to our duties as men and citizens.

The same resources used by the secularists during the past hundred years are still open to *us*. If a sufficient number of dedicated Christians, ministers, and other pro-moral Americans use their influence, energy, and resources, we can return the humanists to private life and replace them with those who truly represent our nation and its best interests.

Never did we need true patriots more than we need them today!

10

THE BIG LIE

I seek to encourage those Americans similarly inclined to help return America to its founding moral imperative. This is neither a cry for religious revolution nor a crusade; it is something else entirely. It is a reminder that we have lost our way. It is a suggestion that we return home again.
DANIEL LAPIN

One of the major reasons for the apathy of so many Christians regarding the moral plight of our nation, particularly among ministers of the gospel, is a gross misunderstanding of the separation of church and state.

By no stretch of the imagination was the "separation" doctrine ever meant to disconnect government from God or to prohibit Christianity from influencing government with truth, righteousness, justice, and mercy.

What Kind of Separation?

Robert L. Cord published one of the most thorough studies ever conducted on this subject. In his *Separation of Church and State: Historical Fact and Current Fiction*, he commented on Supreme Court Justice Harry Blackmun's famous statement, "The First Amendment has erected a wall between church and state. That wall must be kept high and impregnable. We could not approve the slightest breach":

> With those lines of fiction, Mr. Justice Blackmun [the same Justice who wrote the *Roe v. Wade* decision] concluded the first United States Supreme Court opinion that dealt with the meaning and the constitutional mandate of the Establishment of Religion Clause of the First Amendment. "Fiction" is a strong term, but a careful analysis of the early history of the Republic justifies its use. . . . The First Amendment did not, nor was it intended to, create a "high" and "impregnable" wall between Church and State. Rather, its Framer intended it to serve three other purposes.
>
> First, the religious prohibitions of the Amendment were designed to act as a limitation on the new Federal Congress, constitutionally denying to it the power to establish a national church or religion.

Second, the Amendment guaranteed that the right of the individual to exercise freedom of conscience in religious matters was to be safe-guarded against encroachment by the Federal Government.

Third, the Amendment was intended to make certain that the relationship between religion and the state would remain under the control of individual States—several of which in 1791 had established state religions.[1]

The separation doctrine was never intended to wall off Christians from their government but rather to guarantee that no one sect would become the national church. Americans were all too knowledgeable about the Church of England. They intended to make sure there would be no Church of America.

Cord highlights another important point: "With few exceptions, those who fled religious persecution [the Puritans] were no more tolerant of religious dissenters [the Baptists] than were those from whom they had fled."[2] It was bad enough for individual states to have a state religion—ask Roger Williams and the Baptists. Few wanted a federal or national religion or church.

We certainly are not calling for any kind of federal or state religion, either. In fact, we are protesting that Secular Humanism already has *become* America's federally funded religion, while Christianity has been marginalized under the fiction of the separation doctrine.

When I was in Moscow before the fall of the Berlin Wall, my guide proudly proclaimed, "We Russians have the same policy on religion as you Americans—separation of church and state." As I looked around, suddenly I began to realize what an overemphasis on this concept would do to America. The state in Russia was everything, and the church answered to it. Before the fall of communism, the church in Russia had almost zero influence.

We are headed for the same predicament. Every passing week finds the state politicizing something new. First it was taxes, national defense, and education; now morals, especially abortion and homosexuality. Secularists have very cleverly politicized both these latter issues. At one time churches spoke out on these questions based on "thus saith the

Lord." But since abortion and homosexuality have been deemed political, they are out of the jurisdiction of the church—or so the argument has been framed. In some areas, reading from Romans 1 is considered in poor taste. In Canada, one cannot quote Romans 1 over the airwaves.

During a television debate on homosexual rights, my opponent brought up the church-state issue. "The church shouldn't get involved in politics. It will endanger its tax status." That is ridiculous by any legal point of view. In the first place, morals are a major part of the church's business. If the church does not speak out on homosexuality, pornography, drugs, prostitution, abortion, divorce, and so forth, who will?

If the present interpretation of church/state separation is allowed to stand, the church will soon be excluded from everything meaningful in life. Some would, if they could, federalize the raising of our children. Then all 55 million children would become thoroughgoing secularists, willingly obedient to big government.

The Truth About Separation of Church and State

The First Amendment of our Constitution reads, "Congress shall make no law respecting an establishment of religion, or prohibiting the free exercise thereof; or abridging the freedom of speech, or of the press; or the right of the people peaceably to assemble, and to petition the Government for a redress of grievances."

The separation of church and state does not mean that Christian citizens are prohibited from taking an active part in the electoral process. Our forefathers were simply preventing the establishment of a national religion, which Europe had suffered under for centuries. Even today, a state or government-supported church exists in both Germany and England.

Our forefathers never intended government to be isolated from God or the recognition of His existence. Yet with a false interpretation of separation, the humanists have rendered our government almost as secular as Communist China and the former Soviet Union. In fact, in many ways there is more religious freedom in present-day Russia than there is in the United States.

Here, Christians can be put in jail for showing the Campus Crusade–sponsored *Jesus* film in our schools. The same film, however, is welcome in all Russian schools.

Ultimately, the Russians might duplicate the American humanist policies and again expel religion from schools, equate morals with religion, and thus expel morals as well. Just as Judeo-Christian morals and religion have no place in the humanist's scheme of American education, so they have no place in their scheme of government. The method is the same: First, separate religion and politics, then equate religion and morals, and subsequently exclude both.[3]

We believe it is repulsive for Christians to sit back and do nothing while such religious brainwashing takes place. Unless millions of us become vitally involved in changing our present humanistic leadership in government, education, and the media, America cannot help but become a humanist nation in the twenty-first century.

Was Jesus Involved in Politics?

But you can almost hear the refrain: "Jesus never got involved in politics, and therefore we must follow Him and shun that area, too. Let the burly sinners of the world take care of government and the political process."

We beg to differ. Our Lord *was* deeply involved in politics, as anyone can see who cares to read Matthew 23. The Pharisees, Sadducees, high priest, and all those involved with the Jewish temple were the political, religious, and legal rulers of the day.[4] They all heard Jesus tell them: "you devour widows' houses," "you . . . have neglected the weightier matters of the law: justice and mercy and faith," you "strain out a gnat and swallow a camel," you "are full of extortion and self-indulgence," you are "blind," "cleanse the inside of the cup," "inside [you] are full of dead men's bones," "you . . . outwardly appear righteous . . . , but inside you are full of hypocrisy and lawlessness," "you are sons of those who murdered the prophets," and "how can you escape the condemnation of hell?"

Jesus also overturned the tables of the moneychangers in the temple area because they made His father's house a den of thieves. He addressed the political powers of His day in scathing terms, once calling Herod a "fox" (Luke 13:32). He further said, "render therefore to Caesar the things that are Caesar's, and to God the things that are God's" (Matthew 22:21). With a simple and yet profound declaration, our Lord said no to both totalitarianism and anarchy.

Of course the Lord was interested in politics and government. He created it! (See Genesis 9:6.) Besides, He is the King of kings and Lord of lords. One day, all politics and government will be under His control as He reigns and rules (see Psalm 2; Isaiah 9; Revelation 19).

Our nation was not founded independent of God. Our money carries the message "In God We Trust" and our Pledge of Allegiance states that we are "one nation under God." Our Supreme Court, Senate, and House of Representatives open each morning with prayer. This country was built on biblical principles and a clear recognition of God.

Lord of the Cosmos

Without question, preaching the gospel of Jesus the Messiah is the essential ministry of the church. That gospel is a proclamation about Jesus. It tells how the one true God of the universe has "dealt in Jesus Christ with sin, death, guilt, and shame, and now summons men and women everywhere to abandon the idols which hold them captive to these things and to discover a new life, and a new way of life in him."[5]

But it also entails announcing that Jesus is Lord of the cosmos, including this earth. He rules over every area of life. As theologian Tom Wright says, "There is no area of existence or life, including no area of human life, that does not come up for critique in the light of the sovereignty of the crucified and risen Jesus; no area that is exempt from the summons to allegiance."[6] Wright notes that no herald in the ancient world would have said, "Tiberius Caesar has become emperor; accept him if it suits you." It is the same with Jesus, our Lord. He is our Messiah, Savior, Lord, and King.

The Bible further instructs us to preach the whole Word of God (2 Timothy 4:2), which includes being the salt of the earth and asserting a moral influence. To preach the Word of God is to preach the full counsel of God. To preach the full counsel of God includes preaching the whole biblical, Christian worldview.

The Bible has something to say about all of reality, and that, by definition, makes Christianity a worldview. Politics is just as much a part of the Christian worldview as is theology, philosophy, ethics, biology, psychology, sociology, economics, law, and history. The Bible has a lot to say about government, rulership, and legal matters. Voting and politics are simply placing one's privately held values and beliefs into the public arena.

While we lack the space to develop this concept in full, David has written *Understanding The Times*,[7] a 912-page work on this issue, which we highly recommend to our readers. The book presents the case that the Bible is the foundation for all the major aspects of a Christian worldview and that the Messiah of the Gospels is a theologian, teacher-philosopher, ethicist, biologist, psychologist, sociologist, lawyer, king, economist, and Lord of history. He is the human face of the Creator, who created us in His own image.

No wonder Charles Colson and Nancy Pearcey say that "genuine Christianity is a way of seeing and comprehending all reality. It is a worldview."[8] Tom Wright agrees: "Preaching the gospel means announcing Jesus as Lord of the world; and, unless we are prepared to contradict ourselves with every breath we take, we cannot make that announcement without seeking to bring that lordship to bear over every aspect of the world."[9] Elsewhere Wright says, "The language of theology relates intimately and vitally to the whole of life, culture, love, art, politics, and even religion. This could even mean challenging the academic world in a new way by showing how the study of theology is vitally linked to all other disciplines."[10] Further, "the human race was to be shown, invited to, summoned into, and enabled to discover the true way of being human, the way to reflect the very image of God himself in every aspect of life and with every fibre of one's being. If that is what you mean by 'religion' so be it. Jesus and Paul thought of it as Life."[11]

Note how even *Newsweek* magazine portrays Christianity as a worldview:

For Christians Jesus is the hinge on which the door of history swings, the point at which eternity intersects with time, the Savior who redeems time by drawing all things to himself. As the second millennium draws to a close, nearly a third of the world's population claims to be his followers.

But by any secular standard, Jesus is also the dominant figure of Western culture. Like the millennium itself, much of what we now think of as Western ideas, inventions, and values finds its source and inspiration in the religion that worships God in his name. Art and science, the self and society, politics and economics, marriage and the family, right and wrong, body and soul—all have been touched and often radically transformed by Christian influence.[12]

All worldviews, the Christian one included, are awash in ideas, beliefs, issues, and the values of life itself and "are in principle public statements."[13] Maybe that is why the apostle Paul said Christians were to overthrow "[atheist's] arguments and every high thing [e.g., naturalistic science] that exalts itself against the knowledge of God, bringing every thought into captivity to the obedience of Christ" (2 Corinthians 10:5).

Again, Colson and Pearcey: "To engage the world, however, requires that we understand the great ideas that compete for people's minds and hearts. Philosopher Richard Weaver has it right in the title of his well-known book: *Ideas Have Consequences*. It is the great ideas that inform the mind, fire the imagination, move the heart, and shape a culture. History is little more than the recording of the rise and fall of the great ideas—the worldviews—that form our values and move us to act."[14]

Christianity has much to say about the great ideas that inform the mind and move the heart. We must not remain quiet when we step outside the four walls of our sanctuaries. To remain silent is not biblical Christianity or historical Christianity; it is abandonment. Our forefathers were far more courageous. Christianity certainly has something to say about politics and government, because the Bible has much to say about both.

What Can the Church Do?

One fundamental sermon that needs to be preached is that *government is not God!* Nor is the government to play God. Nor is the state to usurp the prerogatives that God has ordained to the family or the church. Nor is the state to ignore biblical morality.

Individuals in their private lives and state officials in their public lives are both to recognize the same morality. Lying and cheating are wrong for individuals; they are equally wrong for public officials. Adultery is wrong for Joe SixPack; adultery is wrong for the president of the United States, too.

At a National Organization of Women convention in Los Angeles years ago, feminist leaders warned their delegates about the rise of the moral majority, who were rapidly awakening from slumber to become activists. They challenged their followers to solve the problem by going home and threatening Christians with "the separation-of-church-and-state issue." They did not care a snap about the church, but they did want to neutralize its influence so they could continue to flood our land with "homosexual rights," "lesbian rights," "prostitute rights," and "abortion rights."

What humanists call *rights,* the church consistently calls *wrongs.* Therefore, if we fail to get involved politically on these moral issues, humanists will pollute our land.

Washington attorney Alan Dye and my San Diego friend James O. Hewitt, both highly respected lawyers, have issued lengthy papers on the church's rights and responsibilities under the law. Both acknowledge that churches cannot endorse political candidates[15] or give money to political campaigns without jeopardizing their nonprofit status.

But when it comes to legislative activity—that is, campaigning for or against legislation, particularly when it concerns morals—churches are permitted to be involved, as long as they do not spend a substantial amount of time or money in the process. "Substantial" is generally considered anything over 5 percent of their annual budget or 5 percent of their activity. As private citizens, ministers are not prohibited from endorsing candidates. Even the most politically active churches would probably not spend half of 1 percent. Consequently, most churches are functioning well within the limits of the law.

Many, however, heed the lie that churches should never get involved in politics. Although churches should not officially endorse candidates for public office, that does not mean that Christians should never run for public office or that churches should not speak out clearly on moral issues. We need to emulate the apostle Paul, leave the safety of the church, and get into the public arena (Acts 17:16ff).

Where Are the Christians?

While attending a meeting of concerned ministers and other Christian leaders in Washington, I met an attorney from Memphis. He had his eyes opened while serving as a federal prosecutor during some hard-core pornography trials. Pornography is a multibillion-dollar business, so its publishers can afford the sharpest humanist lawyers in the nation.

After battling these evil forces for almost three years, this attorney raised an overriding question: "Where are all the Christians who say they are opposed to iniquity?" He concluded, "I believe that pornography floods our land because the Christians refuse to 'get involved' in fighting it."

We would add only one point to that observation: Next to abortion, pornography is the most contaminating scourge in our country.

The Christian community must remain silent no longer.

Enough Is Enough!

When Rick Scarborough moved to Pearland, Texas, a suburb of Houston, in 1990 to pastor the First Baptist Church, not one church member was an elected official at any level in civil government. That is no longer true.

At this writing, three members of his church serve on the city council, and all five on the council profess Christ. Four of his members serve on the school board. The city manager is a member of his church. The police chief is a member of his church. The city attorney is a member of his church. The assistant district attorney of Brazoria County is a member of his church. In addition, his church members serve as volunteers on various committees and commissions throughout the community, county, and state.

As Pastor Scarborough says, "Pearland is not a Christian community, but Christians are serving in leadership and the decisions they make reflect their convictions and moral commitments. . . . Pearland is prospering because godly people are leading by serving. The Scripture instructs us: 'When the righteous are in authority, the people rejoice: but when the wicked beareth rule, the people mourn' (Proverbs 29:2 [KJV]). . . . The changes that have come to Pearland did not come easy, nor did they take place overnight, but I can testify they were worth the effort. Satan does not give back occupied territory without a fight, but he will give it back if you stand in the authority of Jesus Christ and say, 'Enough is Enough.'"[16]

Pastor Scarborough became involved in the moral struggle when a twenty-four-year-old coed spoke to the Pearland high school on the subject of AIDS. It was billed as an "AIDS Awareness Assembly" sponsored by the pro-homosexual organization AIDS Foundation.

He attended the assembly and found that the coed "spoke in the vernacular of her audience, using just enough technical terms to alert everyone that she knew what she was talking about. She proceeded to describe in great detail every form of sexual expression you can imagine. She used humor to diffuse the tension and embarrassment that a mixed crowd of teenagers would feel, as various sexual activities were vividly described. She was careful not to pass moral judgment on any behavior."[17]

The coed then proceeded to describe normal sexual intercourse, anal sex, oral sex, etc. She displayed her condom, "today's amoral solution for the host of afflictions that accompany illicit sex" and then announced, "Condoms are ninety-seven percent effective in combating AIDS when used correctly."[18]

Pastor Scarborough challenged her statistics, and she insisted that the Center for Disease Control in Atlanta, Georgia, was the source for her facts. He opined that, when it comes to illicit sex, three persons dying out of every 100 must be an acceptable price to pay!

But that was not the end of the story. "She informed the students that she was able to continue having sex because she herself used condoms and she believed in their safety. As liberals often do, she concluded with an emotional appeal, asserting, 'I am dying of AIDS [she has since expired], but I am here because I care about you.'"[19]

Pastor Scarborough carried a tape recording of her comments back to his church and allowed his members to hear what she had to say about "safe sex." As he says, "That day, the members of First Baptist Church of Pearland decided enough is enough."

We strongly urge every pastor in America to read Pastor Scarborough's book, *Enough Is Enough: A Call to Christian Involvement*.[20] Such moral activism and courage should be part of the normal Christian life, as it was for the great heroes of the faith. Hear what a few of them endured for the sake of Christ:

> Who through faith subdued kingdoms, worked righteousness, obtained promises, stopped the mouths of lions, quenched the violence of fire, escaped the edge of the sword, out of weakness were made strong, became valiant in battle, turned to flight the armies of the aliens. Women received their dead raised to life again.
>
> Others were tortured, not accepting deliverance, that they might obtain a better resurrection. Still others had trial of mockings and scourgings, yes, and of chains and imprisonment. They were stoned, they were sawn in two, were tempted, were slain with the sword. They wandered about in sheepskins and goatskins, being destitute, afflicted, tormented—of whom the world was not worthy. (HEBREWS 11:33–38)

Some Timely Advice

We close this chapter with some timely advice from Daniel Lapin, a rabbi you've heard from already:

> Why do we now see, as we approach the millennium, America's religious conservatives pushing efforts to pass a school prayer amendment, a defense of marriage act, and other laws codifying moral issues? Until a few decades ago, such acts were not needed. They were part and parcel of what everyone understood to be obviously necessary to American life. The Christians who are leading the above legislative measures are not being proactive—they are being reactive. They are reacting to changes in this country that have not been neutral toward religion, but hostile to it. All of a sudden, Christians in this country have found themselves under selective assault. God has, almost overnight, been removed from the educational, legal, and political institutions of the country.

And what is Rabbi Lapin's advice about how to respond to these appalling developments? What action does he suggest?

> I seek to encourage those Americans similarly inclined to help return America to its founding moral imperative. This is neither a cry for religious revolution nor a crusade; it is something else entirely. It is a reminder that we have lost our way. It is a suggestion that we return home again.[21]

Concerned friend, there *is* a way home; we do *not* have to remain lost. And in the final section of this book we wish to shine a bright light on the path that we believe leads back to life.

PART FOUR:
THE CHALLENGE

11

THE PRO-MORAL MAJORITY

Son of man, I have made you a watchman for the house of Israel;
therefore hear a word from My mouth, and give them warning from
Me: "When I say to the wicked, 'You shall surely die,' and you give
him no warning, nor speak to warn the wicked from his wicked way,
to save his life, that same wicked man shall die in his iniquity;
but his blood I will require at your hand."
Ezekiel 3:17–18

With almost virtual control of the national media, newspapers, magazines, book distribution, education, and government, humanists give the impression that they speak for the majority in America.

They don't.

According to pollster George Barna, only 6 percent of the American people are atheists.[1] One past president of the American Humanist Association, Isaac Asimov, placed the figure of humanists in America at 7.3 million—a small fraction of our nation's population of 270 million.

Yet notice how the press plays up the radical feminists in America, leading one to believe that the majority of American women are feminists. It simply is not true; we guess that fewer than 1 percent of American women are feminists. Most American women are not seeking to destroy patriarchy and establish matriarchy. Most American women prefer that men fight the nation's wars.

A quarter of a century ago pollster George Gallup announced that 50 million Americans claimed to have had a born-again experience and that more than one-third of the adult population reported a life-changing religious experience (60 million of whom identified that experience with Jesus Christ). By 1998, Barna could say, "We have somewhere in the neighborhood of eighty million adult believers in the United States."[2] Beyond that, 86 percent of the American people call themselves Christians or at least describe their religious orientation as Christian.[3]

The True Pro-Moral Majority

By analyzing Barna's and Gallup's statistics, one can conclude that the overwhelming majority of Americans prefer a moral culture in which to raise their children. It is reasonable to assume, therefore, that 80 million Christian adults in this country would vote for morality if the issues were made clear. An additional 60 to 80 million—including Protestants who do not stress a born-again experience, Jews, Catholics, Mormons, Muslims, and others whose moral ideals are either biblically based or at least not hostile to biblically based morality—would also vote the pro-moral cause if they saw it clearly.

Although another one-third of our population does not attend church, we estimate that 50 million or more could be safely classified as "idealistic moralists," who do not consider a Bible-based morality overly burdensome. That is, they were raised in a Christian consensus and possess a God-given, moral conscience. They may not live up to their moral ideals all the time—none of us do—but they hold these values in high regard.

The amoral group is harder to pinpoint. As we have seen, humanists account for only 7.3 million adults, while Barna says there are approximately 15 million atheists and agnostics in America. Add to that number the moral degenerates—gangsters, prostitutes, porn publishers, drug peddlers, militant homosexuals, abortionists, and others without any Bible-based moral values—and we might be able to account for approximately 20 to 30 million adults.

The obvious conclusion is that America is *not* a godless nation of hedonists or humanists without moral values. Consider these interesting statistics:[4]

- 69 million adults hope to "go to heaven only because of their faith in Jesus Christ";

- 124 million adults believe Jesus Christ is divine;

- 65 million adults believe the Bible is inerrant;

- 77 million adults believe that God created Adam and Eve;

- 100 million adults are members of churches or synagogues;

- 40 million adults attend church weekly;

- 17 million adults attend more than once a week;

- 147 million adults believe in God or a universal Spirit;

- 140 million adults believe in life after death;

- 132 million adults (84 percent) believe that the Ten Commandments are valid today.

During the fifty years I have been a minister, I have watched the number of professing Christians double in our country. Years ago the humanists thought they had stifled the American church by founding the Federal, National, and World Council of Churches. But they had not reckoned with the power of the Holy Spirit to work through Bible-believing churches, which have grown enormously during that period.

After World War II, most large denominations were liberal. But these groups have suffered a great decline, whereas fundamental, conservative, more orthodox churches have flourished to such a degree that almost every city in the land boasts a number of dynamic, Bible-believing congregations. Fifty years ago I knew of only two large churches with more than a thousand worshipers in attendance. Today there are scores of such churches, with some "superchurches" running over fifteen thousand in membership. In California alone I know of six churches whose average attendance is close to five thousand each Sunday. One church I know of seats twelve thousand; another requires two and more services to accommodate its fifteen thousand worshipers.

More than a quarter million Bible-believing churches are spread throughout the country. One denomination, the Baptist Bible Fellowship, started fifty years ago; today it numbers over three thousand churches, some of which are among the largest in the nation. The Southern Baptist Convention seems to grow an additional million every three years and now has sixteen million members. In addition, millions of people attend "the electric church" of television every Sunday. This was unknown fifty years ago.

Many of our congregations are also enjoying a refreshing movement of the Holy Spirit. Churches that were spiritually dead just one or two decades ago have come to life, and the Spirit-controlled lifestyle they teach has injected a new vitality and joy into their members. It's contagious! Recently a secular reporter called me to get my view on the number of Generation X young people who are returning to churches even though they were not brought up in church. I mentioned the futility and hopelessness that secularism engenders and how it often leads some to suicide, cults, TM, Wicca, or other equally empty fads. But in the church, these disillusioned young people are finding life and a reason to get out of bed in the morning.

But church growth is not the only fact declaring that Christianity is alive and well. The fastest growing movement in the nation is that of home schools and Christian schools (kindergarten through twelfth grade). That is why secularists oppose any form of tax credits, vouchers, or tuition subsidies for private, religious schools. They would rather subject inner-city children to inferior public schools (which educate no one) than to see them attending religious schools where they would receive a superior education.

Amazingly, there have been some glimmers of hope even in certain public school districts. Legislators in the states of Georgia, Arkansas, and Louisiana recently voted to require that creationism be taught along with evolution. Other states such as Alabama, Oklahoma, and Kansas are warning their students that evolution is a theory of science and not scientific fact. Humanists are becoming quite agitated about the success of the creationist movement in getting fair-minded public school systems to insist that scientific creationism be taught along with the theory of evolution. For two generations they have had it all their way, teaching only evolutionary theory. Being forced to give equal time to creation unnerves them.

And what about the colleges and universities? After my discharge from the air force, I found only a handful of Christian colleges. Today there are scores of good Bible-believing colleges. In addition, most of the older ones have at least doubled in size. While liberal seminaries, totally infiltrated by humanism, have died or have been forced to merge with others, conservative seminaries and Bible institutes have flourished—and new ones continue to start up. Christian colleges and universities are not only multiplying, but many are also full to overflowing, for which we thank God. Our prayer is that these institutions remain faithful to Christ and avoid with all their might the influences of evolutionary teachings, psychobabble, homosexual propaganda, and even theological heresies pertaining to the nature of God and man. We are praying that all Christian colleges become bastions of the biblical Christian worldview and strong opponents of the humanistic, naturalistic, evolutionistic, global government worldviews.

During these same years, one phenomenon has helped to slow the humanist juggernaut: the growth in Christian publishing. Humanists once had such a stranglehold on publishing and the means of distribution that Christians started their own publishing houses, magazines, and periodicals. Today millions of Christian books are produced annually and sold through several avenues:

- sixty-five hundred Christian bookstores across the country;
- large, secular book chains and discount outlets such as Sam's Clubs and Wal*Mart;
- mass market;
- book clubs and catalogs;
- spin racks in airport shops, grocery stores, and other outlets;
- on-line booksellers such as Amazon.com and its competitors.

Largely through these outlets and by the Lord's grace, God has richly blessed my writing ministry, with more than 10 million copies of my books sold. My recent prophetic novel series *Left Behind* (coauthored with Jerry Jenkins) has seen that number increase to over thirty million now in print. These books represent a portion of my calling and pastoral ministry to American believers.

Christian publishers are making such an impact on the marketplace that secular book companies are seeking, and in some cases succeeding, to buy them out. The last time I attended a Christian Bookseller's Convention, three such publishers had agents in attendance to investigate whether any Christian publishers were for sale. When that happens, you can be sure that Christian publishing is profitable! In addition, four secular publishers approached me about writing a book for them. This can only mean that we are getting our message out, despite the secularists' control of newsstands and bookstores, which often refuse to carry Christian literature.

Another powerful factor in the recent harvest of souls is the new openness of Christians to share their faith. Dr. Bill Bright, who founded Campus Crusade for Christ (now with a staff of 16,500), can largely be credited with spearheading the training of thousands of Christians who are storming the spiritual wastelands of college campuses, leading students by the tens of thousands to Christ. If we had sufficient space, we could detail the scores of other parachurch ministries (InterVarsity, The Navigators, etc.); the more than fourteen hundred Christian radio stations; independent Christian broadcasters; and the cable and satellite television outlets that are reaching millions more in our country.

Focus on the Family and Dr. James C. Dobson have been instrumental in reaching millions of homes and alerting parents to the perils that stalk their families. Focus on the Family also supplies great educational literature for the whole family, and Dr. Dobson's books have reached and encouraged millions. Focus also has launched an institute that will strengthen Christian college students for the battle for the family.

Promise Keepers has reached millions of men with the gospel of Christ, emphasizing the importance of family and seeking to help men become better husbands and fathers. Christian families are receiving outstanding instruction on family living and interpersonal relationships, all biblically based.

Chuck Colson and Prison Fellowship have led the way in providing hope and love for those behind bars. Colson's writings also have awakened tens of thousands to the dangers of secularism and evolution. His work (with Nancy Pearcey), *How Now Shall We Live?* contains a powerful defense of the biblical Christian worldview.

The steady growth of Concerned Women for America from zero just two decades ago to its present 650,000 members is another powerful testimony to the faithfulness of God. The National Organization of Women, on the other hand, has dropped from a membership of 300,000 to its present anemic shell. Today it must rely on the liberal news media to get its antifamily message out. Unfortunately, no one from CWA is ever asked to comment.

David's fast-growing Summit Ministries is educating more and more Christian teenagers in their own biblical Christian worldview, preparing them to withstand the tremendous pressures found on today's college campuses to forsake the faith. Summit Ministries is also developing a series of curricula for all ages, including junior high, senior high, and Sunday School, based upon *Understanding the Times*.

There can be no doubt that Christianity is on the rise in America!

Christianity Up—Morals Down

This is all good news, but according to Gallup's latest work, *Surveying the Religious Landscape*, there's a big problem. As he explains, "Americans are as God-loving, churchgoing and Bible believing as ever. But—and it's a big one—their brand of faithfulness is a mile long and an inch deep."[5]

"A mile long and an inch deep" ultimately spells death for the church, the family, the children, the culture, and finally the civilization. This is an appalling situation that must soon change.

Says Barna, "Although most Americans believe they already know the fundamental truths of the Scriptures, our research has discovered that fewer than 10 percent of American Christians actually possess a biblical worldview."[6]

He further says, "In essence, while millions of Americans possess beliefs that qualify them as Christians, assert that the Bible contains practical lessons and principles for life, and claim that they believe God wants to bless their efforts, they ignore their spiritual resources when the rubber meets the road. In short, the spirituality of Americans is Christian in name only. We desire experience more than knowledge. We seek comfort rather than growth. Faith must come on our terms or we reject it. We have enthroned ourselves as the final arbiters of righteousness, the ultimate rulers of our own experience and destiny. We are the Pharisees of the new millennium."[7]

We are both spiritual and immoral, says Charles Colson.

The time has come to take a serious spiritual inventory. According to Barna, Christians can hardly be distinguished from nonbelievers "by the way they live." He says the evidence suggests "that most American Christians today do not live in a way that is quantifiably different from their non-Christian peers, in spite of the fact that they profess to believe in a set of principles that should clearly set them apart."[8]

According to Barna, "The vast majority of Christians do not behave differently because they do not think differently, and they do not think differently because we have never trained them, equipped them, or held them accountable to do so."[9]

We need to hear what Barna says and then reevaluate our own priorities and commitments:

The average Christian spends more time watching television in one evening than he or she spends reading the Bible during the entire week. Only four out of ten people who claim to be Christian also claim they are "absolutely committed" to the Christian faith. Two out of three born-again believers assert that there is no such thing as absolute moral truth. There are other serious consequences as well.

First, millions of Christians view transformation in Christ as a onetime solution to a "crisis" rather than a lifelong "process." Many professing Christians presume that once a person has made peace with God by declaring Christ to be their eternal Protector, their spiritual journey has, for all intents and purposes, come to an end. Faith in God becomes a sort of spiritual "fire" insurance policy for when they die. The ceremonies, rituals, prayers, teaching, and sacraments of the Church are not perceived to have any practical value.

Second, and perhaps as a consequence, many believers stop growing in their faith. When evaluating their life, instead of measuring their performance against God's commands, the standard for comparison is "Did I do better than the next guy?"

Third, many Christians have developed a distorted understanding of what constitutes purposeful or successful living. When asked to describe the ends they live for, the top items most American Christians reported were good health, a successful career, a comfortable lifestyle, and a functional family. The average Christian assumes that when we are happy, God is happy.

Fourth, a large majority of Christians contend that the true meaning of our earthly existence is to simply enjoy life and reap as much fulfillment as we can from our daily pursuits. Even though most believers acknowledge that their blessings come from God, they further contend that the primary purpose of His blessing is to make them happy. Only a relative handful of believers are aware of God's explanation of the reasons for blessing us—namely, that we should become a blessing to others (see Genesis 12:1–3).

Finally, Christians are not prepared to fight the good fight of faith. We've lost sight of how the history of God's creation and people has unfolded, having become fully insulated within a culture that esteems achievement and comfort over sacrifice and suffering. We're not prepared to fight at all; we look for God's hand of deliverance and blessing in the midst of hardships and challenge, rather than seek ways to serve others immersed in similar—or even more difficult—situations.[10]

Those who have watched the deteriorating moral climate of America are alarmed at the increase of kids killing kids, drug use, promiscuity, infidelity, divorce, homosexuality, and abortion—all true signs of a decaying society. The question is, are we decaying by natural historical processes or by design?

A Disastrous Abandonment

While we have been busy building our churches, schools, and ministries, a small but dedicated cadre of humanists has infiltrated the most influential pathways to the minds of our people: education, the media, organizations, and government. We Christians have almost totally abandoned all of these crucial fields of influence. In fact, many Christian leaders have been so busy fighting among themselves over doctrinal or denominational differences that they still do not recognize the true enemy is humanism and its obsession to secularize society.

Unless these Christian leaders open their eyes and see that America is being overrun with the atheistic, amoral religion of humanism and in response mount a united attack based on morality, humanism is sure to triumph.

In the years since I wrote *The Battle for the Mind*, a significant change has taken place in our nation. Media, including the entertainment industry, has all but replaced the church as the most significant influence on society.

I did not believe Ted Turner when, in his private office in 1983, he told my wife, Beverly, and me that "television is more powerful than the government—it elects the government." Numerous presidential elections have passed since that day, and I believe him now!

Without understanding the power of the media, you cannot understand the election of William Jefferson Clinton. How could a draft dodger, a womanizer, a pathological liar, and one who, as a college student, demonstrated against his own country in a foreign land, be elected president of a patriotic, moral country, filled with 80 million evangelical adult Christians and another 100 million pro-moral people, plus 33 million veterans and their families? It cannot be explained without acknowledging the power of the media.

Why, after lying to the American people and being impeached by Congress for perjury, was Clinton not expelled from office? Only one reason: He is the darling of the leftist media. They have protected him at all costs because he promotes their liberal worldview: big government, socialism, UN globalism, feminization of the military, abortion, homosexuality, and multiculturalism. He does whatever the humanist elite tell him to do, including ruling by executive order.

Only an informed church, led by faithful pastor-shepherds, can return moral sanity to our society. But you can rest assured that it will never happen if 52 percent or more of our numbers continue to refuse to study the issues and to vote on election day. If someone is not going to vote for a pro-moral candidate, he certainly is not going to protest the porn shop around the corner or the abortion mill slaughtering thousands daily or the professor stealing his son's or daughter's Christian faith.

Doctrinal Purity Versus Moral Degeneracy

For fifty years I have been a biblical fundamentalist with strong doctrinal convictions. Any pastor or church leader in San Diego, California, where I ministered for twenty-five years, will testify that I never compromised my doctrinal integrity. To this day there remain some Christian groups with whom I cannot work in projects of evangelism.

But the battle against Secular Humanism is a cosmic struggle between worldviews. Listen carefully to Charles Colson: "The culture war is not just about abortion, homosexual rights, or the decline of public education. These are only the skirmishes. The real war is a cosmic struggle between worldviews—between the Christian worldview and the various secular and spiritual [New Age] worldviews arrayed against it. This is what we must understand if we are going to be effective both in evangelizing our world today and in transforming it to reflect the wisdom of the Creator."[11]

Humanists have totally rejected God, creation, Bible-based morality, and the fallen state of man. As such, they represent the most serious threat to our nation in its history. Unless both Christian and non-Christian lovers of virtue stand together as upright citizens, humanists will turn this great land into a modern version of Sodom and Gomorrah.

Let us be honest and confess right now that some of our cities are already there. Says Dennis Prager, "No city in America has so rejected Judeo-Christian norms and traditional conceptions of the holy as has San Francisco."[12] He notes, "The ideas that emanate from the secular [humanist] university and from secular San Francisco, and the chaos in the arts since God was expunged from most artists' lives and works—the most God-oriented of the composers, Bach, wrote the greatest music ever produced, while most of our secular music world produces schlock—are the primary reasons I am religious. I long ago concluded that there is no viable alternative to a God-based value system and society."[13]

When I was assigned to a B-29 flight crew as a waist gunner, I did not ask the other ten men whether they were Catholics, Jews, or Protestants. I merely wanted to know if they could fly the plane or shoot the 50-millimeter machine guns. Later I discovered that the other waist gunner was a Mormon, the turret gunner a Catholic, and the tail gunner a Southern Baptist. We probably never could have worked together on a religious project (in fact, we could not talk about theology without disagreement), but on one fundamental issue we were in 100 percent agreement: We were all Americans interested in preserving our country's freedom.

Today the battle is not physical but moral. Unless a sufficient number of pro-moral Americans acknowledge that fact and are willing to do battle on a basis of common moral conviction, we see no hope for freedom in the twenty-first century. If, however, pro-moral leaders of all religious persuasions are willing to stand together as fellow Americans concerned with preservation of the family and moral decency, we can still win this battle for the minds and hearts of our children.

Salt-and-Light Saints

For two thousand years, the church in the Western world has served as the moral conscience of society. In recent years, many church leaders have been reluctant to speak out on moral issues. Some have addressed particular social problems within the walls of their churches, of course, as if that fulfilled their responsibility, but therein lies the problem. We in the Bible-believing churches have done a reasonably good job of letting our light shine, but that is only half of our Lord's command to His people:

> You are the salt of the earth; but if the salt loses its flavor, how shall it be seasoned? It is then good for nothing but to be thrown out and trampled underfoot by men.
>
> You are the light of the world. A city that is set on a hill cannot be hidden. Nor do they light a lamp and put it under a basket, but on a lampstand, and it gives light to all who are in the house. Let your light so shine before men, that they may see your good works and glorify your Father in heaven. (Matthew 5:13–16)

Society is in a state of moral decay, not because the majority of Americans love degeneracy but because humanism has exercised more influence on our culture than has the church. We can tell thousands of thrilling stories of individuals whose lives have been transformed by a personal experience of faith in Jesus Christ. But we have not been the moral salt and light in our community that we should be. We have failed to give moral leadership to our society. We have permitted, either by ignorance, ineptitude, or laziness, a powerful minority to take over our culture.

David and I are convinced that believing correctly, "walking in the Spirit," or even aggressively sharing our faith with others falls short of our full Christian responsibility. God also expects us to be good parents, responsible citizens, watchmen on the wall, our brother's keeper, and the moral salt and light of the earth. And of course, vote in every election, local, state, and national.

Approximately 55 million school-age children are at stake. They are growing up in an amoral atmosphere, misled by educators who think of them as primates. No wonder our young people fail to distinguish their moral right hand from their left!

God saved Nineveh from destruction after the nation's leaders and adults repented, thus preserving the 120,000 persons who knew not their left hand from their right. We believe He will also save America, if the church will aggressively lead the pro-moral majority to stop this toboggan slide to depravity and return our nation to moral sanity.

That kind of revival will come only if today's faithful ministers and shepherds of the sheep will provide the kind of assertive leadership that John Wesley and George Whitfield brought to colonists in the early eighteenth century, when through their efforts they blessed our nation with the Great Awakening.

Let's Hear It for Morality

We pro-moralists—that is, all who believe in Bible-based morality or moral order—have been silent too long. Except for a few sporadic voices, Christians have been reluctant to voice their political and civic concerns. We have not figured out that politics and voting are merely the public expression of our privately held values and beliefs.

Because you now realize that we really represent the majority in this country, you must raise your voice so that all can hear—from your neighborhood to the state house to the White House. We are convinced that people are waiting for pro-moral leadership.

After carefully analyzing the data taken from grassroots America in "the most comprehensive study we have ever done in the area of religion," George Gallup said, "Americans want a vocal church on spiritual, moral, and ethical matters. People of all faiths want churches and other religious organizations to speak out. However, there is a sharp divergence of opinion among members of various denominations and faiths when it comes to political and economic matters. This, of course, should not surprise us."

The electrifying response of Americans, both Catholic and Protestant, to the Pope's visit to the United States in 1979 and again in 1999 ought to communicate loudly to Christian leaders throughout the country. Wherever he went, crowds appeared in greater numbers than anticipated. Never in our lifetime has an international religious figure spoken out so aggressively on moral issues. The stronger he addressed those issues, the larger the crowds grew.

The pro-moral majority will follow such leadership, but they must hear a call to moral activism from their spiritual shepherds. The editors of *Christianity Today* had this in mind when they added an interesting comment to the George Gallup article:

> The all too obvious failure of liberalism has coincided with a hunger for basic morality and a revitalization of fundamental Christianity. This has created a day of unprecedented opportunity for evangelicals to present the gospel to the world in which we live as well as to effect substantive changes for good within our society. We must now show the world that evangelicals care and know how to translate theology into compassionate action.

We could not agree more! Our caring should be demonstrated in our:

- evangelism—demonstrating our concern for the souls of men;

- brotherly love—proving that we care for them as people (when they hurt, we should be the first to help);
- moral activism—showing that we love their children by voicing our opposition to amoral legislation and advocating pro-morality on the part of government, by the way you vote.

This will also mean that we get involved in the electoral process as faithful citizens, either as candidates or as workers assisting the right kind of candidates. We must be more vocal in letting political leaders know our opinions on pending legislation that involves morals and family values.

To be specific, Christians should raise their voices, from their homes, churches, and places of business, whenever matters come up regarding the following:

- *abortion*—We must forbid the use of tax monies for this form of child abuse.
- *homosexuality*—Our laws are already too weak in this area, and we must never accept homosexual marriages or adoption of children.
- *pornography*—We need laws to eliminate all pornography from our land.
- *prostitution*—This is a blight to any society.
- *gambling*—It is wrong, hurts the poor, and breeds crime.
- *infanticide and euthanasia*—Only God has the right to decide who has the right to live.
- *parents' rights*—God gave parents the right and responsibility to raise their children. Until government figures out a way to bear children, it must refrain from usurping parents' rights.
- *drugs*—Drugs destroy the body, impair the mind, and twist an individual's morals. Substance abuse, as well as efforts to legalize the recreational use of drugs, must continue to be vigorously opposed.

- *world government*—Turning American sovereignty over to the UN should be resisted. Placing U.S. soldiers under UN command should be resisted.

- *Religious or Secular Humanism*—Any and all forms should be vigorously opposed, particularly in government and education.

If a sufficient number of pro-moral Americans speak out and vote accordingly on these issues, more than enough morally minded people in our land would act to stop our descent into an amoral abyss. And we could return our nation to moral self-respect and decency.

12

SUMMER SOLDIERS
AND SUNSHINE PATRIOTS

Onward Christian soldiers! Marching as to war,
With the cross of Jesus, going on before.
SABINE BARING-GOULD

My wife and I have traveled in forty-four countries, including five communist nations, and I can say one thing for certain:

Christianity around the world is *not* dying!

It may surprise you to know that we are experiencing a mighty moving of the Holy Spirit all around the globe. The press says little about it, but Christianity is on the rise. Missionaries report that individuals in Third-World countries—despite repressive regimes, oppressive inflation, and starvation conditions—are turning to Christ in unprecedented numbers. For two decades great numbers of people in South America have been finding Christ. Missionaries in Europe indicate a renewed interest in the gospel. One missionary in France told me that more were converted to Christ in one year than had been saved in his first eleven years there. I could tell you of the work of God in India, Singapore, South Korea, and Taiwan. Reports coming out of both Russia and China indicate a surprising thirst for Christ on the part of the young.

Christianity is *growing* worldwide, not dying. While we cannot precisely assess its growth, we estimate that the church has more than doubled in the last twenty-five years.

The bankruptcy of humanism is rapidly becoming apparent, causing many to return to basics. That often means a return to church and biblical principles for living. Never have we seen a better time for sharing our faith than today! Spirit-filled, salty Christians will reap a mighty harvest.

Why This Book?

Because my wife and I have traveled around the world, spoken face-to-face with over 16 percent of the world's faithful missionaries, and visited the largest Christian radio stations in the world, we have recognized a fundamental fact: 80 to 85 percent of the world's missionaries, most of the technology for preaching the gospel, and most of the money for world missions come from America. The eternal souls of millions of people depend on American Christians to supply them with the good news. If the anti-God, amoral, one-world secularists succeed in enslaving our country, that missionary outlet will be terminated. We are deeply concerned that this ministry be extended.

That is the reason why a minister and a Christian educator have combined forces to vigorously attack the religion of humanism. While we are both patriotic Americans, that is not our dominant concern.[1] We are first and foremost committed Christians.[2] As such, we have a command to preach the gospel to every creature (Colossians 1:23). That is our highest priority. We eagerly answer "Yes!" to the question of the old hymn, "Am I a soldier of the cross?"

Yet in this battle for the mind, the humanist, or pagan, left has been very successful in making words like "war," "battle," and "fight the good fight" politically incorrect. They prefer words like "pluralism," "tolerance," and "celebrate diversity."

In practice, however, secularists turn out to be terribly warlike and intolerant. They allow no opinions that challenge their dogmas. If you doubt that statement, then try to introduce creationism into the classroom. You'll quickly see what the doctrine of diversity really means. Or try to defend the United States in a multicultural course, and you will see what tolerance really means. They brook no competition!

David Horowitz paints the sobering picture: "The fact is that leftists in the universities, through decades of political hiring and promotion, and through systematic intellectual intimidation, have virtually driven conservative thought from the halls of academe. A call made to one of the handful of known conservatives allowed to teach a humanities subject at Princeton confirmed the following suspicion: In Sean Wilentz's history department not a single conservative can be found among its fifty-six faculty members."[3]

That is a perfect illustration of what the humanist left means by pluralism, tolerance, and diversity.

A Call to Arms

We sincerely pray that God will use this book to rouse untold numbers of readers to defend our nation's Bible-based morals. If other ministers of the gospel will use their sphere of influence to similarly oppose humanist thought, we can yet win this battle for the nation's mind and heart. We will yet see the Iron Curtain that surrounds our educational system crumble, just as the Iron Curtain came tumbling down along with the Berlin Wall.

Neither of us wishes to hear the mournful refrain, "No one cares for my soul" (Psalm 142:4). We do care! We believe one soul is worth your time, your effort, your resources, and your very life, as well as the church's time, effort, and resources. Churches need to heed the advice of Chuck Colson and Nancy Pearcey when they say parents "need support from the church, which means local churches need to encourage youth group leaders to go beyond volleyball and pizza parties and begin to teach apologetics and worldview issues."[4]

Nothing in life or death is more important than living for God's truth and righteousness—His moral order, His societal order, His governing order, and His eternal order.

Paul tells us in Colossians that all wisdom and knowledge reside in Christ (2:2–3). Christ is the foundation of all truth.

The Bible tells us that God Himself ordained the family and gave it definition: a married man and woman living together with their children (Mark 10:6–7).

Isaiah the prophet makes it very clear that the Son born in Bethlehem is the proper One to whom we must give our allegiance. Indeed, if it is not Christ, then it will be Plato, Hegel, Marx—statism, collectivism, socialism.

Yet somehow, while Christians do not seem to be tongue-tied when it comes to family values, they do become summer soldiers and sunshine patriots when it comes to government, politics, and political theory.

The left and its media friends simply announce:

- "You can't speak out on abortion, homosexuality, pornography, gambling, prostitution; those are political issues."

- "You can't mention Christ in the public square; that's religious."

- "You can't speak about carrying out the Great Commission; that's hate speech"—and too many Christians shut their mouths, drop their weapons, and walk away.

Do you think the statement about evangelism as hate speech goes too far? Then you haven't heard Joe Lockhart, the official White House spokesman, who declared "that the evangelical Christian notion of carrying out the Great Commission and spreading Christianity . . . equates with perpetuating 'ancient religious hatred.'"[5] As one commentator noted, "In effect, the Clinton administration is now on record as believing that the practice of biblical Christianity is tantamount to a 'hate crime.'"[6]

In addition, the Federal Communications Commission has ruled (FCC Order 99-393) that 50 percent of the programming on noncommercial radio stations "be free of what is their stock in trade: church services, sermons, Bible study, prayer, and all manner of discussion by believers, including syndicated talk shows hosted by the likes of James Dobson and D. James Kennedy."[7] It appears to be "educational" to denounce Christ, while to praise Him is "noneducational."

And still some of our Christian clergy tremble to speak out.

Here is our challenge: Lead! Display godly courage. Go before your congregation and preach the whole counsel of God. Give your flock a detailed defense of the biblical Christian worldview. Start a series of sermons on Matthew 23. You'll quickly see that Christ was not afraid of the religious, political, or legal powers of His time.

Some will say, "Yes, but look at what happened to Him. They crucified Him!"

We know. But that is what biblical Christianity is all about. The Bible tells us that we, too, must suffer for our faith in Him (2 Timothy 3:10–12). Those saints mentioned in Hebrews 11—including the one who was sawed in two—were not tortured because they sat cloistered in the pew, listening to a ten-minute sermon and singing twenty-six verses of "Just As I Am." They were tortured because they left the church grounds and ventured into the public square (Acts 17:16–17), armed with their moral values and biblical beliefs. The world hated them for their truthful statements and for their godly living.

But they determined to follow God's marching orders, whatever the cost.

Of course, whenever you talk about Christians and other morally committed citizens coming to the aid of their country by taking positions of leadership in various fields of influence, the left goes ballistic. They attack us in the press and media as though the social and political involvement of God-fearing Americans is the worst thing that could happen to the nation. They forget, or they were never taught, that Christian involvement in all areas of community life is the heritage of America.

Surprisingly, some opposition to Christian involvement in politics comes from within the church. Even some Bible-believing Christians look askance at their spiritual brothers and sisters who decide to enter the political process.

We think they are in error. And here's why.

Bible Prophecy and Political Involvement

Most knowledgeable, Bible-believing Christians are "looking for the blessed hope and glorious appearing of our great God and Savior Jesus Christ" (Titus 2:13). The return of Christ has been the hope of believers since the first century (1 Thessalonians 4:13–18).

The atheist Bertrand Russell thought the Scriptures erred regarding Matthew 24 and the "this generation" passage (24:34), but he and many others have missed the context. The qualifying expression is "when you see all these things." This expression determines what "this generation" means. It refers to the generation that is present when "all these things" happen: Antichrist, tribulation, signs in heaven, and the return of Christ to the Mount of Olives.

Because present world conditions so closely resemble Bible prophecies of the last days (see 2 Timothy 3:1–7; 2 Peter 3:1–4; Matthew 24:6–7, 37–38), some Christians have concluded that a takeover of our culture by the forces of evil is inevitable. Consequently they do nothing to resist it. They say, "It is necessary that perilous times shall come as we approach the end of the age," so they are unwilling to raise their voices in protest.

This is totally unscriptural! We are commanded to resist the devil and to put on the whole armor of God, that we may be able to withstand in the evil day (Ephesians 6:13).

Christians were never called to be summer soldiers and sunshine patriots. We were called to be active for Christ in season and out of season. We are to emulate the apostle Paul, who left the comfort of the sanctuary and went out into the public square and confronted the humanists of his day (Acts 17:16–34). Centuries earlier Elijah also challenged the humanists of his day (1 Kings 18). And Jesus the Messiah moved into the very headquarters of humanism and took on the Greek and Roman humanists at Mount Hermon (Matthew 16:13ff; 17:1–2).

If we are indeed at the end of the age, we should be raising our voices all the louder in defense of truth and virtue. Should Jesus Christ come for a church full of neutered Christians or for a church on the front lines of the battle for the world's soul, heart, and mind? Jesus Himself asked, "When the Son of Man comes, will He really find faith on the earth?" (Luke 18:8).

William Butler Yeats apparently wondered the same thing in his poem "The Second Coming":

> The best lack all conviction, while the worst
> Are full of passionate intensity.

Robert Bork comments, "When Yeats wrote that in 1919, he may have foreseen that the twentieth century would experience the 'blood-dimmed tide,' as indeed it has. But he can hardly have had any conception of just how thoroughly things would fall apart as the center failed to hold in the last third of this century. He can hardly have foreseen that passionate intensity uncoupled from morality would shred the fabric of

Western culture. The rough beast of decadence, a long time in gestation, having reached its maturity in the last three decades, now sends us slouching towards our new home, not Bethlehem, but Gomorrah."[8]

While we believe in a future seven-year tribulation period in which the Antichrist will rule the world, we do not believe that a humanist takeover of America must be part of that scenario. A humanist takeover of America is neither predestined nor necessary.

But it will deluge the land in the next few years unless Christians become much more assertive in defense of truth, morality, goodness, and decency.

We are not blind to the fact that world conditions are depraved. Adultery, fornication, abortion, pornography, drugs, and homosexuality (see Luke 17: 26–30; Romans 1:24–32) are rampant, and moderns are "lovers of themselves, lovers of money, boasters, proud, blasphemers, disobedient to parents, unthankful, unholy, unloving, unforgiving, slanderers, without self-control, brutal, despisers of good, traitors, headstrong, haughty, lovers of pleasure rather than lovers of God" (2 Timothy 3:2–4). That passage sounds like the front page of most daily newspapers, yet it was written almost two thousand years ago.

But as we watch, wait, prepare, and work until the return of Christ, such a dreadful condition does not have to overwhelm the world. Before Antichrist appears on the scene to set up his kingdom of darkness, Russia will be destroyed by God for attacking Israel (Ezekiel 38–39). The Hebrew prophets foresaw a Western confederation of nations that would mildly oppose Russia. America, Canada, England, a section of Europe, and Australia form part of that Western confederation. But there is no prophetic requirement that this Western confederation be in a state of moral bankruptcy before that day—a day which precedes the seven-year Tribulation.

Sweden and Holland may be closer right now to pre-tribulation moral conditions than any other nations in the Western world. Why is this so? Not because it was predestined but because the godly Christians and pro-moral citizens living there did nothing to stop the socialist, humanist takeover of their universities, media, and government. Consequently, they have turned those delightful lands into moral sewers.

It may be too late for the Christians of Sweden and Holland to oust the humanists from office, but it certainly is not too late in America and Canada. And there may still be time to save England and Australia, although the Fabian Socialists of Great Britain are boasting that twenty of the twenty-three ministers in the present labor government are humanists and socialists.

In order to bring about godly change, however, Christians must get involved in the political process. And they must do so immediately.

A Vision of What It Might Be

In closing this chapter, let us portray how things might look if America took seriously the challenge to once again be the city set on a hill, shining its light on the world.

Christians would seriously repent of their sins and ask the Lord God of the universe to forgive our national sins—cleaning up our moral lives and putting God, the family, the church, our fellowman, our vocations, and our country in proper priority.

Christians would reach out in love to the moral barbarians[9] of our nation and persuade them that they have been deceived about God and his moral order. They would insist that sexual liberation or snorting coke does not lead to an earthly paradise.

Christians would share the loving gospel of Jesus Christ with the empty-hearted victims of our society, leading millions to receive Him.

Christians would take seriously their individual and church responsibilities and thus spiritually and morally turn the world right side up, as did the first-century Christians.

The silence of the churches would be broken, and pastors would no longer be intimidated by politicians, the press, or academia.

The church of Jesus Christ would once again become the moral conscience of the nation and speak out clearly on the issues, as she once did regarding slavery and civil rights, when pulpits were aflame with righteousness and America's conscience was pricked.

Christian youth would be committed to the Word of God, would give honor and respect to their parents, and would obey those in authority.

Elected officials would work to restore our God-given, inalienable rights of life for the born and unborn, freedom of religious expression, and protection from injustice, as well as the freedom to pursue our dreams and earn our keep, independent of government intrusion. The anti-God act of abortion would be seen as the cruel, conscienceless, and immoral practice it is and would be chased from our nation.

Adoption would become a national issue instead of abortion.

The anti-God acts of homosexuality, pedophilia, prostitution, and other perverse sexual practices would be universally viewed as immoral and would be shunned.[10]

Our nation would effectively curtail the $20-billion-a-year pornography business.

Morally minded legislators, voted into office by the Christian and pro-moral community, would take charge of the federally controlled airwaves and establish standards of decency for television, radio, and entertainment and would refuse to license stations and networks that violated that code.

Video and recording studios would be required to produce music and other forms of entertainment that stay within the law. Songwriters and musicians who advocate the murder of police officers, the mutilation and rape of women, illegal drugs, and child abuse would be fined or at least exposed.

Parents would be able to send their children to the school of their choice via private, nongovernmental scholarships or vouchers.[11]

Liberal politicians who send their children to private schools to avoid the rot in a dysfunctional public school would give that same opportunity to the poor families of America.

Liberal politicians would finally admit they were wrong in placing women in combat and sodomizing the U.S. armed forces.

Mothers would be free to stay at home to raise their babies.

Women would realize they were lied to by the radical feminists.

Churches of all sorts would become serious about educating their children academically, spiritually, and morally—providing a quality education with a biblical base.

Fathers would remain in the home and practice what the Scriptures teach about being the spiritual head of the family, including providing for and protecting their wives and children.[12]

Our morally committed legislators would officially recognize that this country is indeed "one nation under God" and would lead the nation to write that fact into law by adding it to the U.S. Constitution.

Voluntary public prayer would be welcomed in public schools, and those who took offense would be free to send their children elsewhere.

God, the Ten Commandments, the Bible, and prayer would be reintroduced into the public schools.

Creationism would be given equal time with Darwinian evolution in our public schools.

The federal government would get out of the educational business altogether, and the federal Department of Education—with its anti-American, one world, evolutionistic, socialistic agenda—would be allowed to pass into oblivion.

Public schools would cancel their explicit sex-education programs (including the federal government's sponsorship of Captain Condom) and choose instead to inspire students to spend more time on academic subjects like reading, writing, and arithmetic, as well as other subjects that would help prepare them for a meaningful and noble life.

Christian schools would ground their students in the biblical Christian worldview.

Christian college faculties would see through the lies of feminism, abortion, multiculturalism, evolution, socialism, globalism, and homosexual marriages.

Seven hundred fifty-five federal judges would be committed to upholding the U.S. Constitution, enabling the U.S. to once again enjoy "justice under law," rather than imposing liberal, humanist interpretations that promote Secular Humanism.

The U.S. Supreme Court would interpret the laws as the Founding Fathers originally intended, rather than according to current whims and personal preferences.

Christians and other morally upright citizens would be represented in our government in proportion to their actual numbers in the general population, so that godly values—not those of the humanist left—guided our nation.

The federal government would return much of its decision-making power to the states, according to constitutional design, thus dramatically reducing the federal tax bite.[13]

Parents would demand that educators stop rewriting history and instead let the facts speak for themselves.[14]

Parents would demand an end to the drug culture and pursue a course of action that would bring all drug pushers to swift justice.

Our children would be taught the role of Christians and others in the founding and development of this country.

Truth, goodness, morality, and righteousness would be subjects of interest.

Art and literature would reflect God's orderly creation instead of man's confused psychological states of disorder, and the federal government would cease funding cultural sewers.[15]

This would be a magnificent start to that "city on a hill" vision of "one nation under God" that most Americans and all Christians would love to see presented to the world. This would be a start toward making sure that the government is resting on Messiah's shoulders (Isaiah 9:6) and not on Plato's.

Our faith is a living, twenty-four-hour-a-day relationship with God through Jesus Christ our Lord, resulting in a life that benefits our churches, homes, culture, country, and our own souls. Now we have to figure out how to wake the sleeping giant and convince him that biblical Christianity demands more of this time than two hours on Sunday morning.

13

WAKING THE SLEEPING GIANT

Why do the nations rage, and the people plot a vain thing?
The kings of the earth set themselves, and the rulers take counsel
together, against the LORD and against His Anointed, saying,
"Let us break Their bonds in pieces and cast away
Their cords from us."
PSALM 2:1–3

efore we can fully awaken the sleeping giant, we must first understand why he fell asleep. And we also need to clarify for what purpose we must awaken him. This requires a brief review of how we arrived at our current situation.

Holes in the Ship

Generally speaking, modern men have not grasped the tremendous holes Charles Darwin and Karl Marx gashed into the hull of Western civilization's ship.

Up to that time the major figure of Western civilization had been Jesus Christ, with the Bible (both Old and New Testaments) its primary textbook. It was a cultural given that God created the universe and everything in it and that man was created in the image of God a little lower than the angels, though far above the animals (Psalm 8:5–6). Man was believed to be so important in God's plans that God descended to earth in the person of Jesus the Messiah and was willing to live and die for the sins of the whole world—a marvelous demonstration of divine love.

This prevailing notion of life and divine love radically changed with Darwin and Marx and their millions of disciples. Instead of placing man under the angels in God's creative scheme of things, man was placed among the animals—no better than an insect, a tapeworm, or a chimp.

"Most people," says Daniel Lapin, "are unaware that the Peabody Museum at Yale University recently reclassified *Homo sapiens* (men and women) so that certain species of chimpanzees are included in the same genus. For the first time in the glorious history of Western civilization the special uniqueness of the human being is being denied."[1]

This is the same Yale University that returned $20 million dollars to Lee Bass because it could not abide by his stipulation for the gift. Bass, a Yale alumnus, wanted his grant to be used for the study of Western civilization. The university wanted to use it for a multicultural curriculum,[2] not one "that favored Western Civilization."[3] That any university would return $20 million because it would not teach Western Civ is proof that the hour is late . . . very late.

Is man created in the image of God, with a mind, soul, spirit, and moral nature? Or is he an evolving animal with no soul, no spirit, a physical brain, and an evolving moral and legal structure to match? Much of Western history over the last 150 years has chronicled the struggle over this question.

Daniel Lapin summarizes our point: "If we got here by a process of unaided materialistic evolution [the humanist position], then we are not significantly different from animals, and everyone knows that animals do not have moral choice. We do not punish a cougar for snatching a rancher's sheep for dinner. That is what cougars do. We may find a way of protecting the farmer's assets but we do not consider the cougar wicked. If we are qualitatively animals, then mugging little old ladies is just what some people do. Labeling their actions as wicked makes no sense and you cannot punish humans who have done nothing wicked any more than you can punish cougars."[4]

Hence the West's dilemma: Is man created in God's own image, or is he the product of evolution with a simultaneously evolving morality?

The bulk of the twentieth century writhed under the conflict caused by this dilemma. Mussolini and Fascism—based on evolution, socialism, and statism—sought to create the "New Fascist Man." Hitler and Nazism—based on evolution, socialism, and statism—sought to create the "New Aryan Man." Stalin and Communism—based on evolution, socialism, and statism—sought to create the "New Soviet Man."

Those three "isms" dominated the last century and accounted for the deaths of tens of millions of human beings. "But the intransigent facts," says *The Black Book of Communism*, "demonstrate that Communist regimes have victimized approximately 100 million people in contrast to the approximately 25 million victims of the Nazis."[5]

R. J. Rummel places the death count in the twentieth century at 172 million human beings, with the possibility of approaching 320 million.[6] This figure does not include the millions of abortions committed under the watchful eye of the humanists and their Planned Parenthood organizations. Without question, the twentieth century was the bloodiest of all centuries. Yet the West, in general, and America, in particular, are still struggling over the question of man's origins—God or nature!

One cannot read about the slaughter of the twentieth century without noting that all the "isms" responsible for the butchery looked upon man as an evolving animal. "In Communism there exists a sociopolitical eugenics, a form of social Darwinism. In the words of Dominic Colas, 'As master of the knowledge of the evolution of the social species, Lenin decided who should disappear by virtue of having been condemned to the dustbin of history.'"[7] Indeed, Lenin always animalized his opponents before he killed them, referring to them as "harmful insects," "lice," "scorpions," and "bloodsuckers."[8]

Today, the humanists—who, as we have seen, number only 7 to 10 million, with perhaps 15 to 20 million fellow travelers in the whole country—have captured, for all intents and purposes, the major power centers of American society. Where is the other 85 to 90 percent of the nation?

Sleeping—sleeping right through the greatest siege of the mind in history.

Who's Really "Pro-Moral"?

Humanists have very cleverly worked the expression "pro-moral" to their advantage by pointing out the human foibles (sin, if you will) of those who defend the pro-moral position.

But just because we have all sinned and come short of the glory of God (Romans 3:23) does not mean that we cannot defend the pro-moral position. The pro-moral position says that God, the creator of the universe, has a moral order as well as a physical order. His moral order is reflected in the conscience of the creatures He made in His own image. The fact that man fell into sin and marred this image, twisting his conscience, in no way detracts from the ability and responsibility of fallen man to defend a pro-moral position.

In the same vein, we can defend a pro-family position (one married man, one married woman, children) and still recognize that divorce is a reality, even that adultery is a reality. Fallen mankind can defend positions that he himself has tarnished by his own sinful behavior.

Yet such lapses do make it more difficult to defend the pro-moral position and do give humanists plenty of ammunition for the media.

Several years ago a reporter was overheard admitting that if the head of the National Council of Churches fell into adultery, he would cover it up, but if Jerry Falwell or Billy Graham fell into adultery, he would splash it all over the front pages of the newspaper. Why? Because Falwell and Graham live and preach a definite moral code, while the liberal clergy have no such code.

(Shortly after this conversation took place, it just so happened that the president of the National Council of Churches *did* commit adultery—and the report was indeed buried by the media.)

Humanists will always defend such activity, and they will always protect their own practitioners of it. But when those who advocate a pro-moral position are discovered to have violated their own code, they are either ridiculed or hounded out of office. Humanists have no problems with employing such a double standard because they operate from an amoral, anti-God ethic. Morality is whatever advances their position.

Do pro-moral people sin? Of course they do. And when they sin, they should repent and ask for God's forgiveness. But pro-moral people also know it is important to maintain a moral standard, even though they themselves sometimes fall short of it.

The amoral ethic may sound good, even very good. In fact, Paul Kurtz in the *Humanist Manifesto 2000* sounds almost like Billy Graham. He says we "ought" to tell the truth, keep promises, be honest, sincere, reliable, and dependable. How he arrives at these moral "oughts" is interesting in itself—we guess that he stole most of them from Christianity—but it's important to remember that these nice-sounding dos and don'ts are only temporary and expedient. They are not fixed. They change according to the situation.

Today, Paul Kurtz and his fellow humanists can afford to be nice, even "love thy neighbor" nice.[9] But when the secularists gain the power to launch America into a global government, you can be sure that these nice sounding moral expressions will change immediately and radically. We will be told that because evolving mankind is entering a new era, a new ethic is required. And the new ethic will exactly mimic the horrors described in *The Black Book of Communism*. At that moment Christians will be termed mentally ill, or as the former UN specialist Dr. Brock Chisholm insists, they will be held accountable for all the social maladjustment and unhappiness in the world and judged accordingly.[10] For resisting the new social and political order, Christians will again face what they faced in the French Revolution, the Russian Revolution, and what George Bernard Shaw termed "execution in a kindly manner."[11]

Pro-moral forces must awaken *now* and resist this threat, or they will witness a worldwide dictatorship without boundaries. This is what the psalmist described when he said, "Why do the nations rage, and the people plot a vain thing? The kings of the earth set themselves, and the rulers take counsel together, against the LORD and against His Anointed, saying, 'Let us break Their bonds in pieces, and cast away Their cords from us'" (Psalm 2:1–2).

Thankfully, the psalmist also tells us that the Lord "sits in the heavens and laughs." Just imagine! Here is puny man, who cannot find his way to the bathroom at 2 A.M., telling the God of the universe how to run things and how to instruct mankind in what is morally and spiritually best.

A modern poet, Steve Turner, put into verse exactly what Christians and the pro-moral forces are up against. His 1978 poem is titled simply "Creed."

> We believe in Marxfreudanddarwin.
> We believe everything is OK
> as long as you don't hurt anyone,
> to the best of your definition of hurt,
> and to the best of your knowledge.

We believe in sex before, during, and after marriage.
We believe in the therapy of sin.
We believe that adultery is fun.
We believe that sodomy is OK.
We believe that taboos are taboo.

We believe that everything is getting better
despite evidence to the contrary.
The evidence must be investigated.
And you can prove anything with evidence.

We believe there's something in
horoscopes, UFOs and bent spoons;
Jesus was a good man
just like Buddha, Mohammed, and ourselves.
He was a good moral teacher
although we think His good morals were bad.

We believe that all religions are basically the same—
at least the one that we read was.
They all believe in love and goodness.
They only differ on matters of
creation, sin, heaven, hell, God, and salvation.

We believe that after death comes the Nothing.
Because when you ask the dead what happens they say nothing.
If death is not the end, if the dead have lied,
then it's compulsory heaven for all
excepting perhaps Hitler, Stalin, and Genghis Khan.

We believe in Masters and Johnson.
What's selected is average.
What's average is normal.
What's normal is good.

We believe in total disarmament.
We believe there are direct links between warfare and bloodshed.
Americans should beat their guns into tractors
and the Russians would be sure to follow.

We believe that man is essentially good.
It's only his behavior that lets him down.
This is the fault of society.
Society is the fault of conditions.
Conditions are the fault of society.

We believe that each man must find the truth that is right for him.
Reality will adapt accordingly.
The universe will readjust.
History will alter.

We believe that there is no absolute truth
excepting the truth that there is no absolute truth.

We believe in the rejection of creeds,
and the flowering of individual thought.

"Chance" a post-script

If chance be the Father of all flesh,
disaster is his rainbow in the sky,
and when you hear

State of Emergency!
Sniper Kills Ten!
Troops on Rampage!
Whites Go Looting!
Bomb Blasts School!

It is but the sound of man worshiping his maker.

Christians and (we hope) all pro-moral Americans believe in something, too. We believe in God. We believe He is the Creator and Redeemer of mankind. We believe that the earth is God's gift to us to preserve and to husband. We believe Jesus Christ is the most dominant figure of Western culture. We believe that family, church, and country are gifts of God. We believe in the moral order and that right and wrong are determined by the Bible. We believe that 3–6 percent of the population should not be able to dictate school curriculum. We believe that prayer, the Bible, the Ten Commandments, and God should be returned to our public schools, government—and for some—our churches as well. We believe that America's founding documents—the Declaration of Independence, U.S. Constitution, Northwest Ordinance Treaty—should be returned to our public school curriculum.

We are in a desperate situation, and we need to awaken the 85 to 90 percent of Americans—Protestant, Catholic, Jew, Mormon, Muslim—to the true condition of their country. If we fail, the last great experiment in free government will perish from the earth. It is either a Bible-based moral order—the pro-moral position—or it is chaos and despair—the amoral position.

Looking for Heroes

One of America's great theologians is Dr. Carl F. H. Henry. In his book *Twilight of a Great Civilization*, he says, "The real heroes of our time are those who in a faithless age hold, live, and share their faith in God. Genuine revolutionary courage belongs to those who remain true to God even if atheistic rulers force them underground or punish citizens simply for being Christians. The true immortals will be those who seek to apply the principles of the Bible concretely to the complicated realities of modern life, who preserve a devout and virtuous family life, who are faithful to the abiding values of yesterday, today, and tomorrow."[12]

It was Joshua who said: "Choose for yourselves this day whom you will serve. . . . As for me and my house, we will serve the LORD" (Joshua 24:15).

Join us! It is not merely a siege of the mind; it is a siege of the twenty-first century. This is one battle where Christians cannot afford to stand on the sidelines. If they do, their children will soon be repeating the New School Prayer:

> Now I sit me down in school
> Where praying is against the rule

For this great nation under God
Finds mention of Him very odd
If Scripture now the class recites
It violates the Bill of Rights
And anytime my head I bow
Becomes a federal matter now
Our hair can be purple or orange or green
That's no offense, it's the freedom scene
The law is specific, the law is precise
Prayers spoken aloud are a serious vice
For praying in a public hall
Might offend someone with no faith at all
In silence alone we must meditate
God's name is prohibited by the State
We're allowed to cuss and dress like freaks
And pierce our noses, tongues and cheeks
They've outlawed guns; but first the Bible
To quote the Good Book makes me liable
We can elect a pregnant Senior Queen
And the unwed daddy, our Senior King
It's "inappropriate" to teach right from wrong
We're taught that such "judgments" do not belong
We can get our condoms and birth control
Study witchcraft, vampires and totem poles
But the Ten Commandments are not allowed
No Word of God must reach this crowd
It's scary here I must confess
When chaos reigns the school's a mess
So, Lord, this silent plea I make
Should I be shot, My soul please take.[13]

If this prayer disturbs you as much as it does us, read the next chapter and ask God what He would have you do in this centuries-old war between the wisdom of God and the wisdom of man. How can you help to save America for the sake of your children and grandchildren?

14

WHAT YOU CAN DO

When the church is doggedly and strategically fulfilling its biblical mandate, there is no group of people in the world that has as significant an impact on humanity.
GEORGE BARNA

If America is going to be saved from Secular Humanism, it will take the combined efforts of the pro-moral majority—and particularly the evangelical Christian community.

"Those of us who venerate freedom," says Daniel Lapin, "be we Jewish or Christian, be we religious or secularized, have no option but to pray for the health of Christianity in America. No other group possesses both the faith and the numbers sufficient to hold back the ever-encroaching, sometimes sinister, power of the [humanist] state."[1]

We evangelical Christians are certainly not the only ones interested in morality, the family, and the church. But most likely we will be the ones motivated to speak out on these issues. If we do, millions of other pro-moralists will follow. Many in mainline churches, who are sick of the liberalism of their denominations, will gladly follow our lead, if they can but hear our voice. Millions more in the Roman Catholic Church are certainly a significant part of the pro-moral majority. The Catholic constituency has been in the forefront of the abortion issue for years, even though major portions of Catholic higher education have fallen for humanism, and liberation theology has drawn many Catholics into the Marxist camp.[2]

We are in a gigantic, cosmic war for the soul of our country—and it takes armies to win wars. We need an army of pro-moral activists, encouraged by their Bible-believing ministers, who will provide America with the spiritual and moral leadership for which this country yearns.

You, dear reader, are only one person—but you are one! You cannot decide for 80 million evangelicals, but you can decide, with God's help, to use whatever gifts, talents, and energy you possess to steer this country away from the rocky coasts of secularism. Each one of us can be a lighthouse of sorts.

Strategies for Action

The following strategies, both short term and long term, are given for your consideration. Please evaluate each carefully and act accordingly. The secret is that *everyone* has to do *something!* No one can do everything, but everyone can do at least one thing. May our gracious God provide us with the insight to know what we can do and grant us the desire to do it.

1. *Know Your Biblical Christian Worldview*

"Then Paul stood in the midst of Mars' hill, and said, Ye men of Athens, I perceive that in all things ye are too superstitious. For as I passed by, and beheld your devotions, I found an altar with this inscription, 'TO THE UNKNOWN GOD.' Whom therefore ye ignorantly worship, him declare I unto you. God that made the world and all things therein, seeing that he is Lord of heaven and earth, dwelleth not in temples made with hands" (Acts 17:22–24, KJV).

It is just as impossible to beat a worldview with no worldview, as it is to defeat the Green Bay Packers with no football team.

Says Charles Colson, "The church's singular failure in recent decades has been the failure to see Christianity as a life system, or worldview, that governs every area of existence. This failure has been crippling in many ways."[3] And again, "A debilitating weakness in modern evangelicalism is that we've been fighting cultural skirmishes on all sides without knowing what the war itself is about. We have not identified the worldviews that lie at the root of cultural conflict—and this ignorance dooms our best efforts."[4]

George Barna has arrived at the same conclusion. He says, "Roughly one-quarter of all American adults claim that their worldview is inherently founded on biblical principles. And yet, when asked to describe the content of that worldview, or to explain how they arrived at their understanding of truth, meaning, and appropriate behavior, less than one in ten were able to do so. The research suggests that most people's worldview is little more than a collection of fragmented ideals mindlessly adopted from pop culture."[5]

Colson and Pearcey develop the Christian worldview in their excellent work *How Now Shall We Live?* which we recommend to our readers. David has likewise spelled out what is entailed in a biblical Christian worldview. He defines it as any set of ideas or beliefs that speaks to a theology, philosophy, ethics, biology, psychology, sociology, law, economics, politics, and history. Readers are urged to study David's work.[6]

But can we realistically get a handle on this issue of worldview? Barna says yes and explains his thinking as follows:

> We have somewhere in the neighborhood of eighty million adult believers in the United States. Since perhaps 10 percent currently possess a biblical world view, they become our foundation upon which we will build. Let's imagine that each of those individuals took on just three people to coach in worldview development over the course of the next two years. After twenty-four months, we'd jump from 10 percent to 40 percent of the Christian population possessing a biblical worldview. Repeat the process, using that 40 percent as the new base of coaches. Let's lighten the load and say each worldview Christian took two believers under his or her wing. There would not even be enough worldview-starved believers to team with all the coaches available. Most important, within four years we could theoretically wipe out biblical illiteracy and indifference among the body of Christ.[7]

2. Pray!

On June 28, 1787, Benjamin Franklin addressed one of his peers at the Constitutional Convention in Philadelphia. He said, "I have lived, Sir, a long time; and the longer I live the more convincing Proofs I see of this Truth, That God governs in the Affairs of Men!—And if a Sparrow cannot fall to the Ground without his Notice, is it probable that an Empire can sire without his Aid?—We have been assured, Sir, in the Sacred Writings, that 'except the Lord build the House, they labor in vain that build it.' I firmly believe this;—and I also believe that without his concurring Aid we shall succeed in this political Building no better that the Builders of Babel."[8]

And how do we secure the aid and direction of God in our efforts? Through prayer!

> If my people, which are called by my name, shall humble themselves, and pray, and seek my face, and turn from their wicked ways; then will I hear from heaven, and will forgive their sin, and will heal their land. (2 Chronicles 7:14, KJV)

> Pray without ceasing. (1 Thessalonians 5:17)

> Be anxious for nothing, but in everything by prayer and supplication, with thanksgiving, let your requests be made known to God; and the peace of God, which surpasses all understanding, will guard your hearts and minds through Christ Jesus. (Philippians 4:6)

And for whom shall we pray? Although you have probably prayed for America many times, we encourage you specifically to entreat the Lord for the sixteen people whom you elect to office. Praying for those in authority over you is a command of Scripture (1 Timothy 2:1–2). And it is not as overwhelming a task as you might think! You elect only five people nationally, five in your state, and six locally. You pay their salaries through your taxes, and they make the decisions that largely determine how you and your children will live. So pray for them![9]

Therefore I exhort first of all that supplications, prayers, intercessions, and giving of thanks be made for all men, for kings and all who are in authority, that we may lead a quiet and peaceable life in all godliness and reverence. For this is good and acceptable in the sight of God our Savior, who desires all men to be saved and to come to the knowledge of the truth (1 Timothy 2:1–4).

3. Share Your Faith

About half of this nation's 80 million evangelicals share their faith once a week; 5 million do so once or more daily. If the rest of our evangelicals would share their faith effectively, we could easily solve the moral problems of our age by sheer numbers of converts—provided, of course, that these new believers develop a firm commitment to moral absolutes.

The new millennium provides an unprecedented opportunity for Christians to disseminate their faith in Christ. Humanism has brought about so much moral anarchy that people are looking for something real to believe in. In Christ we have the answer to troubled hearts. Let us not keep Him to ourselves!

4. Show Compassion for the Victims of Humanism

History shows that Christians have been the most humanitarian of peoples. Our Lord teaches us through the story of the Good Samaritan to care deeply for others. We need to assist the poor, the refugees, and the troubled victims of humanism's libertine ways. We are impelled to cry out against abortion, homosexuality, and adultery, but we must also reach out loving arms to unwed mothers, AIDS patients, divorced partners, and children being raised by one parent.

Thank God for those Christian men who lovingly shared some of their time and energy with me and my brother after the death of our father! Those Christians provided the proper role models that we so desperately needed during our crisis.

Concerned Women for America has taken a strong position against abortion, homosexuality, and other so-called human rights issues. In addition, through a relatively new organization, CWA is trying to put together a local abortion counseling program for unwed mothers so that young girls can receive the proper kind of love and advice during their time of need. Concerned citizens should provide moral and emotional support as these girls cope with the biggest decision of their lives. It is our hope that this counseling ministry will follow CWA's prayer chains all over the country.

5. Protect Your Children

Charles Colson says the culture war is particularly directed at our youth. "The naturalistic view of life pervades every area of Western culture, but nowhere with greater effect than among young people."[10]

In this cosmic struggle, you must not lose your children to the forces of darkness (Matthew 18). Toward that end, for nearly forty years David has been conducting two-week summer camps for teens. These Summit Ministries programs are tailored to prepare Christian teenagers not only to survive but flourish on our Secular Humanist, Marxist, postmodern campuses. We cannot recommend these programs too highly. They will establish teens in a biblical Christian worldview and expose the Secular Humanist worldview for the cancer that it is.[11]

6. Reach the Campus

The source of most humanistic teaching in our culture may be found in the educational arena, primarily at the college and university level. What heartbreak it has caused! Note the anguish of one mother: "Our daughter was raised in Christian schools and in a Christian home where we taught her Christian values and morals and where she learned that Jesus Christ is the way of salvation. Two years out of high school at twenty years of age, she enrolled at the University of Oregon. We were apprehensive but trusted her judgment as she had always shown clear vision. We did not know this is one of the most liberal universities in the nation. Unfortunately, she was overwhelmed by her professors and began to believe their philosophies. She graduated two years ago with a political science and English degree and has turned her back on all that she believed in. We are trusting God to bring our girl back. The wait is sometimes difficult, but we are on bended knee."

Or listen to the outrage of a concerned father over his daughter's experience at Southern Oregon University: "My daughter was very nearly thrown out of SOU, a tax-financed school near here, midway through her first quarter as a college student this past month. After a serious argument with university officials, she is being permitted to complete the academic year—but has been told in no uncertain terms, not to return as a student next year. She is a shy eighteen-year-old who enrolled in September and is taking calculus, physics, chemistry (all at the 200 sophomore level) and organ classes.

"She made the honor roll first quarter with grades of A in calculus, physics and organ, and B in chemistry. It is true that she lacks the drugs, alcohol, sexual promiscuity, nose, ear, and tongue rings, tattoos, arrogant lack of respect for older adults, dishonesty, and profanity of speech that are characteristic of many of her fellow students. Her demeanor is recognizably different as a result. Her lack of social graces is not, however, the reason that university officials first demanded that she leave. Her sin is that she has refused to take the university's three-quarter, four-unit-per-quarter, total-immersion indoctrination course in the Oregon State Religion."

This father identifies the course as the university's own brand of "atheistic secular humanism." He notes, "The Oregon State Religion being promulgated here is indeed different from other religions. A great religion emphasizes the higher human traits. The Oregon religion is based primarily upon the lowest aspects of human nature. The course text opens with a thirteen-page article on rape, including detailed descriptions of actual rapes—which sets the stage for teaching feminism—and goes downhill from there."

Summit Ministries is preparing to go onto the campuses in conjunction with the organization Students for America to distribute tens of thousands of books to students. We are even heading for Harvard University campus—the center of humanism in America.

We are calling this outreach "Operation: Campus Book Distribution." We plan to place tens of thousands of copies of works such as *Mind Siege*, Phillip E. Johnson's *Reason in the Balance*, Michael Behe's *Darwin's Black Box*, C. S. Lewis's *Mere Christianity*, Charles Colson and Nancy Pearcey's *How Now Shall We Live?*, David Noebel's *Understanding the Times*, Nancy Pearcey and Charles Thaxton's *The Soul of Science*, among others. The books will be given away, free of charge, to students who promise to read them. Full- and half-page ads will be taken out in the campus newspaper promoting the book and telling where it may be obtained.

You can become actively involved by

- purchasing books for distribution;
- sending us the names of Christian students on various campuses across America who might be willing to help with the distributions;

- praying for a specific campus, especially how you might help us reach its students and faculty.[12]

A number of years ago students at Charles University in Prague announced to their professors that they had had it up to their foreheads with communist propaganda. You saw what happened as the Iron Curtain began to crumble. It would be wonderful if American students finally had had enough of humanist propaganda and rose up to say, "Enough is enough!"

And if you are looking for a classic example of how sick the campus situation is, check out Tufts University. On one hand "a Christian group at Tufts University has been banned from using campus facilities and stripped of university funding after it refused to consider a lesbian member for a senior leadership position."[13] On the other hand, Tufts University was the site of a gay and lesbian "Teach Out," which conducted sexually explicit workshops for teenagers "in the art of injecting positive homosexual themes into public school materials—down to the elementary school level."[14] Enough said?

7. Read, Read, Read

Christianity always has been a worldview of the Bible, books, study, and learning. Just consider the example set by the Bible itself:

Study to shew thyself approved unto God, a workman that needeth not to be ashamed, rightly dividing the word of truth. (2 Timothy 2:15, KJV)

Bring the cloak that I left with Carpus at Troas when you come—and the books, especially the parchments. (2 Timothy 4:13)

Today must be no exception. We are all too aware of the awful statistics: "Almost half of all adults do not read even one book during a typical year."[15]

We are challenging each of you to turn off the television for a few hours every day and begin reading some of the works we have listed in the bibliography. Be assured that the information you receive via television will be slanted toward humanism.

You will not find on national television a defense of the creationist point of view. You will search forever for a program defending intelligent design in the universe. You will not find the word "purpose" used in any program dealing with nature. You will not find a broadcast on the stylidium orchid, the bombardier beetle, the coelacanth fish, or even the latest information on the pepper moth scandal. You will not find a meaningful defense of the father-mother-child family. Never will you happen upon a program defending moral absolutes or Bible-based morality. You will not find a production showing the Christian roots of America's constitutional republic. In fact, you will never find anything on America's republican form of government, since "republic" is a politically incorrect word. Finally, you will not see an art show on television with images you could actually recognize.

So why not pick up a book and read about these things instead?

8) De-fund the Humanist Left

If the religious right had a pipeline into your wallet through the national tax structure, the howl from the humanist left and their media pets would be heard around the world. The left would be on the airwaves every night and day, arguing for the separation of church and state.

Yet the humanist left *does* have a direct pipeline into your wallet through the federal tax structure, and not one word of protest is raised. Federal monies going to the Department of Education, the National Academy of Sciences, the National Legal Services, the National Endowment of the Arts, the National Endowment of the Humanities, Planned Parenthood, UNESCO, and literally hundreds (and more likely thousands) of other left-wing organizations are advancing the humanist worldview.

All such funding should cease as a true violation of the First Amendment, which prohibits the establishment of a national religion. But this will not happen until a pro-moral majority sits in Congress, and that will not happen until Christians get serious about their obligations of citizenship.

9. *National Drive to Register Christians*

Seventeen percent of adult Christians have not registered to vote.[16] That is nearly 15 million votes. Every Bible-teaching church should designate at least one special Christian Citizenship Sunday for registration of all its members. This is nonpartisan, nonpolitical, positive citizenship, so it should be pursued with diligence.

Each church also should appoint one or two members to keep track of all political and governmental issues that impact biblical morality, family, and the church and to report periodically to the congregation. Churches already have mission committees, evangelism committees, education committees, and social committees; now they need a community committee (Salt-and-Light groups) to keep an eye on Big Brother (government) and Little Brother (colleges and universities).

After making sure you're registered to vote yourself, offer to become the registrar of voters for your church. After a short period of training, you can help others prepare for election day.

The importance of registering millions of Christians and enabling them to exercise their God-given right to vote for their country's leaders cannot be overemphasized. A political forecaster indicated that fewer people go to the polls than ever before, and that phenomenon is expected to get worse. Cities in New York, New Jersey, and Connecticut recently elected officials with less than 25 percent of the vote.

We can understand why the general population has grown disillusioned with politicians. They seem so unresponsive to the people who elected them, cooperating instead with amoral activists and pressure groups. But such disillusionment should only increase the determination of the discerning, morally minded voter who backs the candidate representing moral decency and pro-American ideals.

10. *Help in the Campaign of Pro-Moral Candidates*

Volunteer workers are the most significant single factor in winning elections on all levels—and that is often where Christians are the weakest. Few have the foresight to realize that a few weeks of work on behalf of the right candidate will save hours and years of turmoil.

According to former Congressman John Conlan, three hundred precinct workers can elect almost any good candidate to Congress. With only 435 congressional districts, 130,500 of our 80 million Christians—a little more than one per church—could easily change the complexion of Congress in just a few elections.

One politician we know was converted while serving as a state assemblyman. After losing a bid for Congress, he ran the following year for mayor of one of the twenty largest cities in the country. With the heavy backing of the Christian community and others concerned for moral decency, he was elected. Today the porn shops of that city are closed, degenerate movies are not permitted, and other secularist trends have been halted. A sister city, just forty-five miles away, still groans under all these evil things.

If we are going to turn this country around, it will be at the voting booth. Because our press is so dominated by liberals, we have to make up the difference through a massive army of volunteer workers. We have more than enough manpower; now we need to educate and activate it.

On the local level, it is often not difficult to get people elected. Many offices are won by only a few votes. A former governor of Ohio, for example, worked energetically to get humanists off the backs of Christian parents who chose to send their children to Christian schools. He was elected by a little more than eleven thousand votes in a state with well over one million eligible Christian voters.

A deacon in a neighboring church announced his candidacy for a city council seat. I invited a group of pastors to breakfast to hear his testimony, and they organized an ad hoc group called Ministers Concerned for Moral Decency. Sixteen of them let their names be used to endorse that good man, as is their right as free citizens. The letter was circulated far and wide, and he was elected by 691 votes. Even his opponent acknowledged that the letter was largely instrumental in the outcome.

Christians seriously err when they insist that a candidate be a committed Christian before he is worthy of their support. We must learn that Christians are not the only ones with strong moral convictions. We need politicians sincerely committed to moral principles, with the character to stand up for them.

Personally, we would rather elect a man or woman committed to biblical morality than one who loudly proclaims allegiance to Christ but who refuses to define his or her moral position. Candidates are better judged by the company they keep and the kind of advisors they select than by their politically motivated statements of faith.

Morally minded people should heed one word of caution with respect to politicians: Ignore what they say, and carefully examine what they do. Remember, a professional politician will say anything to get elected. His voting record speaks more loudly than his rhetoric, for it reveals what he really believes, and it demonstrates how he responds to pressure.

Any elected official who has voted for abortion-on-demand, for partial-birth abortion, for leniency on pornography, for special rights for homosexuals, for decriminalization of prostitution, and for children's rights at the expense of parents' rights is dangerous at best and amoral at worst. Consequently, he should be exposed and replaced, regardless of his party, race, or religion. Until we pro-moralists remove some of these people from office and return them to private life, Washington, Sacramento, Albany, and other capitals will not take us seriously.

Atheistic, amoral humanists will not rest until they have managed to separate America from God. This is particularly true of our judges.[17] Because most judgeships are appointed positions, it will take several years to change that picture. The only way to bring morality back into our judicial system is to elect strong, pro-moral candidates to all federal offices, particularly in the key positions of president, senator, and governor. Remember, most federal judges are appointed by the president on the recommendation of the senators from his party, and a similar approach is used for lesser judicial posts.

The only hope for America politically is that millions of the silent pro-moral majority will become militant about their morality and elect men of conviction and character to public office. If we are diligent in exercising our right and responsibility to vote such representatives into government leadership, we could see a rebirth of moral and spiritual sanity.

11. Expose Amoral Candidates and Incumbents

Carefully examine the voting record of the key sixteen who represent you or are candidates for those offices. Any who are liberal, amoral, or weak on morality can be defeated, if you inform as many voters as possible about what they really stand for. Voters need to know the truth about politicians. A few hours spent in research and a few dollars invested at your local printer can render your community a favor by exposing amoral candidates to the voting public.

One reason that local politicians do not tend to stay in office as long as national leaders is that voters keep better track of their voting records. National politicians often think we do not know what they are voting for or against. But because we have to live under their decisions, those of us who care should uncover their voting record, print it, and circulate it. Every politician should be confronted with his voting record on election day.

The bottom line? *No humanist is fit to hold office.* Those who have failed the minimum morals test should be replaced. They are known by their voting records. The sooner the millions of pro-moral voters realize this and rise up, replacing secularists with those who hold strong moral convictions, the better off this country will be.

Anyone who could vote in favor of partial-birth abortion should be replaced immediately. Any politician who could vote in favor of making homosexuality an alternative lifestyle should be rejected at the ballot box. Any politician who favors surrendering American sovereignty to the United Nations should be removed from office. Any politician who rejects the Bible as the moral standard of right and wrong should be retired.

Party affiliation is not an adequate criterion to determine worthiness for the job. More important than party is a political leader's position on the ethical and political spectrum. Currently the pro-moralists—those who can always be counted to vote in favor of decency and family protection—number approximately 25 percent (based on the voting record of Congress). Another 10–15 percent vote all or some of the time with pro-moralists. The humanist left and "bought" politicians—that is, politicians paid for by the feminists, homosexual lobby, the gaming interests, Hollywood, or Communist China—can usually be counted on to vote the amoral cause.

By replacing the two groups—the humanist left and the "bought" politicians—we could return moral sanity to the United States Senate, the House of Representatives, and ultimately to America. We do not need to replace all of Congress. An additional 15 to 20 percent of pro-moralists would suffice, because with a solid group of 40 percent who would always vote for morality and the family, many of the middle-of-the-roaders would swing to the moral position, providing a majority. Just two elections could dramatically change the climate of our national government.

12. Enlighten Your Friends and Neighbors

It is important to keep abreast of religious, political, moral, and cultural affairs. We highly recommend *World* magazine, *Human Events*, the *Washington Times*, Focus on the Family's *Citizen* magazine, and Concerned Women for America's monthly *Family Voice*. We also recommend that you listen to Beverly LaHaye, Phyllis Schlafly, James C. Dobson, Charles Colson, Rush Limbaugh, Ollie North, and other pro-American, pro-moral, and pro-family voices. We recommend that you read at least the following books that will bring you up to date on the issues facing our nation: (1) David A. Noebel, *Understanding the Times: The Religious Worldviews of Our Day and the Search for Truth;* (2) Charles Colson and Nancy Pearcey, *How Now Shall We Live?* (3) James C. Dobson and Gary L. Bauer, *Children at Risk: The Battle for the Hearts and Minds of our Kids;* (4) Daniel Lapin, *America's Real War;* and (5) Balint Vazsonyi, *America's 30 Years War.*

It is not enough to be informed personally. You must communicate pertinent information to your friends. Start with this book by passing it on to a friend. Check to see if your pastor has read it. If not, make a gift of it, with the request that he read it. Instead of throwing away your pro-moral newsletters, loan them to your friends, duplicating key sections for those who need to know what is really taking place in our nation and around the world. While we have life and freedom, let us use it to preserve our lives and freedom. Someone has said, "It is better to light one candle than to curse the darkness."

The right kind of book is a wonderful candle.

13. Consider Running for Public Office

Every Christian should consider the possibility of running for office. Obviously, God does not want 80 million of us to run for office, but He could use 200,000. (See Proverbs 29:2.)

First, identify your moral convictions. After that, evaluate the office, the need, your speaking ability, and the coterie of friends who would help you. Start with small offices—school boards—and work your way up. It is definitely something to pray about.

We also need to become more active in recruiting godly men to run for public office, where their moral influence can be felt. We are in a moral quagmire today because gospel ministers have failed to recruit "ministers of God" (Romans 13:1–7, KJV) from their congregation to run for office.

In the 1940s my godly pastor echoed the unwise advice of many Christians when he taught, "Politics is a dirty business. Rather than getting involved in politics, we Christians should stick to preaching the gospel and let the nice civic-minded people run the country." I do not condemn him for this, for I was equally as apathetic during the '50s and early '60s. Until then I had never recruited anyone for public office. God used my life and that of my church—which during my pastorate grew ten times in size and sent 300 of her young people into the ministry or to the mission field—but I never actively solicited candidates for political office.

Then, in the providence of God, I was subjected to a painful educational experience when our church attempted to get a zoning variance passed by the city council. After two hundred thousand dollars and three years of effort, we lost, 6 to 2. For the first time I realized that men and women largely hostile to the church controlled our city.

Gradually that has changed. Christians, backed by fellow believers throughout the city, have won elections, while others who value high morals have replaced humanists or those influenced by humanists. These pro-moral additions have helped to crack down on massage parlors and porn shops, and churches are now given a fair hearing for their growth needs.

Let us show you one simple method by which ministers could change in a heartbeat the moral climate of our age. If all 250,000 ministers in our country would ask God to use them to recruit just two members each year to run for public office, starting with school boards, city councils, and so forth, that would total nearly half a million candidates for office (assuming elections every other year). With adequate support from their friends, church associates, and neighbors, a significant portion would be elected. Many would gain name recognition and proceed to state and national office, and eventually a majority of the 500-plus now misrepresenting us in Washington, D.C., would be replaced by those who would truly represent the pro-moral majority.

We believe this plan is so practical and feasible that we are praying for and looking forward to the day that we can enter the voting booth and have the luxury of choosing between two Christian candidates for the same national office.

One city in Indiana, in which my wife and I held a Family Life Seminar, has already enjoyed that privilege. Two Christian attorneys, members of the same Baptist church, became outraged at the district attorney for failing to prosecute the porn peddlers of their community. With their pastor's approval, they ran in their respective parties' primaries for DA—and won. On election day the community had a choice between a Democrat and a Republican, both of whom were committed to morality. Now, that is true Christian citizenship in action!

After a seminar in Illinois where I had spoken on the need for churches to start Christian schools, the seminar chairman drove me to the airport. To my surprise he announced, "We don't have that problem in our community. Four of our five school-board members are born-again Christians, and we refuse to hire humanists in our system or use harmful textbooks." He then related their agreement that no member could leave the board until he recruited another pro-moral

Christian candidate to take his place. If all sixteen thousand school districts in America were run that way, we could break the stranglehold that the humanists now have on the minds of America's youth.

Dr. D. James Kennedy, pastor of the famed Coral Ridge Presbyterian Church, told us that eleven of his members were currently running for office in that community and that he was praying for the day when fifty would do so. If half the Bible-believing pastors had his vision and courage, America would not be facing the current cultural breakdown.

14. Join Local, State, and National Pro-Moral Organizations

Become active in one or more of the groups we have mentioned or others of like mind in your community. The moral tone of the new millennium will be determined by the feminists, humanists, homosexuals, and liberal-humanist left—or by pro-moral, pro-American Christians. It is up to you. If there is no group in your area, start one.

15. Speak Out and Write Vigorously on Moral Issues

Barna discovered that only 9 percent of evangelical Christians sent a letter to a company protesting their ethics in the past year; only 41 percent contacted a public official to express their opinion in the past year; only 41 percent had a discussion with someone about politics in the past year; only 47 percent tried to influence someone's opinion on an issue in the past year; only 37 percent attended a community meeting on a local issue in the past year; and only 24 percent gave money to a homeless or poor person in the past year.[18]

No government leader is deaf to the concerns of his or her constituency. Several of our victories—stopping the ERA, for example—have been due to letter-writing campaigns. Put each leader's address on your "key sixteen" prayer card, and let him hear from you on important moral and family-life issues.

This is a day of pressure politics. Unfortunately, the high-pressure tactics of the human-rights activists give our leaders the impression that they speak for the majority, when just the opposite is true. The only way to change that is to write concise, kind, respectful, but forthright letters, stipulating your reasons for favoring or opposing certain legislation or government activities. Such epistles are more effective than you think.

Perhaps you remember how in early 1999 the ACLU filed lawsuits against a number of counties in Kentucky and Ohio that had allowed the posting of the Ten Commandments on public buildings. Instead of running away from the battle, a group of Christians formed the "Adams County for the Ten Commandments" and went on the offensive. Here is how James C. Dobson described what happened:

Rather than turn a blind eye to the situation, a group called Adams County for the Ten Commandments began offering blue and white yard signs—each printed with the Ten Commandments—for a donation of $2 each. Thousands of the signs began showing up in yards throughout Adams County. The movement quickly spread from southern Ohio to northern Kentucky, where citizens had heard about the signs and began asking about them. Judy Sears, owner of the Sonshine Christian Bookstore in Corbin, Kentucky said, "As a Christian majority, we have let people walk all over us and we haven't spoken up . . . it's time for us to take the country back for God."[19]

And the results of their grass-roots effort? Judge for yourself:

- The Ohio legislature passed a resolution of "support, understanding and sympathy" for the Adams County School District's fight against the ACLU.

- The movement swept beyond Ohio and Kentucky, and according to the Associated Press, those famous blue-and-white signs have now been spotted in twenty-four states and four foreign countries.[20]

- According to the Cincinnati Inquirer, students nationwide are wearing T-shirts displaying the Ten Commandments to "show their faith and protest the nineteenth anniversary of the Stone v. Graham Supreme Court ruling, which outlawed the reading of the Ten Commandments in Kentucky Schools."[21]

16. *Fund Good, Pro-Moral, Pro-Family Causes*

It takes an enormous amount of money to fight amoral, government-backed, foundation-sponsored programs and legislation. Take the ERA, for example. Five million federal dollars were provided for the Houston fiasco called the IWY (International Women's Year, an idea that originated in the Kremlin in Moscow, according to *U.S. News & World Report*). It turned out to be little more than a rallying call to pass the ERA.

Now additional dollars are provided by presidential staff personnel (paid by taxpayers), and even the prestige of the presidency is used to gain passage for something that will bring great harm to the families and morals of America. To fight this and other humanist programs, we need to provide after-tax-dollar donations.

Give whatever you can afford. We can not think of any better causes to support than Concerned Women for America, Eagle Forum, Focus on the Family, Family Research Council, Prison Fellowship, WallBuilders, or Summit Ministries, to name a few.

17. *Assist Other Pro-Moral, Pro-Family Organizations*

When you hear of other groups that share your convictions, lend your moral and financial support. Remember, we are in a war that the enemy has been planning for over one hundred years. "In late nineteenth-century England, several small groups of scientists and scholars organized under the leadership of Thomas H. Huxley to overthrow the cultural dominance of Christianity—particularly the intellectual dominance of the Anglican Church. Their goal was to secularize society, replacing the Christian worldview with scientific naturalism, a worldview that recognizes the existence of nature alone."[22]

Only dedication, hard work, sacrifice, and cooperation with other pro-moral and pro-American activists will ensure victory. After our triumph over humanism and its dreadful effects, there will be ample time to voice our theological and other differences. But for the time being, we are obliged to fight a common enemy, and it will take the combined efforts of every morally concerned and informed American—Protestant, Catholic, Jew, Mormon, and Muslim. It is time to vote into office only those leaders who share our moral values and who will return our laws to the biblical principles on which they were founded. We owe no less to our children and grandchildren.

18. Capture the Culture

"Conservative political victories will always be tenuous and fragile unless conservatives recapture the culture."[23]

The Christian life should never be dull or boring. There is plenty to do in all spheres of life. The importance of Christians entering the cultural sphere (art, music, popular entertainment, theater, media, law, religion, education) cannot be overlooked or underestimated.

As Robert Bork makes very clear in his work, conservatives who hold to a pro-moral point of view might control the White House and the Congress, but still "they cannot attack modern liberalism in its fortress . . . Hollywood, the network evening news, universities, church bureaucracies, the *New York Times* and the *Washington Post*."[24] Modern liberals, says Bork, "captured the government and its bureaucracies because they captured the culture."[25]

Christians need to ponder this point carefully. Christian parents need to prepare their sons and daughters to invade this fortress of the left. Someday the major newscasters will retire, and there is nothing amiss in believing that well-prepared Christians can replace them.

Christian teens need to realize a simple fact of life—it may be more important to the kingdom of Christ to be a biology professor at Harvard than a preacher, or to be a songwriter or a film producer than a missionary or a president. In other words, each Christian needs to pray for guidance on where God can most use him or her in this cosmic struggle of the ages.

Listen carefully to Robert Bork again: "Perhaps the most promising development in our times is the rise of an energetic, optimistic, and politically sophisticated religious conservatism. It may prove more powerful than merely political or economic conservatism because religious conservatism's objectives are cultural and moral as well. Thus, though these conservatives can help elect candidates to national and statewide offices, as they have repeatedly demonstrated, their more important influence may lie elsewhere. Because it is a grass roots movement, the new religious conservatism can alter the culture both by its electing local officials and school boards (which have greater effects on culture than do national politicians), and by setting a moral tone in opposition to today's liberal relativism."[26]

19. Vote in Every Election

Make being a responsible Christian citizen a priority and vote in every election. One thing that has provided more freedom for more people for a longer period of time than in all of human history is the government "of the people" given to us by our predominantly Christian forefathers. That is, by giving the people the right to vote for those who would make the decisions of government, they gave us our freedom. In short, it was a republic. In fact, in Colonial Virginia they considered voting in every election so important they fined non-voters "five shillings" for failing to show up at the polls. They considered voting not only a right but a duty.

So, too, should Christians today. The main reason we have lost influence in our culture is because so many Christians do not vote. Think of it: Only 48 percent of Christians bother to vote, even in presidential elections. If we could motivate another 20 percent of our brethren to exercise even this minimum standard of Christian citizenship—voting in every election—we would exercise more influence over who represents us in Washington, DC, than do the humanists, whom we outnumber two to one or more. Yet for the last fifty years, they have had more influence in who appoints our judges and government bureaucrats than we do, simply because 52 percent of Christians do not vote, and the humanists vote with a vengeance. For Christians living in a free society, not to vote is, in our opinion, a sin against God, our families, and future generations. In the year 2000, the U.S. Supreme Court rendered several anti-Christian, anti-moral decisions, often by a vote of five to four. Whose fault is that? The Christians who did not bother to vote in past election.

When you pray for America, pray that more of our numbers will become voters in future elections. For if we are ever to bring the

"Christian consensus" that Dr. Francis Shaeffer talked about back to America, it will be through the ballot box.

20. *Do Not Gain the World but Lose Your Soul*

Jesus asked an unsettling question that is as relevant today as it was two millennia ago: "For what profit is it to a man if he gains the whole world, and loses his own soul? Or what will a man give in exchange for his soul?" (Matthew 16:26).

All Bible-believing Christians know that political-governmental issues are first of all matters of the soul and its values. Politics is merely placing one's values into the public square. Therefore, the heart, mind, and soul of each of us must be conformed to the will of God (Romans 12:1–2). Such conforming is possible only through a personal relationship with Jesus Christ. George Barna puts it like this: "We must preach the Word of God, for it is only by hearing the truth about God's holiness, our sinfulness, and Jesus' atoning death and resurrection that people can be restored into a proper and lasting relationship with God" (see 2 Timothy 4:2).[27]

Each of us is responsible for what we do with God's Son—the very One whom the humanists are seeking to replace with Foucault, Derrida, Russell, Huxley, Freud, Rorty, Dewey, Wundt, Darwin, Marx, or Nietzsche.

We urge each of our readers to read their Bibles and discover what it says about Jesus the Messiah. In the meantime, ponder Barna's challenge: "Someday God will ask you to give an account for your time on earth. What report of your commitment to practical, holy, life-transforming service will you be able to give Him?"[28]

Let's Be About Our Father's Business

Let us as Christian adults be about our Father's business of protecting and defending our children (Matthew 18). Let us contend earnestly for the faith (Jude 3). Let us declare the gospel of Jesus Christ as Messiah and Lord (Romans 1:3–17; 1 Corinthians 15:1–4). Let us understand the times in which we live so we will know what to do (1 Chronicles 12:32).

Let us judge every idea by bringing it to Christ (2 Corinthians 10:5).

And let us not be deceived by vain and deceitful worldviews (Colossians 2:8).

That should keep us occupied, challenged, satisfied, and living victoriously until our lives are over or He comes for His family!

And just in case you read or hear that Christians want to turn back the clock of progress, let us remind you that Jeremiah faced the same issue a few thousand years ago. His response to Israel: "Thus says the LORD: Stand in the ways and see, and ask for the old paths, where the good way is, and walk in it; then you will find rest for your souls" (Jeremiah 6:16). Unfortunately, Israel responded with a curt, "We will not walk in it."

Let us pray that America has learned a lesson from Israel's tragic history.

15

TIME TO CHOOSE

This book was written primarily to believers in our Lord Jesus Christ. It was designed to warn about the powerful forces assembled against them, forces that seek to throw off the moral cords of God (Psalm 2) and declare themselves liberated—only to find themselves slaves to their own passions and ideas (2 Peter 2:19).

The same pagan forces that opposed Elijah on Mount Carmel (Baal and Asherah, 1 Kings 18), that fought our Lord at Mount Hermon (Pan and Caesar, Matthew 16), and that battled Paul at Mount Mars (Stoics and Epicureans, Acts 17) are among us still . . . more powerful than ever.

The religion of Baal and Asherah promoted worship of nature and sex and celebrated through child sacrifice. The same kind of worship today is called radical environmentalism, sex ed or Sangerism, and is celebrated through abortion.[1]

The religion of Pan and Caesar worshiped the state. The same kind of worship today is called statism, Big Government, Big Brother, one-world government or the coming new world order.

Stoicism and Epicureanism promoted the religions of pantheism and atheism. The same kind of religion exists today through New Age teachings, liberalism, Scientific Humanism, Secular Humanism, Marxism, cultural Marxism, socialism, or postmodernism.

Different names but still the same pagan dogmas.

We have sought to alert Christians to this battle for their hearts, minds, souls, and spirits.

We have attempted to motivate and encourage Christians not to sit on the sidelines or be spectators in the stands while this battle rages.

We are hoping, of course, that you will respond much differently than did the people of Israel in Elijah's day: "the people said nothing" (1 Kings 18:21, NIV). Rather, we are praying that you will respond with Christian maturity and spirituality—*and enter the battlefield.*

Your battlefield may be your church, your school or college, your workplace, the government, the media, or the voting booth. Wherever it is, we pray that God will give you the courage, knowledge, and wisdom to carry on this battle for the mind.

Even if you lose in this life, you still win! For you will have been faithful and obedient to the King of kings and Lord of lords. You will have understood the times in which you live; you will have known what must be done (1 Chronicles 12:32). And you will be about your Father's business, protecting and defending your faith, your family, your friends, and your freedom.

Every believer knows that some day the kingdoms of this world will "become the kingdoms of our Lord and of His Christ, and He shall reign forever and ever" (Revelation 11:15). It is each Christian's moral duty to live, wait, watch, and work for such a time and especially to manifest the character of Christ in our present circumstances. He is our Savior, Lord, and King, and His love needs to be shed abroad in our hearts and in our world—*now*.

You could not ask for more adventure in one lifetime! Try to imagine the moment when this life is over and you stand before the bema and hear from the lips of Jesus Christ, "Well done, thou good and faithful servant. You have been My lighthouse to the world."

It will indeed be worth it all when we see Jesus!

But can you imagine what it will be like for the Christian couch potatoes who never made an effort to live the exciting Christian life?

A Place for You

Two hundred thousand individuals make up the leadership of America. It is our aim to make sure that a significant number of that 200,000 are either mature Christians or at least not hostile to Christ and His people. Surely, out of a constituency of 80 million evangelical adults, we can find 200,000 leaders! And if not, perhaps the church should rethink its priorities. Perhaps time needs to be set aside for a course in courage.

Let us not fool ourselves. If we refuse to engage in the battle for the mind and heart, we stand to lose all—our families, our churches, our country, our civilization. Remember, tens of thousands already have lost their children to humanist education and pop culture. Churches already have come under the gun for speaking out against abortion, homosexuality, pornography, and gambling.

Our country stands at the crossroads, unsure if private morality and public morality mix. Western civilization is certainly under the gun, with shouts of "Hey, hey, ho, ho, Western civ has got to go" ringing out from our university campuses. Can anyone dispute that we are slouching toward Gomorrah?

We agree that it is better to fight and lose than never to have fought at all. We also would not mind being part of that company "of whom the world was not worthy" (Hebrews 11:38). Those great saints "obtained a good testimony through faith," but "did not receive the promise, God having provided something better for us, that they should not be made perfect apart from us" (Hebrews 11:39–40).

They've handed the gauntlet to us. It's now our turn.

Get Involved!

The only way we will be able to reclaim our country and our culture is through hard work—as in blood, sweat, and tears.

That means prayer.

Prayer that God will send a moral and spiritual revival over our land, as He did to Nineveh of old. Prayer that God will change the hearts and minds of His people through a relationship with Himself. Prayer that God will open the eyes of His people to the need to know and defend the one worldview that speaks to reality—to the real world—namely, biblical Christianity.

And prayer that God's people will not shirk their duty and responsibilities regarding Christian citizenship. That means more hard work—study, thought, evangelism, discipleship, grounding in our own Christian worldview, and, yes, the ballot box!

Historically, Christians vote more than 80 percent of the time for the candidate of either party that is most committed to moral values. An additional block of 20 percent voting Christians would be more than enough to return a majority of God-conscious justices to the Supreme Court, senators and representatives to Congress, and even a man of Christian principles to the White House. We owe no less to our God and our children and grandchildren.

A Word to Pastors

You probably noticed that we dedicated this book to the pastor-shepherds of this country. Our reason is clear. We are convinced that if the men of God who fill the pulpits of this country would actively urge their members to become responsible Christian citizens by voting for pro-moral men and women in every election, we could easily return our government to the moral base upon which it was founded.

History shows that it was the pastors of early America who rallied the people to throw off the tyranny of England. It also shows that ministers of the gospel later rallied the people to oppose slavery and bring freedom to a whole race.

Today our country is faced with the most cruel enemy it has ever confronted, the religious forces of Secular Humanism. Ministers of the gospel and their constituencies make up the only group in this country with sufficient followers to vote the rascals out of office and to reform the courts, media, entertainment, and education.

If pastors hide behind false excuses such as, "I don't want to become controversial" or "I just preach the gospel, brother" (a freedom they will soon lose if they do nothing) or "separation of church and state" (two words that cannot be found in the U.S. Constitution), we will lose all our freedoms to the one-world government that is the obsession of secularists.

One of the best illustrations of responsible Christian citizenship I ever saw occurred the Sunday before a national election.

Forty-four hundred people worshiped that day in one of the most evangelistic churches in America. After his message and a compelling invitation to accept Jesus Christ as one's Savior and Lord, the pastor stepped down from the pulpit and told the congregation, "I want to have a special time of prayer before you leave today for the national election on Tuesday. As you know, it is a very important time for our nation, and I am concerned that all Christians become responsible citizens, know the issues, and get out to vote. The Bible says that 'righteousness exalts a nation, but sin is a reproach to any people' (Proverbs 14:34). Before we pray, I want to tell you that at my request, on Tuesday you will receive a call from one of the members of our church, urging you to vote. We are not telling you who to vote for, but we urge all our members to vote. Oh yes, please vote early so they will not have to call you so many times."

That great congregation laughed heartily, probably because many in the audience had heard rumors that a particular party's election strategy involved paying voters to vote early and often! Anyway, the pastor led the congregation in prayer for our nation and its future leadership.

A month later I asked him how many complaints he received for doing such a patriotic act.

"Not one," he replied.

If every pastor in America did something like that and taught his congregation that freedom is a gift from God and not from the government, America would not be facing the death of freedom and morality, which looms over it today. And the church of Jesus Christ could continue to be the bastion of world evangelism.

And Now, to the Battle!

If you have a pastor like the man described above, encourage him, volunteer to help him, and pray for him daily.

If you do not have such a shepherd, pray for him and give him a copy of this book.

Whether the ministers of America will rise to the challenge of the twenty-first century remains to be seen. History will reveal the answer. If they do, we will continue to enjoy the freedoms we have known in our personal, religious, and political lives. If they don't, Americans— and particularly Christian Americans—will lose all vestiges of their freedom.

We shall soon see if America's Christian leadership includes men and women of vision and courage or men and women of compromise, neutrality, and defeat. Vigilance is always the price of freedom, whether religious or political. And as James Russell Lowell reminds us:

> Once to every man and nation
> Comes the moment to decide,
> In the strife of Truth with Falsehood
> For the good or evil side.
> Then it is the brave man chooses
> While the coward stands aside.

APPENDIX A

Preliminary Questions for Candidates to Determine
Their Position on Morals

1. Do you agree that this country was founded on a belief in God
   and the moral principles of the Bible? Do you concur that it has
   been departing from those principles and needs to return to them?

   Yes_____   No_____

2. Do you approve of abortion-on-demand when the life of the
   mother is not in danger?

   Yes_____   No_____

3. Do you favor voluntary prayer in the public schools if led by
   students?

   Yes_____   No_____

4. Would you favor stricter laws relating to the sale of pornography?

   Yes_____   No_____

5. Do you favor stronger laws against the use and sale of hard
   drugs?

   Yes_____   No_____

6. Are you in favor of legalizing marijuana?

    Yes_____ No_____

7. Would you favor legalizing prostitution?

    Yes_____ No_____

8. Do you favor laws that would increase homosexual rights?

    Yes_____ No_____

9. Would you vote to permit known homosexuals to teach in schools?

    Yes_____ No_____

10. Do you favor the right of parents to send their children to private schools?

    Yes_____ No_____

11. Do you favor more federal government involvement in education?

    Yes_____ No_____

12. Do you favor capital punishment for capital offenses?

    Yes_____ No_____

13. Do you favor removal of the tax-exempt status of churches?

    Yes_____ No_____

14. Do you believe that government should be able to remove children from parental care even when there is no physical abuse?

    Yes_____ No_____

15. Do you favor sex education, contraceptives, or abortions for minors without parental consent?

    Yes_____ No_____

16. Except in wartime or dire emergency, would you vote for government spending that exceeds revenues?

     Yes_____   No_____

17. Do you favor a reduction in taxes to allow families more spendable income?

     Yes_____   No_____

18. Do you favor a reduction in government?

     Yes_____   No_____

APPENDIX B

Christianity and Science

Don't think for a moment that only the "common" man or one of mediocre intelligence finds faith acceptable. That is a misconception made popular by secularists. Historically, it just is not true! Some of the most brilliant, well-educated individuals in history have been men and women of faith.

Consider such luminaries as John Wycliffe (1320–1384), Martin Luther (1483–1546), John Calvin (1509–1564), Sir Isaac Newton (1642–1727), and Jonathan Edwards (1703–1758). Consider that nearly all the men who founded the various sciences—Joseph Lister, Louis Pasteur, Johannes Kepler, Robert Boyle, Georges Cuvier, Charles Babbage, Lord Rayleigh, James C. Maxwell, Michael Faraday, Ambrose Fleming, Lord Kelvin, Jean-Henri Fabre, William Herschel, Gregor Mendel, Louis Agassiz, James Simpson, Blaise Pascal, William Ramsay, John Ray, Bernhard Riemann, Matthew Maury, David Brewster, John Woodward, Rudolf Virchow, Carolus Linnaeus, and Humphry Davy—were men of faith. Modern-day Secular Humanists claim science as their own domain[1] but fail to mention that the father of the modern scientific method itself, Sir Francis Bacon, was a committed Christian.

Dr. Schaeffer calls Bacon (1561–1626) "the major prophet of the scientific revolution." A lawyer, essayist, and lord chancellor of England, Bacon stressed careful observation and a systematic collection of information to unlock nature's secrets. He took the Bible seriously, including the historic Fall.[2]

Johannes Kepler (1571–1630), a German astronomer known as the father of modern astronomy, was the first to show that the planets' orbits are elliptical, not circular. His faith is clearly expressed in the preface of his book *The Mystery of the Universe*: "Since we astronomers are priests of the highest God in regard to the book of nature, it befits us to be thoughtful, not of the glory of our minds, but rather, above all else, of the glory of God."[3]

Robert Boyle (1627–1691), known as the father of modern chemistry, was renowned for his careful observation. According to the *Encyclopedia Britannica*, Boyle viewed nature as "a mechanism that has been made and set in motion by the Creator at the beginning and now functioned according to secondary laws, which could be studied by science."[4] He stressed that scientific research "helped to reveal the greatness of the Creator."[5] Though a member of the Royal Society and a dedicated scientist, he was equally committed to propagating the gospel abroad, translating the Scriptures into Irish and Turkish and writing material on the harmony of his scientific and Christian positions. Even the endowment provided in his will for the Boyle lectures stipulated that they persist "for proving the Christian Religion against notorious infidels."[6]

Sir Isaac Newton (1642–1727) is famous for his discovery of the law of gravity. But we often forget that he also invented calculus and in 1687 published *The Mathematical Principles of Natural Philosophy*, which became

one of the most influential books in the history of human thought. By experimenting in Neville's Court in Trinity College at Cambridge University, he was also able to work out the speed of sound by timing the interval between the sound of an object which he dropped, and the echo coming back to him from a known distance.

Throughout his lifetime, Newton tried to be loyal to what he believed the Bible teaches. It has been said that seventeenth century scientists limited themselves to the how without the interest in the why. This is not true. Newton, like any other early scientist, had no problem with the why because he began with the existence of a personal God who had created the universe.

In his later years, Newton wrote more about the Bible than about science, though little was published. Humanists have said that they wish he had spent all his time on his science. They think he wasted the hours he expended on biblical study, but they really are a bit blind when they say this. As Whitehead and Oppenheimer stressed, if Newton and others had not had a biblical base, they would have no base for their science at all.[7]

Blaise Pascal (1623–1662), a brilliant mathematician, invented the barometer and is considered by some a major writer of French prose.

An outstanding Christian, he emphasized that he did not see people lost like specks of dust in the universe (which was now so much larger and more complicated than people had thought), for people—as unique—could comprehend something of the universe. People could comprehend the stars; the stars comprehend nothing. And besides this, for Pascal, people were special because Christ died on the cross for them.[8]

Michael Faraday (1791–1867) never had the benefit of formal education, yet he invented the electric transformer, motor, and generator. He developed the concept of electromagnetic fields. He engaged in experimental organic chemistry by separating benzene from heating oil. Faraday was a Christian who belonged to a small religious order that believed "the Bible, and that alone, with nothing added to it nor taken away from it by man, is the sole and sufficient guide for each individual, at all times and in all circumstances."[9] Faraday's scientific but thoroughly Christian search for truth was based upon belief in biblical creation and salvation through Jesus Christ.

James Clerk Maxwell (1831–1879), a physicist, is one of the most respected men of science. A man who extended Faraday's research in magnetic fields and electricity, he united the concept of force fields (forces acting through a distance) into a set of four equations. His electromagnetic theory was instrumental in advancing experimentation in optics and electronics. Raised in a Christian home, by eight years of age "he memorized all 176 verses of Psalm 119. Maxwell lived during the period of Charles Darwin, when evolutionary faith was spreading rapidly. He saw through this counterfeit to true faith immediately, and opposed it."[10]

The advanced educational and technological levels unique to the Western world would never have occurred had it not been for the believing men who shaped the Industrial and Scientific Revolutions. Theistic scientists assumed the universe was designed to follow dependable, even rational laws. Imagine where we would be if atheistic humanists, obsessed with unguided and continual change, had been in charge! They would have sent us back to the Dark Ages.

Francis Schaeffer points out that many scientists acknowledge science's debt to Christianity—rather than to theories of atheism and scientific naturalism and universal randomness.

Indeed, at a crucial point the Scientific Revolution rested upon what the Bible teaches. Both Alfred North Whitehead (1861–1947) and J. Robert Oppenheimer (1904–1967) have stressed that modern science was born out of the Christian world view.[11] Whitehead was a widely respected mathematician and philosopher, and Oppenheimer, after he became director of the Institute for Advanced Study at Princeton in 1947, wrote on a wide range of subjects related to science, in addition to writing in his own field on the structure of the atom and atomic energy. As far as I know, neither of the two men were Christians, or claimed to be Christians, yet both were straightforward in acknowledging that modern science was born out of the Christian world view.

Oppenheimer, for example, described this in an article "On Science and Culture" in *Encounter* in October 1962. In the Harvard University Lowell Lectures entitled *Science and the Modern World* (1925), Whitehead said that Christianity is the mother of science because of "the medieval insistence on the rationality of God." Whitehead also spoke of confidence "in the intelligible rationality of a personal being." He also says in these lectures that because of the rationality of God, the early scientists had an "inexpugnable belief that every detailed occurrence can be correlated with its antecedents in a perfectly definite manner, exemplifying general principles. Without this belief the incredible labors of scientists would be without hope." In other words, because the early scientists believed that the world was created by a reasonable God, they were not surprised to discover that people could find out something true about nature and the universe on the basis of reason.[12]

Schaeffer further argues that though not all the scientists of the Age of Enlightenment were committed Christians, all lived within what he calls a Christian consensus. Consequently, their theories were heavily influenced by a universe of order and design. He says:

Living within the concept that the world was created by a reasonable God, scientists could move with confidence, expecting to be able to find out about the world by observation and experimentation. This was their epistemological base—the philosophical foundation with which they were sure they could know. (*Epistemology* is the theory of knowledge—how we know, or how we know we can know.) Since the world had been created by a reasonable God, they were not surprised to find a correlation between themselves as observers and the thing observed—that is between the subject and the object. This base is normative to one functioning in the Christian framework, whether he is observing a chair or the molecules, which make up the chair. Without this foundation, Western modern science would not have been born.

Here one must consider an important question: Did the work of the Renaissance play a part in the birth of modern science? Of course it did. More than that, the gradual intellectual and cultural awakenings in the Middle Ages also exerted their influence. The increased knowledge of Greek thought—at Padua University, for example— opened new doors. Certainly, Renaissance elements and those of the

Greek intellectual traditions were involved in the scientific awakening. But to say theoretically that the Greek tradition would have been in itself a sufficient stimulus for the Scientific Revolution comes up against the fact that it was not. It was the Christian factor that made the difference. Whitehead and Oppenheimer are right. Christianity is the mother of modern science because it insists that the God who created the universe has revealed himself in the Bible to be the kind of God he is. Consequently, there is a sufficient basis for science to study the universe. Later, when the Christian base was lost, a tradition and momentum had been set in motion, and the pragmatic necessity of technology, and even control by the state, drives science on, but . . . with a subtle yet important change in emphasis.[13]

Men of Faith and Men of Science

It has taken a Hungarian refugee living in the United States to make the most obvious observation: "For the century ends as it began, and as the case has been for many centuries. It may be unfair; it may be cruel; it may be embarrassing; but the fact is that discoveries, inventions, creative activities of all kinds continue to pour forth from the accustomed source: the headliner countries of Western civilization."[14] He then says, "Goodness knows, everybody has been bending over backward to cover up the uncomfortable reality. We invented an entire mind game called multiculturalism. We wrote entire fictitious histories. We are 'celebrating diversity' day and night. Like children, we cover our eyes and pretend no one can see us."[15]

Few want to admit there is a relationship between Western civilization, Christianity, and science!

Daniel Lapin observed, "Virtually every major discovery in physics, medicine, chemistry, mathematics, electricity, nuclear physics, mechanics and just about everything else has taken place in Christian countries."[16]

His comment "and just about everything else" could well refer to the host of inventions made by Christians and in Christian lands. For example, actuarial tables and the calculating machine by Charles Babbage; chloroform by James Simpson; the electric motor by Joseph

Henry; the kaleidoscope by David Brewster; the discovery of inert gases by William Ramsay; pasteurization by Louis Pasteur; and the telegraph by Samuel Morse.

Space and time do not permit us to describe the many other scientists of faith,[17] such as John Philoponus, Robert Grosseteste, Roger Bacon, Dietrich von Frieberg, Thomas Bradwardine, Nicole Oresme, Georgius Agricola, Jan van Helmont, Francesco Grimaldi, John Ray, Isaac Barrow, Antoni van Leeuwenhoek, Niels Steno, James Bradley, Ewald von Kleist, Carolus Linnaeus, Leonhard Euler, John Dalton, Thomas Young, William Buckland, Adam Sedgwick, Augustin Cauchy, John Herschel, Matthew Maury, Philip Grosse, Asa Gray, James Dana, George Boole, Humphry Davy, Lord Rayleigh, Ambrose Fleming, Jean-Henri Fabre, George Stokes, William Herschel, James Joule, Georg Riemann, Bernhard Riemann, John Woodward, Rudolf Virchow, Edward Morley, Pierre Duhem, Georges Lemaître, George Washington Carver, Sir Arthur Eddington, and the hundreds of competent men of science today who believe in a personal God of design and order and who reject the false claims of atheistic humanism. Not until what Dr. Schaeffer calls the age of "contemporary science" did a number of scientists begin to sink into skepticism, atheism, amorality, and socialism.

Humanists love to identify the great scientists of the past as either their kin or as their forerunners. Particularly, they wish to claim credit for both the Age of Enlightenment and the Scientific Revolution. They fail to point out that the free thinkers—the true forerunners of atheism and ultimately of the humanists themselves—labored predominantly in the nonscientific fields of philosophy, sociology, psychology, the humanities, and behavioral studies. Few of them are to be found in the fields of "hard" science.

Yet even though this is true, millions today have been duped into thinking that only dim bulbs could swallow Christianity. In the past forty years alone, however, Christian men of science have founded several creationist organizations, such as the Creation Research Center, with more than six hundred scientists as members. Christian colleges have grown tremendously in the past five decades, and many of their scholars have gone on to secular graduate schools with such thorough undergraduate training in biblical truth that they have remained uncor-rupted by humanist brainwashing.

This groundswell of Christian scholarship, so antagonistic to humanism, has served as the catalyst for many new books, magazines, and movies, all exposing man-centered religion as a fraud. Such exposés, disseminated at a time when the theories of humanism are proving themselves to be socially chaotic, are creating a tidal wave of national concern large enough to frighten the humanists. They realize that if enough Christian citizens become informed of the dangers implicit in the secularists' unscientific theories, they will be challenged every day in their classrooms, until at retirement they will be replaced by a new generation of nonevolutionists who have decided it is time to regain their country and culture.

BIBLIOGRAPHY

Recommended Reading List

Ackerman, Paul, and Bob Williams. *Kansas Tornado: 1999 Science Curriculum Standards Battle*. El Cajon, Calif.: Institute for Creation Research, 1999.

Adams, Charles. *For Good and Evil: The Impact of Taxes on the Course of Civilization*. New York: Madison Books, 1993.

_____. *Those Dirty Rotten Taxes: The Tax Revolts that Built America*. New York: The Free Press, 1998.

Alcorn, Randy C. *Christians in the Wake of the Sexual Revolution*. Sisters, Oreg.: Multnomah Press, 1985.

Amos, Gary, and Richard Gardiner. *Never Before in History: America's Inspired Birth*. Dallas: Haughton, 1998.

Anderson, Martin. *Impostors in the Temple: American Intellectuals Are Destroying Our Universities and Cheating Our Students of Their Future*. New York: Simon and Schuster, 1992.

Ankerberg, John, and John Weldon. *Darwin's Leap of Faith: Exposing the False Religion of Evolution*. Eugene, Oreg.: Harvest House, 1998.

Barna, George. *The Second Coming of the Church: A Blueprint for Survival*. Nashville: Word, 1998.

Barton, David. *Original Intent: The Courts, the Constitution, and Religion*. Aledo, Tex.: WallBuilders Press, 1997.

_____. *Benjamin Rush: Signer of the Declaration of Independence*. Aledo, Tex.: WallBuilders Press, 1999.

Bauer, P. T. *Equality, the Third World, and Economic Delusion*. Cambridge, Mass.: Harvard University Press, 1981.

Bauman, Michael, and David Hall. *God and Caesar*. Camp Hill, Pa.: Christian Publications, 1994.

Bauman, Michael, David Hall, and Robert Newman. *Evangelical Apologetics*. Camp Hill, Pa.: Christian Publications, 1996.

Bauman, Michael, and Martin I. Klauber. *Historians of the Christian Tradition*. Nashville: Broadman and Holman, 1995.

Beckwith, Francis J., and Michael E. Bauman. *Are You Politically Correct? Debating America's Cultural Standards*. Buffalo, N.Y.: Prometheus Books, 1993.

Beckwith, Francis J., and Stephen E. Parrish. *See the Gods Fall*. Joplin, Mo.: College Press, 1997.

Beckwith, Francis J., and Gregory Koukl. *Relativism: Feet Firmly Planted in Mid-Air*. Grand Rapids, Mich.: Baker Books, 1998.

Behe, Michael J. *Darwin's Black Box: The Biochemical Challenge to Evolution*. New York: The Free Press, 1996.

Beisner, E. Calvin. *Prosperity and Poverty: The Compassionate Use of Resources in a World of Scarcity*. Wheaton, Ill.: Crossway Books, 1988.

Bennett, William J. *The Death of Outrage: Bill Clinton and the Assault on American Ideals*. New York: The Free Press, 1998.

Bethell, Tom. *The Noblest Triumph: Property and Prosperity Through the Ages*. New York: St. Martin's Press, 1998.

Bird, Wendell R. *The Origin of Species Revisited*. 2 vols. New York: Philosophical Library, 1989.

Black, Jim Nelson. *When Nations Die: America on the Brink.* Wheaton, Ill.: Tyndale House, 1994.

Breese, David. *Seven Men That Rule the World from the Grave.* Chicago: Moody Press, 1993.

Bright, Bill. *God: Discover His Character.* Orlando, Fla.: New Life Publications, 1999.

Bork, Robert H. *The Tempting of America: The Political Seduction of the Law.* New York: The Free Press, 1990.

_____. *Slouching Towards Gomorrah: Modern Liberalism and American Decline.* New York: HarperCollins, 1996.

Buchanan, Patrick J. *A Republic, Not an Empire: Reclaiming America's Destiny.* Washington, D.C.: Regnery, 1999.

Carson, D. A. *The Gagging of God.* Grand Rapids, Mich.: Zondervan, 1996.

Chalfant, John W. *Abandonment Theology: The Clergy and the Decline of American Christianity.* Winter Park, Fla.: America: A Call to Greatness, Inc., 1999.

Clark, Gordon H. *A Christian Philosophy of Education.* Jefferson, Md.: The Trinity Foundation, 1988.

Clark, Kelly James, ed. *Philosophers Who Believe: The Spiritual Journeys of 11 Leading Thinkers.* Downers Grove, Ill.: InterVarsity Press, 1993.

Collier, Peter, and David Horowitz. *Destructive Generation: Second Thoughts About the '60s.* New York: Summit Books, 1989.

Colson, Charles. *Kingdoms in Conflict.* Grand Rapids, Mich.: Zondervan, 1989.

Colson, Charles, and Jack Eckerd. *Why America Doesn't Work.* Dallas: Word, 1991.

Colson, Charles, and Nancy Pearcey. *How Now Shall We Live?* Wheaton, Ill.: Tyndale House, 1999.

Cord, Robert L. *Separation of Church and State: Historical Fact and Current Fiction*. Grand Rapids, Mich.: Baker Book House, 1988.

Courtois, Stephane, ed. *The Black Book of Communism: Crimes, Terror, Repression*. Cambridge, Mass.: Harvard University Press, 1999.

Craig, William Lane. *Reasonable Faith: Christian Truth and Apologetics*. Wheaton, Ill.: Crossway Books, 1994.

Crane, Philip M. *The Democrat's Dilemma*. Chicago: Henry Regnery Company, 1964.

Crozier, Brian. *The Rise and Fall of the Soviet Empire*. Rocklin, Calif.: Prima, 1999.

Davis, Percival, and Dean H. Kenyon. *Of Pandas and People: The Central Question of Biological Origins*. Dallas: Haughton, 1998.

Davis, Walter W. *God in Man's World*. Maggie Valley, N.C.: Biblical Standards Publications, 1999.

Dembski, William A. *The Design Inference: Eliminating Chance Through Small Probabilities*. Cambridge, Eng.: Cambridge University Press, 1998.

————. *Intelligent Design: The Bridge Between Science and Theology*. Downers Grove, Ill.: InterVarsity Press, 1999.

Denton, Michael. *Evolution: A Theory in Crisis: New Developments in Science Are Challenging Orthodox Darwinism*. Bethesda, Md.: Adler and Adler, 1996.

DeVos, Rich. *Compassionate Capitalism: People Helping People Help Themselves*. New York: Penguin Books, 1993.

Dobbs, Zygmund, ed. *The Great Deceit: Social Pseudo-Sciences*. West Sayville, N.Y.: Veritas Foundation, 1964.

Dobson, James C. *Life on the Edge: A Young Adult's Guide to a Meaningful Future*. Dallas: Word, 1995.

————. *Solid Answers: America's Foremost Family Counselor Responds to Tough Questions Facing Today's Families*. Wheaton, Ill.: Tyndale House, 1997.

Dobson, James C., and Gary L. Bauer. *Children at Risk*. Dallas: Word, 1990.

Donohue, William. *The Politics of the American Civil Liberties Union*. Piscataway, N.J.: Transaction, 1985.

D'Souza, Dinesh. *Illiberal Education: The Politics of Race, and Sex on Campus*. New York: The Free Press, 1991.

Eakman, B. K. *Cloning of the American Mind: Eradicating Morality Through Education*. Lafayette, La.: Huntington House, 1998.

Ellis, John M. *Literature Lost: Social Agendas and the Corruption of the Humanities*. New Haven, Conn.: Yale University Press, 1997.

Ellis, Richard J. *The Dark Side of the Left: Illiberal Egalitarianism in America*. Lawrence, Kans.: University of Kansas Press, 1998.

Ericson, Edward E., Jr. *Solzhenitsyn and the Modern World*. Washington, D.C.: Regnery Gateway, 1993.

Evans, M. Stanton. *The Liberal Establishment*. New York: The Devin-Adair Company, 1965.

_____. *The Theme Is Freedom: Religion, Politics, and the American Tradition*. Washington, D.C.: Regnery, 1994.

Feder, Don. *A Jewish Conservative Looks at Pagan America*. Lafayette, La.: Huntington House, 1993.

_____. *Who's Afraid of the Religious Right?* Ottawa, Ill.: Jameson Books, Inc., 1996.

Federer, William J. *America's God and Country Encyclopedia of Quotations*. Coppell, Tex.: Fame, 1996.

Friedman, Milton, and Rose Friedman. *Free to Choose*. New York: Harcourt, Brace, Jovanovich, 1980.

Furet, Francois. *The Passing of an Illusion: The Idea of Communism in the Twentieth Century*. Chicago: University of Chicago Press, 1999.

Geisler, Norman L. *Christian Apologetics*. Grand Rapids, Mich.: Baker Book House, 1988.

_____. *Christian Ethics: Options and Issues*. Grand Rapids, Mich.: Baker Book House, 1989.

_____. *Creating God in the Image of Man? The New "Open" View of God*. Minneapolis: Bethany House, 1997.

_____. *Baker Encyclopedia of Christian Apologetics*. Grand Rapids, Mich.: Baker Book House, 1999.

Geisler, Norman L., and William E. Nix. *A General Introduction to the Bible*. Chicago: Moody Press, 1986.

Geisler, Norman L., and Ron Brooks. *When Skeptics Ask: A Handbook on Christian Evidences*. Grand Rapids, Mich.: Baker Book House, 1995.

Geisler, Norman L., and Frank Turek. *Legislated Morality: Is It Wise? Is It Legal? Is It Possible?* Minneapolis: Bethany House, 1998.

Geisler, Norman L., and Thomas Howe. *When Critics Ask: A Popular Handbook on Bible Difficulties*. Grand Rapids, Mich.: Baker Book House, 1999.

Gilder, George. *Wealth and Poverty*. New York: Basic Books, 1981.

_____. *Men and Marriage*. Gretna, La.: Pelican, 1986.

Gish, Duane T. *Evolution: The Challenge of the Fossil Record*. El Cajon, Calif.: Institute for Creation Research, 1985.

_____. *Teaching Creation Science in Public Schools*. El Cajon, Calif.: Institute for Creation Research, 1993.

Grant, George. *Grand Illusions: The Legacy of Planned Parenthood*. Franklin, Tenn.: Adroit Press, 1992.

Groothuis, Douglas. *Truth Decay: Defending Christianity Against the Challenges of Postmodernism*. Downers Grove, Ill.: InterVarsity Press, 2000.

Habermas, Gary, and Antony Flew. *Did Jesus Rise from the Dead?* New York: Harper and Row, 1987.

Henry, Carl F. H. *Twilight of a Great Civilization: The Drift Toward Neo-Paganism*. Wheaton, Ill.: Crossway Books, 1988.

_____. *God, Revelation and Authority*. Reprint (6 vols.), Wheaton, Ill.: Crossway Books, 1999.

Herman, Arthur. *The Idea of Decline in Western History*. New York: The Free Press, 1997.

_____. *Joseph McCarthy: Reexamining the Life and Legacy of America's Most Hated Senator*. New York: The Free Press, 2000.

Hollander, Paul. *Anti-Americanism: Irrational and Rational*. New Brunswick, N.J.: Transaction, 1995.

Horowitz, David. *Radical Son: A Generational Odyssey*. New York: The Free Press, 1997.

Johnson, Phillip E. *Darwin on Trial*. Downers Grove, Ill.: InterVarsity Press, 1993.

_____. *Reason in the Balance: The Case Against Naturalism in Science, Law and Education*. Downers Grove, Ill.: InterVarsity Press, 1995.

_____. *Objections Sustained: Subversive Essays on Evolution, Law and Culture*. Downers Grove, Ill.: InterVarsity Press, 1998.

Kennedy, D. James, and Jim Nelson Black. *Character and Destiny: A Nation in Search of Its Soul*. Grand Rapids, Mich.: Zondervan, 1994.

Kennedy, D. James, and Jerry Newcombe. *What If Jesus Had Never Been Born?* Nashville: Thomas Nelson, 1994.

_____. *The Gates of Hell Shall Not Prevail: The Attack on Christianity and What You Need to Know to Combat It*. Nashville: Thomas Nelson, 1996.

_____. *What If the Bible Had Never Been Written?* Nashville: Thomas Nelson, 1998.

Koster, John P. *The Atheist Syndrome*. Brentwood, Tenn.: Wolgemuth and Hyatt, 1989.

Kreeft, Peter. *A Refutation of Moral Relativism: Interviews with an Absolutist*. San Francisco: Ignatius, 1999.

Kutchins, Herb, and Stuart A. Kirk. *Making Us Crazy: DSM–The Psychiatric Bible and the Creation of Mental Disorders*. New York: The Free Press,1997.

LaHaye, Tim. *Faith of Our Founding Fathers*. Brentwood, Tenn.: Wolgemuth and Hyatt, 1987.

_____. *A Nation Without a Conscience: Where Have All the Values Gone?* Wheaton, Ill.: Tyndale House, 1994.

_____. *Power of the Cross: Real Stories, Real People, A Real God*. Sisters, Oreg.: Multnomah Books, 1996.

Lapin, Daniel. *America's Real War*. Sisters, Oreg.: Multnomah, 1999.

Lewis, C. S. *Mere Christianity*. New York: Macmillan, 1952.

Limbaugh, Rush. *The Way Things Ought to Be*. New York: Pocket Books, 1992.

Lutzer, Erwin W. *Hitler's Cross: The Revealing Story of How the Cross of Christ Was Used As a Symbol of the Nazi Agenda*. Chicago: Moody Press, 1995.

Marsden, George M. *The Soul of the American University: From Protestant Establishment to Established Nonbelief*. New York: Oxford University Press, 1994.

Martin, Jobe. *The Evolution of a Creationist*. Reprint, Rockwall, Tex.: Biblical Discipleship Publishers, 1996.

Martin, Malachi. *The Keys of This Blood*. New York: Simon and Schuster, 1990.

MacArthur, John F., Jr. *The Vanishing Conscience*. Dallas: Word, 1994.

McDowell, Josh. *The New Evidence That Demands a Verdict*. Nashville: Thomas Nelson, 1999.

McDowell, Josh, and Bob Hostetler. *Right from Wrong*. Dallas: Word, 1994.

McDowell, Josh, and Norman Geisler. *Love Is Always Right: A Defense of the One Moral Absolute*. Dallas: Word, 1996.

McDowell, Josh, and Bob Hostetler. *The New Tolerance*. Wheaton, Ill.: Tyndale House, 1998.

Milton, Richard. *Shattering the Myths of Darwinism*. Rochester, Vt.: Park Street Press, 1997.

Moreland, J. P. *Scaling the Secular City*. Grand Rapids. Mich.: Baker Book House, 1987.

_____. *Christianity and the Nature of Science: A Philosophical Investigation*. Grand Rapids, Mich.: Baker Book House, 1989.

_____. *Love Your God with All Your Mind*. Colorado Springs, Colo.: NavPress, 1997.

_____, ed. *The Creation Hypothesis: Scientific Evidence for an Intelligent Designer*. Downers Grove, Ill.: InterVarsity Press, 1994.

Moreland, J. P., and Scott B. Rae. *Body and Soul: Human Nature and the Crisis in Ethics*. Downers Grove, Ill.: InterVarsity Press, 2000.

Morris, Henry M. *The Biblical Basis for Modern Science*. Grand Rapids, Mich.: Baker Book House, 1984.

_____. *The Long War Against God: The History and Impact of the Creation/Evolution Conflict*. Grand Rapids, Mich.: Baker Book House, 1990.

_____. *That Their Words May Be Used Against Them: Quotes from Evolutionists Useful for Creationists*. San Diego: Institute for Creation Research, 1997.

Muggeridge, Malcolm. *Jesus Rediscovered*. Wheaton, Ill.: Tyndale House, 1969.

Murphree, Jon Tal. *Divine Paradoxes: A Finite View of an Infinite God*. Camp Hill, Pa.: Christian Publications, 1998.

Murray, Michael J. *Reason for the Hope Within*. Grand Rapids, Mich.: Eerdmans, 1998.

Nash, Ronald H. *Christian Faith and Historical Understanding*. Dallas: Probe, 1984.

_____. *Poverty and Wealth: The Christian Debate Over Capitalism*. Westchester, Ill.: Crossway, 1987.

_____. *Faith and Reason: Searching for a Rational Faith*. Grand Rapids, Mich.: Zondervan, 1988.

_____. *The Closing of the American Heart*. Dallas: Probe Books, 1990.

_____. *Worldviews in Conflict*. Grand Rapids, Mich.: Zondervan, 1992.

_____. *Why the Left Is Not Right: The Religious Left: Who They Are and What They Believe*. Grand Rapids, Mich.: Zondervan, 1996.

_____. *The Meaning of History*. Nashville: Broadman and Holman, 1998.

_____. *Life's Ultimate Questions: An Introduction to Philosophy*. Grand Rapids, Mich.: Zondervan, 1999.

Noebel, David A. *Understanding the Times: The Religious Worldviews of Our Day and the Search for Truth*. Eugene, Oreg.: Harvest House, 1991.

Noebel, David A., J. F. Baldwin, and Kevin J. Bywater. *Clergy in the Classroom: The Religion of Secular Humanism*. Manitou Springs, Colo.: Summit Press, 1995.

Olasky, Marvin. *Fighting for Liberty and Virtue*. Wheaton, Ill.: Crossway Books, 1995.

Overman, Dean L. *A Case Against Accident and Self-Organization*. New York: Rowman and Littlefield, 1997.

Pearcey, Nancy R., and Charles B. Thaxton. *The Soul of Science: Christian Faith and Natural Philosophy*. Wheaton, Ill.: Crossway Books, 1994.

Perloff, James. *Tornado in a Junkyard: The Relentless Myth of Darwinism*. Arlington, Mass.: Refuge Books, 1999.

Plantinga, Alvin. *Warranted Christian Belief.* New York: Oxford University Press, 2000.

Reisman, Judith A. *Kinsey: Crimes and Consequences.* Arlington, Va.: Institute for Media Education, Inc., 1998.

Rueda, Enrique T. *The Homosexual Network: Private Lives and Public Policy.* Old Greenwich, Conn.: Devin Adair Company, 1982.

Satinover, Jeffrey. *Homosexuality and the Politics of Truth.* Grand Rapids, Mich.: Baker Book House, 1996.

Scarborough, Rick. *Enough Is Enough: A Call to Christian Involvement.* Lynchburg, Va.: Liberty House, 1996.

Schaeffer, Francis A. *A Christian Manifesto.* Wheaton, Ill.: Crossway Books, 1982.

_____. *The Complete Works of Francis A. Schaeffer: A Christian Worldview.* 5 vols. Westchester, Ill.: Crossway Books, 1982.

_____. *How Should We Then Live?* Wheaton, Ill.: Crossway Books, 1983.

Schlossberg, Herbert. *Idols for Destruction: The Conflict of Christian Faith and American Culture.* Wheaton, Ill.: Crossway Books, 1990.

Schwarz, Fred C. *Beating the Unbeatable Foe: One Man's Victory Over Communism, Leviathan, and the Last Enemy.* Washington, D.C.: Regnery, 1996.

Sowell, Thomas. *Inside American Education: The Decline, the Deception, the Dogmas.* New York: The Free Press, 1993.

_____. *The Vision of the Anointed: Self-Congratulation as a Basis for Social Policy.* New York: HarperCollins, 1995.

_____. *Conquests and Cultures: An International History.* New York: Basic Books, 1998.

_____. *The Quest for Cosmic Justice.* New York: The Free Press, 1999.

Stormer, John A. *None Dare Call It Education: What's Happening in Our Schools.* Florissant, Mo.: Liberty Bell Press, 1998.

Sykes, Charles J. *Dumbing Down Our Kids: Why American Children Feel Good About Themselves but Can't Read, Write, or Add.* New York: St. Martin's Press, 1995.

Thaxton, Charles B., Walter L. Bradley, and Roger L. Olsen. *The Mystery of Life's Origin.* New York: Philosophical Library, 1984.

Thomas, Cal. *Occupied Territory.* Brentwood, Tenn.: Wolgemuth and Hyatt, 1987.

_____. *The Things That Matter Most.* New York: HarperCollins, 1994.

Titus, Herbert W. *God, Man, and Law: The Biblical Principles.* Oak Brook, Ill.: Institute in Basic Life Principles, 1994.

Vazsonyi, Balint. *America's 30 Years War.* Washington, D. C.: Regnery, 1998.

Veith, Gene Edward, Jr. *Postmodern Times: A Christian Guide to Contemporary Thought and Culture.* Wheaton, Ill.: Crossway Books, 1994.

Vitz, Paul C. *Psychology As Religion: The Cult of Self-Worship.* Grand Rapids, Mich.: Eerdmans, 1994.

_____. *Faith of the Fatherless: The Psychology of Atheism.* Dallas: Spence Publishing, 1999.

Von Kuehnelt-Leddihn, Erik. *Leftism Revisited: From deSade and Marx to Hitler and Pol Pot.* Washington, D.C.: Regnery Gateway, 1990.

Wilson, Bill, ed. *The Best of Josh McDowell: A Ready Defense.* Nashville: Thomas Nelson, 1993.

Wolfe, Christopher, ed. *Homosexuality and American Public Life.* Dallas: Spence Publishing, 1999.

Wright, N. T. *What Saint Paul Really Said: Was Paul of Tarsus the Real Founder of Christianity?* Grand Rapids, Mich.: Eerdmans, 1997.

NOTES

INTRODUCTION

1. George Barna, *The Second Coming of the Church: A Blueprint for Survival* (Nashville: Word, 1998), 148. "We have somewhere in the neighborhood of eighty million adult believers in the United States."

2. Brad Scott, *Streams of Confusion: Thirteen Great Ideas That Are Contaminating Our Thought and Culture* (Wheaton, Ill.: Crossway Books, 1999).

3. As Tim LaHaye was the original author of this book two decades ago, we will continue to preserve his first-person perspective in this edition of the work. Therefore all illustrations told in first person—"I did this or that"—should be understood as coming from Tim. When personal stories are told from coauthor David Noebel's experience, we use the third person—"When David did this or that."

CHAPTER 1

1. For a discussion of the brain/mind issue see David A. Noebel, *Understanding the Times: The Religious Worldviews of Our Day and the Search for Truth* (Eugene, Oreg.: Harvest House, ninth printing, 1999), 178–180; 401f. Also, see Sir John Eccles and Daniel N. Robinson, *The Wonders of Being Human: Our Brain and Our Mind* (Boston, Mass.: New Science Library, 1984) and

J. P. Moreland and Scott B. Rae, *Body and Soul* (Downers Grove, Ill.: InterVarsity Press, 2000).

2. See Tim LaHaye, *Why You Act the Way You Do* (Wheaton, Ill.: Tyndale House, 1985).

3. Cal Thomas, *The Things That Matter Most* (New York: HarperCollins, 1994), 53.

4. "The Gangsta Next Door," Gene Edward Veith, *World* (September 23, 2000) 15.

5. From an email to the author (September 25, 2000).

6. Thomas, 49.

7. Allen Charles Kors, "The Contradiction Inherent in Social Responsibility," *Academic Questions* 12, no. 4 (fall 1999): 21: "There is no social justice; there is only justice. Social justice is a denial of justice itself." Or Thomas Sowell, *The Quest for Cosmic Justice* (New York: The Free Press, 1999), 77: "Envy was once considered to be one of the seven deadly sins before it became one of the most admired virtues under its new name 'social justice.'"

8. Timothy J. Dailey, Family Research Council, "'Hate Crime' Laws Mean Unequal Protection," *In Focus* (4 October 1999): 1: "Federal 'hate crime' legislation, such as the Hate Crimes Protection Acts (HCPA), would mean that an eight-year-old girl has less protection under the law than a homosexual college student."

9. The U.S. Navy is planning to place women on submarines since they are the last bastion of maleness in the armed forces. This is in spite of the fact that most feminists hate the military.

10. "In the world it is called Tolerance, but in hell it is called Despair . . . the sin that believes in nothing, cares for nothing, seeks to know nothing, interferes with nothing, enjoys nothing, hates nothing, finds purpose in nothing, lives for nothing, and remains alive because there is nothing for which it will die." Dorothy Sayers as quoted in Charles Colson and Ellen Santilli Vaughn, *Against the Night: Living in the New Dark Ages* (Ann Arbor, Mich.: Servant Books, 1989), 93.

11. See Concerned Women for America, "Outcome-Based Education: Remaking Your Children through Radical Educational Reform."

12. Product of conception.

NOTES

CHAPTER 2

1. N. T. Wright, *The New Testament and the People of God* (Minneapolis: Fortress Press, 1992), 132–133 says the Christian response to, who are we? ("We are humans, made in the image of the Creator"), where are we? ("We are in a good and beautiful, though transient world, the creation of the God in whose image we are made"), what is wrong? ("Humanity has rebelled against the Creator"), and what is the solution? ("The Creator has acted, is acting, and will act within his creation to deal with the weight of evil . . . focused upon Jesus") "constitute an articulated ground-plan of the mainline or traditional Christian worldview."

2. Arthur Herman, *The Idea of Decline in Western History* (New York: The Free Press, 1997), 357.

3. Ibid.

4. At the present time the Society has six hundred voting members and more than two thousand sustaining members.

5. Henry M. Morris, *The Long War Against God: The History and Impact of the Creation/Evolution Conflict* (Grand Rapids, Mich.: Baker Book House, 1989), 320–321. Also see Morris's *The Biblical Basis for Modern Science* (Grand Rapids, Mich.: Baker Book House, 1984).

6. For readers interested in this subject, we recommend the following: all books published by the Institute for Creation Research; Walter Brown's *In the Beginning*: *Compelling Evidence for Creation and the Flood*: all works by Phillip E. Johnson on the subject of evolution; Norman Macbeth's *Darwin Retried: An Appeal to Reason*; Luther D. Sunderland's *Darwin's Enigma*; J. P. Moreland's *Christianity and the Nature of Science*; Walter James ReMine's *The Biotic Message: Evolution Versus Message Theory*. And for our atheist readers we recommend Richard Milton's *Shattering the Myths of Darwinism*. Milton is an atheist who sees through the myths of Darwin.

7. Phillip E. Johnson, "The Church of Darwinism," *Human Events* (27 August 1999): 16.

8. Francis J. Beckwith and Gregory Koukl, *Relativism: Feet Firmly*

317

Planted in Mid-Air (Grand Rapids, Mich.: Baker Book House, 1998), 61–69.

9. Ibid., 69.

10. Erik von Kuehnelt-Leddihn, *Leftism Revisited: From deSade and Marx to Hitler and Pol Pot* (Washington, D.C.: Regnery Gateway, 1990), 334.

11. See Josh McDowell and Norm Geisler, *Love Is Always Right: A Defense of the One Moral Absolute* (Dallas: Word, 1996).

12. Charles Colson and Nancy Pearcey, *How Now Shall We Live?* (Wheaton, Ill.: Tyndale House, 1999), 376.

13. For a detailed summary of this point see D. James Kennedy and Jerry Newcombe, *What If Jesus Had Never Been Born?* (Nashville: Thomas Nelson, 1994).

14. David A. Noebel, *Understanding the Times: The Religious Worldviews of Our Day and the Search for Truth* (Eugene, Oreg.: Harvest House, 1991).

15. Ibid. We also recommend Josh McDowell's *The New Evidence That Demands a Verdict* (Nashville: Thomas Nelson, 1999) for further study on worldview.

16. Since this work is primarily an examination and exposé of Secular Humanism, we want our readers to know that they can obtain the "wisdom of God" in great detail elsewhere. See (a) The Holy Bible; (b) Norman L. Geisler, *Baker Encyclopedia of Christian Apologetics* (Grand Rapids, Mich.: Baker Book House, 1999); (c) Josh McDowell, *The New Evidence That Demands a Verdict* (Nashville: Thomas Nelson, 1999); and (d) Carl F. H. Henry, *God, Revelation and Authority*, 6 vols. (Wheaton, Ill.: Crossway Books, 1999).

CHAPTER 3

1. See chapter 8 for documented confirmation that Secular Humanism is a religion in the very same sense that Christianity is a religion.

2. Alvin Plantinga, *Warranted Christian Belief* (New York: Oxford University Press, 2000), 436.

3. See Joseph Epstein's "Light As Ayer: The Illogical Life of a Logical Positivist," *The Weekly Standard* (31 January 2000): 29–30 for an inside look at the moral life of A. J. Ayer. Ayer "played women" as other men "played golf." Ayer's friend Stuart Hampshire had a child with Ayer's first wife while Ayer was still married to her. Ayer's comment upon his work in *Language, Truth and Logic* was, "Well, I suppose that the most important defect is that all of it was false." Since this work is required reading in America's colleges, we are hoping that Ayer's own comment on his work will also be relayed to students.

4. See David A. Noebel, *Understanding the Times: The Religious Worldviews of Our Day and the Search for Truth* (Eugene, Oreg.: Harvest House, 1991) for an additional five tenets of Secular Humanism, including its view of psychology, sociology, law, economics, and history.

5. John Dewey's influence on American education cannot be overstated. He was heavily involved with Norman Thomas in the Fabian Socialist organization, the League for Industrial Democracy. It was this organization that published Dewey's *Education and the Social Order* in 1934. Dewey worked toward establishing a "new social order," by which he meant a socialistic order. As Zygmund Dobbs's *The Great Deceit* puts it, "Dewey masterminded the spreading of socialist propaganda through the schools in order to prepare for revolution" (p. 260).

6. See the Corliss Lamont Web site—"dedicated to the work of Corliss Lamont and the Philosophy of Humanism." The Web site lists his relationships to Columbia University, Harvard University, *Free Inquiry,* and a great deal more.

7. See George Grant, *Grand Illusions: The Legacy of Planned Parenthood* (Franklin, Tenn.: Adroit Press, 1992) for the radical background of Sanger.

8. Ted Turner's estranged wife, Jane Fonda, has shown interest in the Christian faith, and Christians are praying that Ted Turner will follow her example. If Mr. Turner should retire from managing the team, Harvard's Alan M. Dershowitz would be an immediate

successor. See Alan M. Dershowitz, "Taking Disbelief Out of the Closet," *Free Inquiry* 19, no. 3 (summer 1999): 6.

9. Zygmund Dobbs, ed., *The Great Deceit: Social Pseudo-Sciences* (West Sayville, N.Y.: Veritas Foundation, 1964), 327: "Felix Frankfurter organized the American Civil Liberties Union (ACLU) in 1920, in company with Morris Hillquit (head of the American Socialist Party), Laski, Roger N. Baldwin, Jane Addams, Harry F. Ward, A. J. Muste, Scott Nearing and Norman Thomas. This organization was a socialist front pure and simple. The Communist Party had then only recently split off from the Socialist movement, and the ACLU allowed a number of red partisans such as William Z. Foster and Elizabeth G. Flynn to serve on its national committee. The socialists hoped that they would be officially recognized by Lenin's Communist International, and were trying to coalesce all leftist forces into one political movement."

10. See the Corliss Lamont Website for his relationship to the Emergency Civil Liberties Union.

11. Samuel L. Blumenfeld, *NEA: Trojan Horse in American Education* (Boise, Idaho: The Paradigm Company, 1990). Also, G. Gregory Moo, *Power Grab: How the National Education Association Is Betraying Our Children* (Washington, D.C.: Regnery Publishing, 1999).

12. See J. Michael Waller, "Funding Subversion of National Security," *Insight* (21 August 2000): 16.

13. See Ann Coulter, "The Democrat Philosophy," *Human Events* (4 August 2000): 6: The "Playboy Foundation is a big contributor to the National Organization for Women, the Women's Action Alliance, Emily's List (for electing liberals to office), Feminists for Free Expression, Voters for Choice, Planned Parenthood, the National Abortion Rights Action League, the American Civil Liberties Union, and People for the American Way."

14. See Rene A. Wormser, *Foundations: Their Power and Influence* (New York: Devin-Adair Company, 1958). Frank J. Gaffney, Jr., *Commentary* magazine (January 2000): 27: "Thanks in particular to the sustained generosity of the MacArthur, Ford, W. Alton

Jones, Ploughshares, Hewlett, Carnegie, Merck, and Rockefeller foundations, thousands of professors and graduate students have been trained to . . . promote the necessity of global governance." William Rusher, *Washington Times* (26 December 1999): B4: "In other words, it is relentlessly liberal. Mr. Freeman cites one estimate that out of the 50,000 foundations of all kinds, just nine are explicitly conservative." Carroll Quigley, *Tragedy and Hope: A History of the World in Our Time* (New York: The MacMillan Company, 1966), 946–47 refers to the influence of the foundations and how Corliss Lamont and his parents funded "a score of extreme Left organizations, including the Communist Party itself." Incidentally, while Quigley is hostile to Senator Joseph McCarthy, the Radical Right and ex-Communists, he agrees with the findings of Rene A. Wormser's work on foundations.

15. Charles Colson and Nancy Pearcey, *How Now Shall We Live?* (Wheaton, Ill.: Tyndale House, 1999), 119.

16. Carroll Quigley, *Tragedy and Hope: A History of the World in Our Time* (New York: The MacMillan Company, 1966), 945–46 summarizes Corliss Lamont's support of "extreme Left organizations, including the Communist Party itself." Lamont was recognized among the humanists as "the chief figure in 'fellow traveler' circles and one of the chief spokesmen for the Soviet point of view."

17. Corliss Lamont, *The Philosophy of Humanism* (New York: Frederick Ungar Publishing Co., 1977), 12–13.

18. Ibid., 116.

19. Ibid., 30.

20. Nancy R. Pearcey and Charles B. Thaxton, *The Soul of Science: Christian Faith and Natural Philosophy* (Wheaton, Ill.: Crossway Books, 1994), 19: "In the late nineteenth-century England, several small groups of scientists and scholars organized under the leadership of Thomas H. Huxley to overthrow the cultural dominance of Christianity—particularly the intellectual dominance of the Anglican church."

21. Lamont, op cit., 45.

22. Paul Kurtz, "Is Everyone a Humanist?" in *The Humanist Alternative*, ed. Paul Kurtz (Buffalo, NY: Prometheus Books, 1973), 177.

23. Bertrand Russell, "Why I Am Not a Christian," in *The Basic Writings of Bertrand Russell*, ed. Robert E. Egner and Lester E. Denonn (New York: Simon and Schuster, 1961), 586.

24. Francis Bacon, "Of Atheism," in *Selected Writings of Francis Bacon*, ed. Hugh G. Dick (New York: Random House, 1955), 44.

25. Henry M. Morris, *The Troubled Waters of Evolution* (San Diego: Creation-Life Publishers, 1974). Also, see Henry M. Morris, *Evolution in Turmoil* (San Diego: Creation-Life Publishers, 1982) and Henry M. Morris and Gary E. Parker, *What Is Creation Science?* (El Cajon, Calif.: Masters Books, 1987).

26. Lamont, op. cit., 83.

27. Ibid., 249.

28. Ibid., 110.

29. Henry M. Morris, *Education for the Real World* (San Diego: Creation Life Publishers, 1977), 82. This is the same Julian Huxley who took up Lord Morley's challenge to create a new religion based on science. Huxley called it "evolutionary humanism." See Norman L. Geisler, *Baker Encyclopedia of Christian Apologetics* (Grand Rapids, Mich.: Baker Book House, 1999), 346.

30. See David A. Noebel, *Understanding the Times*, chapter 12 on Secular Humanist biology.

31. Homer Duncan, *Secular Humanism* (Lubbock, Tex.: Christian Focus on Government, 1979), 16.

32. Ibid., 17.

33. Ibid., 16. For further information on this point see Walt Brown, *In The Beginning* (Phoenix, Ariz.: Center for Scientific Creation, 1995) and Richard Milton, *Shattering the Myths of Darwinism* (Rochester, Vt.: Park Street Press, 1997). Also, see all the works by Phillip E. Johnson on the subject of Darwinism.

34. See John P. Koster, *The Atheist Syndrome* (Brentwood, Tenn.: Wolgemuth and Hyatt, 1989) for an in-depth look at the influence of Charles Darwin, Thomas Henry Huxley, Friedrich Nietzsche, Sigmund Freud, and Scientific Atheism.

35. John W. Whitehead and John Conlan, "The Establishment of the Religion of Secular Humanism and Its First Amendment Implications," *Texas Tech Law Review* 10 (winter 1978): 54. See chapter 7 for a full look at Secular Humanism as a religion.

36. S. S. Chawla, "A Philosophical Journey to the West," *The Humanist* (September–October 1964): 151.

37. Paul Kurtz, *Humanist Manifesto II* (Buffalo, N.Y.: Prometheus Books, 1973), 18.

38. See David A. Noebel, *Understanding the Times*, chapter 9, entitled "Secular Humanist Ethics." There Lester Kirkendall is quoted as saying, "Humanists have had an important role in the sexual revolution." For background on the roles of Margaret Sanger and Alfred C. Kinsey in the sexual revolution, we recommend George Grant, *Grand Illusions: The Legacy of Planned Parenthood* (Franklin, Tenn.: Adroit Press, 1992) and Judith A. Reisman, *Kinsey: Crimes and Consequences* (Arlington, Va.: Institute for Media Education, Inc., 1998).

39. Enrique T. Rueda, *The Homosexual Network: Private Lives and Public Policy* (Old Greenwich, Conn.: Devin Adair Company, 1982); Boris Sokoloff, *The Permissive Society* (New Rochelle, N.Y.: Arlington House, 1972); Jeffrey Satinover, *Homosexuality and the Politics of Truth* (Grand Rapids, Mich.: Baker Book House, 1996); Robert H. Bork, *Slouching Towards Gomorrah: Modern Liberalism and American Decline* (New York: HarperCollins, 1996); Christopher Wolfe, ed., *Homosexuality and American Public Life* (Dallas: Spence Publishing, 1999).

40. B. K. Eakman, *Cloning of the American Mind: Eradicating Morality Through Education* (Lafayette, La.: Huntington House, 1998), 146 gives the background of Bolshevik Georg Lukacs and his "aggressive sex education programs" in the Soviet Union and Hungary. His goal was to undermine Christian morality and "archaic family structure."

41. Daniel Horowitz, *Betty Friedan and the Making of the Feminine Mystique: The American Left, the Cold War, and Modern Feminism* (Amherst, Mass.: University of Massachusetts Press, 1998), 93.

42. Cal Thomas, *The Things That Matter Most* (New York: HarperCollins, 1994), 84.

43. Lamont, op. cit., 235. Paul Kurtz in *Humanist Manifesto 2000* says, "Although humanists have called for liberation from repressive puritanical codes, they have likewise defended moral responsibility." Puritanical codes is the buzz word for adultery, fornication and homosexuality. In a humanist publication *A New Bill of Sexual Rights and Responsibilities* by Lester Kirkendall, the following sexual practices were advocated: extramarital sexual relationships, premarital sexual relationships, homosexuality, bisexuality and genital associations. Interestingly, Kurtz in *Manifesto 2000* does agree that humanists "accept the Golden Rule that 'we should not treat others as we would not like to be treated.'"

44. Ibid., 229.

45. Paul Johnson, *Intellectuals* (New York: HarperCollins, 1988), chapter 1.

46. Balint Vazsonyi, *America's 30 Years War* (Washington, D. C.: Regnery, 1998), 95.

47. Katherine A. Kersten, "To Hell with Sin," *Wall Street Journal* (17 September 1999): W15.

48. Lamont, op. cit., 227.

49. Ibid., 14.

50. Francis A. Schaeffer, *How Should We Then Live?* (Old Tappan, N.J.: Fleming H. Revell, 1976), 224.

51. See David A. Noebel, *Understanding the Times*, chapter 24, entitled "Secular Humanist Politics."

52. Julian Huxley, "A New World Vision: Selections from a Controversial Document," *The Humanist* (March–April 1979): 35.

53. When humanists use the word "democracy," keep in mind America's state-run educational system, where there is no freedom of choice for creationism. Would a world government ruled by humanists be any different? And even though a majority of Americans favor the teaching of creationism alongside evolution, that means nothing to humanists. Recently when the Kansas Board

of Education decided to downgrade the teaching of evolution, the humanists proved to be poor sports and found it difficult even to tell the truth about the situation. A democratic vote meant nothing to the humanists. It is either their way or no way. And we want them to rule a one-world government?

54. Lamont, op. cit., 281.
55. See Noebel, *Understanding the Times*, chapter 27, entitled "Secular Humanist Economics" for a summary of the humanists' latest thinking on economics.
56. See Igor Shafarevich, *The Socialist Phenomenon* (New York: Harper and Row, 1980) for such a history of failure.
57. Lamont, op. cit., 281.
58. See Georgi Shakhnazarov, *The Coming World Order* (Moscow: Progress Publishers, 1981). Shakhnazarov has been a longtime aide to Mikhail Gorbachev, both inside and outside government. His book is the blueprint for a one-world socialist government, and not a humanist alive would fail to buy into it. Paul Kurtz in *Humanist Manifesto 2000* calls for an international system of taxation. Says Kurtz, "This would not be a voluntary contribution but an actual tax. The existing vital agencies of the United Nations would be financed by the funds raised. This includes UNESCO, UNICEF, the World Health Organization, the World Bank, the International Monetary Fund, and other organizations."
59. Claire Chambers, *The SIECUS Circle* (Belmont, Mass.: Western Islands, 1977), 87.
60. Ibid., 69–70.
61. Lamont, op. cit., 281–82.
62. Ibid., 257–58.
63. "Cronkite Champions World Government," *Washington Times* (3 December 1999): A2. Taken from a speech by Walter Cronkite before the World Federalist Association at the United Nations, 19 October 1999.
64. Ibid., 82.

65. Humanist Society of San Francisco, *Humanism: What Is It?* (San Francisco: Humanist Society of San Francisco, 1949), 3.

CHAPTER 4

1. Alexis de Tocqueville, *Democracy in America* (New Rochelle, N.Y.: Arlington House, n.d.), 1:294.

2. Ibid., 297.

3. Achille Murat, *A Moral and Political Sketch of the United States* (London: Effingham Wilson, 1833), 113, 132, quoted in David Barton, *Original Intent: The Courts, the Constitution and Religion* (Aledo, Tex.: WallBuilders Press, 1997), 121.

4. The Unitarians of Jefferson and Adams's day are not to be confused with present-day Unitarians. As David Barton notes, the *Theological Dictionary* of 1823 described Unitarians in these words: "In common with other Christians, they confess that He [Jesus] is the Christ, the Son of the Living God; and in one word, they believe all that the writers of the New Testament, particularly the four Evangelists, have stated concerning him." Barton also quotes other Unitarian sources stating their belief in the Bible "admitting no standard of Christian truth, nor any rule of Christian practice, but the words of the Lord Jesus and his Apostles." See Barton, *Original Intent*, 314.

5. Lester J. Cappon, *The Adams-Jefferson Letters* (Chapel Hill, N.C.: University of North Carolina Press, 1987), 339–40.

6. See David Barton in *Original Intent*, chapter 16, for the humanistic revisionism occurring in our educational institutions today. Barton answers each charge with historical fact and data. Also, see socialist Barbara Ehrenreich, "Why the Religious Right Is Wrong," *Time* (7 September 1992) for her attack on America's founders.

7. Gary DeMar, *America's Christian History: The Untold Story* (Atlanta, Ga.: American Vision Publishers, Inc., 1993), 5.

8. Daniel Lapin, *America's Real War* (Sisters, Oreg.: Multnomah Publishers, 1999), 95.

9. Ibid., 12.

10. Barton, op. cit., 81.

11. Ibid., 82.
12. Ibid., 83.
13. Ibid., 84.
14. Ibid.
15. Ibid., 85.
16. Ibid., 137.
17. Ibid.
18. David Barton, *Benjamin Rush: Signer of the Declaration of Independence* (Aledo, Tex.: WallBuilders Press, 1999), 123.
19. Barton, *Original Intent*, 167.
20. Ibid., 169. Also, see Tim LaHaye, *Faith of our Founding Fathers* (Brentwood, Tenn.: Wolgemuth and Hyatt, 1987). The 1988 edition published by New Leaf Press.
21. Ibid., 131.
22. Ibid., 336.
23. Ibid., 165.
24. Ibid., 167.
25. Ibid.
26. Ibid.
27. Ibid., 32.
28. Lapin, op. cit., 12.
29. Balint Vazsonyi, *America's 30 Years War* (Washington, D.C.: Regnery, 1998), 46: "All [Greek philosophy, Roman law, French Enlightenment] were noted, all [Luther, Calvin, Zwingli] played a part, all entered the thought processes of America's founders. But the sole book that originated beyond the English Channel, and which they retained in its entirety, was the Bible."
30. Francis A. Schaeffer, *How Should We Then Live?* (Wheaton, Ill.: Crossway Books, 1983), 105.
31. William F. Buckley Jr., "The Meaning of Heritage," *National Review* 51, no. 22 (22 November 1999): 46.
32. See David A. Noebel, *Understanding the Times: The Religious Worldview of Our Day and the Search for Truth* (Eugene, Oreg.: Harvest House, 1991), chapter 29, entitled "Biblical Christian Economics."

CHAPTER 5

1. See George M. Marsden, *The Soul of the American University: From Protestant Establishment to Established Nonbelief* (New York: Oxford University Press, 1994); B. K. Eakman, *Cloning of the American Mind: Eradicating Morality Through Education* (Lafayette, La.: Huntington House, 1998); and Zygmund Dobbs, ed., *The Great Deceit: Social Pseudo-Sciences* (West Sayville, N.Y.: Veritas Foundation, 1964) for historical data on how the humanists captured America's educational system.

2. Cal Thomas, *The Things That Matter Most* (New York: HarperCollins, 1994), 82: "One out of every five Americans [is] now infected with a viral, sexually transmitted disease. That's 56 million people."

3. William F. Buckley Jr., "Head to Toe Exam: USA, 1999," *National Review* 51, no. 24 (20 December 1999): 71. In this same article Buckley says, "The central social problem is, of course, illegitimate births."

4. Ibid.

5. David Popenoe and Barbara Dafoe Whitehead, "The State of Our Unions: The Social Health of Marriage in America," (The National Marriage Project, Rutgers University, 1999) 2, quoted in James C. Dobson's "Family News from Focus on the Family," (November 1999) 2.

6. Cheryl Wetzstein, "Marriage Will Be Multiple in the Coming Millennium," *Insight* 15, no. 46 (13 December 1999): 30.

7. Cal Thomas, *The Things That Matter Most* (New York: HarperCollins, 1994), 118.

8. Francis A. Schaeffer, *How Should We Then Live?* (Old Tappan, N.J.: Fleming H. Revell, 1976), 51–52. Also see Robert William Fogel, *The Fourth Great Awakening* (Chicago, Ill.: University of Chicago Press, 2000), 117f.

9. Ibid.

10. See Matt Labash, "Among the Pornographers," *The Weekly Standard* 4, no. 2 (21 September 1998): 20–25 for a summary of present-day humanism and pornography. Vern Bullough, a senior editor of *Free Inquiry* magazine, is up to his eyebrows in porn.

"We hope," says Bullough, "to get more [pornography] deposits from the industry—so we'll have the biggest porn collection in the country. . . . The porners love their new academic cachet. The Cal State types have taken to calling them 'Adult Entertainers.'" Bullough's Center for Sex Research is located at California State University, Northridge—"a sort of Left Coast Kinsey Institute."

11. Will Durant, *The Story of Philosophy*, 2nd ed. (New York: Pocket Books, 1961), 203.

12. Schaeffer, op. cit., 122–24.

13. Frederic Bastiat, *Selected Essays on Political Economy* (Princeton, N.J.: D. Van Nostrand Company, 1964), 292.

14. William F. Buckley Jr., "The Meaning of Heritage," *National Review* 51, no. 22 (22 November 1999): 42, "It was in one of his [Albert Jay Nock] essays, I think, that I first saw quoted John Adams's admonition that the state seeks to turn every contingency into an excuse for enhancing power in itself, and of course Jefferson's adage that the government can only do something for the people in proportion as it can do something to the people."

15. See John A. Stormer, *None Dare Call It Education: What's Happening in Our Schools* (Florissant, Mo.: Liberty Bell Press, 1998); Charles J. Sykes, *Dumbing Down Our Kids: Why American Children Feel Good About Themselves but Can't Read, Write, or Add* (New York: St. Martin's Press, 1995); and B. K. Eakman, *Cloning of the American Mind: Eradicating Morality Through Education* (Lafayette, La.: Huntington House, 1998).

16. Balint Vazsonyi, *America's 30 Year War* (Washington, D.C.: Regnery, 1998), 179. Vazsonyi's book is a litany of freedoms that Americans have lost over the past thirty years alone.

17. Dennis Prager, "Levi Strauss and the Condom Christmas Tree," *The Prager Perspective* (1 January 1999): 3. Also, see Charles Colson and Nancy Pearcey, *How Now Shall We Live?* (Wheaton, Ill.: Tyndale House, 1999), 426.

18. On average, Americans spend $7,000 per student per year, and there are approximately 55 million students. Education is the third largest industry today, behind health care and government itself.

19. For an excellent summary on how this happened, see Zygmund

Dobbs, ed., *The Great Deceit: Social Pseudo-Sciences* (West Sayville, N.Y.: Veritas Foundation, 1964). Harvard people did the research and writing for this volume, which makes it even more interesting. Also, see B. K. Eakman, *Cloning of the American Mind: Eradicating Morality Through Education* (Lafayette, La.: Huntington House, 1998).

20. Eakman, op. cit., 109–10: "How, in a single generation, did the culture change from a character-directed focus revolving around restraint, industriousness, and self-sacrifice, to a peer-oriented, self-obsessed society preoccupied with eternal youth, sexual gymnastics, and immediate gratification? . . . Much of American thought and culture were more profoundly influenced by the likes of Wundt, Neil, Ellis, Owen, Gross, Steckel, Fromm, Reich, Adorno, Freud, Marx, Lewin, Marcuse, Gramsci, Rees, Orage, Chisholm, Lunacharsky, and Lukacs [than even John Dewey and the Progressives]."

21. M. Margaret Patricia McCarran, *Fabianism in the Political Life of Britain*, 1919–1931 (Chicago: The Heritage Foundation, Inc., 1954). Christopher Story, ed., *Soviet Analyst* (October 1999): 2: "There are 23 members of Mr. [Tony] Blair's Cabinet: In January 1999, the Secretary of the Fabian Society wrote to Mr. Christopher Gill, the Conservative MP for Ludlow, Shropshire, saying that he was proud to be able to inform him that 20 members of the Blair Cabinet belonged to the Fabian Society. The Fabians are 'gradualist' revolutionaries or 'change agents'—with the same ultimate objectives as the Leninist revolutionaries."

22. Paul A. Kienel, *The Philosophy of Christian School Education* (Whittier, Calif.: Western Association of Christian Schools), 169.

23. Association for Supervision and Curriculum Development, *A New Look at Progressive Education* (Washington, D.C.: ASCD, 1972), 2.

24. Gordon H. Clark, *Dewey* (Philadelphia: The Presbyterian and Reformed Publishing Co., 1960), 15.

25. Keep in mind Julian Huxley's quest to use science to create a new religion. He called it "evolutionary humanism" and defended it as

a religion. See Norman L. Geisler, *Baker Encyclopedia of Christian Apologetics* (Grand Rapids, Mich.: Baker Book House, 1999), 346.

26. See B. K. Eakman, *Cloning of the American Mind.*

27. U. S. Supreme Court decision dated June 19, 1961 titled *Torcaso v. Watkins.* Said the Court: "Among religions in this country which do not teach what would generally be considered a belief in God are Buddhism, Taoism, Ethical Culture, Secular Humanism and others."

28. Eakman, op. cit.

29. Cal Thomas, "Republicans Can Help Kids with Choice," *Colorado Springs Gazette* (31 August 1999) N7.

30. George F. Will, "The Censoring of Zachary" *Newsweek* (20 March 2000) 82.

31. Julie Foster, "Banned in Kentucky: God, Country, Etc.," *World Net Daily,* 17 May 2000.

32. Paul Johnson, "The Real Message of the Millennium," *The Reader's Digest* (December 1999) 65.

33. Cal Thomas, *The Things That Matter Most* (New York: HarperCollins, 1994), 112.

34. Rush H. Limbaugh, III, *The Way Things Ought to Be* (New York: Pocket Books, 1992), 302.

CHAPTER 6

1. For example, Leo Pfeffer wrote an article titled "The Triumph of Secular Humanism" in which he boasted, "In this [college] arena, it is not Protestantism, Catholicism, or Judaism which will emerge the victor, but Secular Humanism, a cultural force which in many respects is stronger in the United States than any of the major religious groups or any alliance among them." Leo Pfeffer, "The Triumph of Secular Humanism," *Journal of Church and State* 19 (spring, 1977): 211.

2. *Humanist Manifesto I* and *II* (Buffalo, N.Y.: Prometheus Books, 1977), 3.

3. Ibid., 13.

4. Ibid., 8.

5. Ibid., 16.

6. Ibid.

7. Paul Kurtz, "Humanist Manifesto 2000: A Call for a New Planetary Humanism," *Free Inquiry* (fall 1999): 8–9.

8. *Humanist Manifesto I and II*, op. cit., 8.

9. Ibid.

10. Ibid.

11. Ibid., 17.

12. Kurtz, op. cit., 9.

13. *Humanist Manifesto I and II*, op. cit., 17.

14. See Barbara Dafoe Whitehead, *The Divorce Culture* (New York: Alfred A. Knopf, 1997) for a study of our present divorce culture.

15. Ibid., 18–19.

16. Kurtz, op. cit., 10, 13. Kurtz is very careful not to be too specific, lest he arouse the sleeping "religionists." He insists that "Society should not deny homosexuals, bisexuals, or transgendered and transsexuals equal rights. . . . Same-sex couples should have the same rights as heterosexual couples." Kurtz does throw a few bones to the radical right fundamentalists, e.g., humanists accept the Golden Rule and the biblical injunction to accept the aliens within our midst. "Thou shalt not commit adultery," however, is just too difficult a pill to swallow.

17. *Humanist Manifesto I and II*, op. cit., 17.

18. Ibid.

19. Ibid., 19.

20. Ibid., 18.

21. Kurtz, op. cit., 13–14. Kurtz maintains that "Children, adolescents, and young adults should have exposure to different viewpoints and enjoy encouragement to think for themselves." We know he really doesn't mean it, since the Christian worldview has been systematically deleted from the educational curriculum and Kurtz has said nothing in protest. Only a humanist worldview is allowed in our schools, and Kurtz knows that. If one suggests that creation be taught along with evolution, the howls would be heard

around the world. The Pledge of Allegiance to the flag of the United States is also under attack for mentioning "under God." This is "exposure to different viewpoints"?

22. *Humanist Manifesto I* and *II,* op. cit., 9.
23. Ibid., 21.
24. Ibid., 22.
25. Kurtz, op. cit., 16–17.
26. See Ludwig von Mises, *Socialism* (Indianapolis: Liberty Classics, 1981); Igor Shafarevich, *The Socialist Phenomenon* (New York: Harper and Row, 1980); and Tom Bethell, *The Noblest Triumph: Property and Prosperity Through the Ages* (New York: St. Martin's Press, 1998).
27. *Humanist Manifesto I* and *II,* op. cit., 20.
28. Ibid., 21.
29. Ibid., 7.
30. Ibid., 15–16.
31. Ibid., 13.
32. Ibid., 16–17.
33. Ibid., 8.
34. Ibid., 14.
35. Ibid., 9–10.
36. See David A. Noebel, *Understanding the Times: The Religious Worldviews of Our Day and the Search for Truth* (Eugene, Oreg.: Harvest House, 1991) for a systematic study of ten humanist doctrines taught in our public educational establishment today. Another in-depth study of the basic tenets of humanism in our public schools is B. K. Eakman, *Cloning of the American Mind: Eradicating Morality Through Education.* Charles Colson and Nancy Pearcey, *How Now Shall We Live?* contains a great deal of material being taught in the public schools.

CHAPTER 7

1. Sharon Begley, "Science Finds God," *Newsweek* (20 July 1998) 48.
2. Ibid., 49.
3. Ibid.

4. Paul Amos Moody, *Introduction to Evolution* (New York: Harper and Row, 1970), 497–98.

5 Henry Margenau, "Modern Physics and the Turn to Belief in God," *The Intellectuals Speak Out About God*, ed. Roy Abraham Varghese (Dallas: Lewis and Stanley, 1984), 43.

6. See "The Mysteries of the Bible: Archaeology's Amazing Finds in the Holy Land," *U.S. News and World Report* (17 April 1995) 60–61.

7. See David A. Noebel, *Understanding the Times: The Religious Worldviews of Our Day and the Search for Truth* (Eugene, Oreg.: Harvest House, 1991), chapters 5 and 8. See Norman L. Geisler's works in general and *Philosophy of Religion* (Grand Rapids, Mich.: Baker Book House, 1988) and *Baker Encyclopedia of Christian Apologetics* (Grand Rapids, Mich.: Baker Book House, 1999) in particular. Also Josh McDowell, *The New Evidence That Demands a Verdict* (Nashville, Tenn.: Thomas Nelson, 1999).

8. See Charles B. Thaxton, Walter L. Bradley, and Roger L. Olsen, *The Mystery of Life's Origin* (New York: Philosophical Library, 1984).

9. See Michael Denton, *Evolution: A Theory in Crisis* (Bethesda, Md.: Adler and Adler, 1986). Also, see Richard Milton, *Shattering the Myths of Darwinism* (Rochester, Vt.: Park Street Press, 1997) and Henry M. Morris, *That Their Words May Be Used Against Them: Quotes from Evolutionists Useful for Creationists* (San Diego: Institute for Creation Research, 1997).

10. Luther D. Sunderland, *Darwin's Enigma: Fossils and Other Problems* (Santee, Calif.: Master Book Publishers, 1988), 27.

11. David Raup, "Conflicts Between Darwinism and Paleontology," *Chicago Field Museum of Natural History Bulletin* 50 (January 1979), quoted in Sunderland, op. cit., 10.

14. Karl Popper, *Unended Quest* (Glasgow: Fontana Books, 1976), quoted in Sunderland, op. cit., 28.

13. See Duane Gish, *Evolution: The Challenge of the Fossil Record* (El Cajon, Calif.: Institute for Creation Research, 1985).

14. Carl Wieland, "Goodbye, Peppered Moths: A Classic Evolutionary Story Comes Unstuck," *Creation* 21, no. 3 (June–August 1999): 22.

15. "Feathers for *T. rex*?" *National Geographic* 197, no. 3 (March 2000) forum 2.

16. George Wald, "The Origin of Life," in *The Physics and Chemistry of Life* (New York: Simon and Schuster, 1955), 9, quoted in Morris, op. cit., 51.

17. Ibid., 12.

18. Richard Bliss, "It Takes a Miracle for Evolution," *Christian Heritage Courier* 1 (March 1979): 4.

19. See Michael J. Behe, *Darwin's Black Box: The Biochemical Challenge to Evolution* (New York: The Free Press, 1996) for an extensive study of the living cell.

20. Paul Davies, *God and the New Physics* (New York: Simon and Schuster, 1983), 145.

21. Phillip E. Johnson, *Objections Sustained: Subversive Essays on Evolution, Law and Culture* (Downers Grove, Ill.: InterVarsity Press, 1998), 9.

22. Nancy Pearcey, "Creation Mythology," *World* (24 June 2000) 23.

23. Ibid.

24. See Thomas Roder, Volker Kubillus, and Anthony Burwell, *Psychiatrists: The Men Behind Hitler* (Los Angeles: Freedom Publishing, 1995) and Bruce Wiseman, *Psychiatry: The Ultimate Betrayal* (Los Angeles: Freedom Publishing, 1995).

25. See Francis A. Schaeffer and C. Everett Koop, *Whatever Happened to the Human Race?* (Old Tappan, N.J.: Fleming H. Revell, 1979), 102–10.

26. Cal Thomas, *The Things That Matter Most* (New York: HarperCollins, 1994), 82.

27. "New Study Challenges Theory of 'Gay Gene' in Homosexuals," *Washington Times* (23 April 1999) A3. For further material on the subject see Jeffrey Satinover, *Homosexuality and the Politics of Truth* (Grand Rapids, Mich.: Baker Book House, 1996), Christopher Wolfe, ed., *Homosexuality and American Public Life* (Dallas: Spence Publishing, 1999), *The Weekly Standard*, 17 June 1996 and *The Prager Perspective*, 1 March 1997 and 15 March 1997.

28. Jennifer Kabbany, "Scientific Studies Fail to Corroborate 'Gay Gene' Theory," *Washington Times* (1 August 2000): 2.

29. Don Feder, "A City Goes to Pot," *The Weekly Standard* (13 December 1999): 19.

30. Ibid., 18.

31. Ibid., 19.

32. *Education Update* 3, no. 3 (summer 1979).

33. Ibid.

34. Ibid.

35. Ibid.

36. Cheryl Wetzstein, "Most Girls in Best Friends Program Avoid Sex, Drugs, Booze, Survey Finds," *Washington Times* (27 November 1999): A2.

37. Ibid.

38. Tim LaHaye, *The Battle for the Mind* (Old Tappan, N.J.: Fleming H. Revell, 1980), 118.

39. Nancy Pearcey, "Darwin's Dirty Secret," *World* (25 March 2000): 15.

40. Stephane Courtois, ed., *The Black Book of Communism: Crimes, Terror, Repression* (Cambridge, Mass.: Harvard University Press, 1999), 72.

41. Carroll Quigley, *Tragedy and Hope: A History of the World in Our Time* (New York: The MacMillan Company, 1966), 255.

42. Ibid., 27.

43. R. J. Rummel, *Death by Government* (New Brunswick, N.J.: Transaction Publishers, 1994), 9.

44. Ibid.

45. Yet neither Darwin nor Dewey were scientists! Darwin's degree was in theology and Dewey's in philosophy.

CHAPTER 8

1. Ian S. Markham, ed., *A World Religions Reader,* 2nd ed. (Malden, Mass.: Blackwell Publishers, 2000).

2. Roy Wood Sellars, *The Next Step in Religion* (New York: The Macmillan Company, 1918), foreword.

3. Roy Wood Sellars, *Religion Coming of Age* (New York: The Macmillan Company, 1928), vi.

4. Ibid., 270.

5. Charles Francis Potter, *Humanism: A New Religion* (New York: Simon and Schuster, 1930), 3.

6. Ibid., 128.

7. Charles Francis Potter, *Humanizing Religion* (New York: Harper and Brothers Publishing, 1933), 1.

8. John Dewey, *A Common Faith* (New Haven, Conn.: Yale University Press, 1934), 87.

9. See Samuel L. Blumenfeld, *NEA: Trojan Horse in American Education* (Boise, Idaho: The Paradigm Company, 1990).

10. Tolbert H. McCarroll, "Religions of the Future," *The Humanist* (November–December 1966): 51.

11. Lloyd Morain and Mary Morain, *Humanism As the Next Step* (Boston: The Beacon Press, 1954), 4.

12. Claire Chambers, *The SIECUS Circle* (Belmont, Mass.: Western Islands, 1977), 92.

13. Paul Kurtz, ed., *The Humanist Alternative* (Buffalo, N.Y.: Prometheus Books, 1973), 18.

14. Curtis W. Reese, *Humanism* (Chicago: The Open Court Publishing Company, 1926).

15. Curtis W. Reese, *Humanist Religion* (New York: The MacMillan Company, 1931), 5.

16. Henry Nelson Wieman and Bernard Eugene Meland, *American Philosophies of Religion* (Chicago: Willett, Clark and Company, 1936), 258–59.

17. Herbert Wallace Schneider, *Religion in 20th Century America* (Cambridge, Mass.: Harvard University Press, 1952), 141.

18. Leo Pfeffer, "Issues That Divide: The Triumph of Secular Humanism," *Journal of Church and State* 19, no. 2 (spring 1977): 211.

19. Julian Huxley, *Religion Without Revelation* (New York: The New American Library, 1957), 208.

20. Norman L. Geisler, *Baker Encyclopedia of Christian Apologetics* (Grand Rapids: Baker Book House, 1999), 346.

21. Chambers, op. cit., 60–61.
22. Ibid., 92.
23. Barbara M. Morris, *Change Agents in the Schools* (Ellicott City, Md.: The Barbara Morris Report, 1979), 19.
24. Abby Van Buren, *Cincinnati Enquirer* (6 September 1999): D4.
25. Selwyn Crawford, "Atheists Need Fellowship, Too," *Dallas Morning News* (8 July 2000): G1.
26. Ibid., G6.
27. *Humanist Manifestos I and II* (Buffalo, N.Y.: Prometheus Books, 1977), 3. This is Paul Kurtz's opening statement as he introduces the two *Manifestos*.
28. Paul Kurtz, "The New Inquisition in the Schools," *Free Inquiry* 7, no. 1 (winter 1986–87): 5.
29. Paul Kurtz, "The Two Humanisms in Conflict: Religious vs. Secular," *Free Inquiry* 11, no. 4 (fall 1991): 50.
30. Debra Bradley Ruder, "Humanist Chaplain Serves Ethical 'Nonbelievers,'" *Harvard Gazette* 88, no. 42: 10.
31. See David A. Noebel, J. F. Baldwin, and Kevin J. Bywater, *Clergy in the Classroom: The Religion of Secular Humanism* (Manitou Springs, Colo.: Summit Press, 1995), 93 for a photocopy of the directory listing humanism amongst the campus ministries. Summit Ministries also has a video on the book *Clergy in the Classroom*.
32. Ibid., 111.
33. Corliss Lamont, *The Philosophy of Humanism* (New York: Frederick Ungar Publishing Co., 1977), 24. Also see Noebel, op. cit., 75–76.
34. John W. Whitehead and John Conlan, "The Establishment of the Religion of Secular Humanism and Its First Amendment Implications," *Texas Tech Law Review* 10 (winter 1978): 19.
35. See David A. Noebel, *Understanding the Times: The Religious Worldviews of Our Day and the Search for Truth* (Eugene, Oreg.: Harvest House, 1991), chapter 3. Noebel also defines the Secular Humanist worldview in philosophy, ethics, biology, psychology, sociology, law, politics, economics, and history. Secular or

Planetary Humanism is a total worldview—and a religious world-view at its theological core.

36. Whitehead and Conlan, op. cit., 30–31.
37. Lamont, op. cit., 283.
38. Irving Kristol, "The Future of American Jewry," *Commentary* (August 1991): 22–23.
39. Ibid., 23.
40. Ibid., 25.
41. Lamont, op. cit., 6.
42. Chambers, op. cit., 82.
43. Lamont, op. cit., 53.
44. James. M. Parsons, *The Assault on the Family* (Melbourne, Fla.: Pro/Media, 1978), 10.
45. John J. Dunphy, "A Religion for a New Age," *The Humanist* (January–February 1983): 26.
46. Lester Mondale was a signatory to *Humanist Manifesto I* (1933).
47. Whitehead and Conlan, op. cit., 33.

CHAPTER 9

1. Stephen Moore, "The Greatest Century That Ever Was," *Human Events* 56, no. 1 (14 January 2000): 7.
2. Daniel Lapin, *America's Real War* (Sisters, Oreg.: Multnomah, 1999), 57.
3. See Rael Jean Isaac and Erich Isaac, *The Coercive Utopians: Social Deception by America's Power Players* (Chicago: Regnery Gateway, 1983); Richard John Neuhaus, *The Naked Public Square: Religion and Democracy in America* (Grand Rapids, Mich.: William B. Eerdmans, 1984); Richard Bernstein, *Dictatorship of Virtue: Multiculturalism and the Battle for America's Future* (New York: Alfred A. Knopf, 1994); Balint Vazsonyi, *America's 30 Years War* (Washington, D.C.: Regnery, 1998); Charles Colson and Nancy Pearcey, *How Now Shall We Live?* (Wheaton, Ill.: Tyndale House, 1999); Thomas Sowell, *A Conflict of Visions* (New York: William Morrow, 1987); and Boris Sokoloff, *The Permissive Society* (New Rochelle, N.Y.: Arlington House, 1972).

4. Cal Thomas, *The Things That Matter Most* (New York: HarperCollins, 1994), 108.

5. Colson and Pearcey, op. cit., 319.

6. Reed Irvine, Joseph C. Goulden, and Cliff Kincaid, *The News Manipulators: Why You Can't Trust the News* (Smithtown, N.Y.: Book Distributors, Inc., 1993), xiv–xix.

7. Marvin Olasky, "Remarkable Providences: Hypocrisy Watch," *World* (11 December 1999): 34.

8. Since Christians believe that all wisdom and knowledge reside in Christ (Colossians 2:2–3) and that Jesus the Messiah is the word or logos of God (John 1:1), he certainly merits the titles of philosopher or lover of wisdom, as well as Savior, Lord, King, Head, Light, and Alpha and Omega.

9. Olasky, op. cit., 34.

10. Ibid.

11. David Horowitz, *Hating Whitey and Other Progressive Causes* (Dallas: Spence Publishing, 1999), 188.

12. See Michael Medved, *Hollywood vs. America: Popular Culture and the War on Traditional Values* (New York: HarperCollins, 1992).

13. See Kenneth Lloyd Billingsley, *Hollywood Party: How Communism Seduced the American Film Industry in the 1930s and 1940s* (Rocklin, Calif.: Prima Publishing, 1998). How Hollywood reacted to an award given Elia Kazan also tells us a great deal about the lay of the land.

14. Medved, op. cit., 10.

15. *San Diego Union,* 28 December 1979.

16. Claire Chambers, *The SIECUS Circle* (Belmont, Mass.: Western Islands, 1977), 62.

17. For a detailed study of these interlocking efforts we recommend Claire Chamber's five-hundred-page, well-documented book *The SIECUS Circle.* Zygmund Dobbs's *The Great Deceit: Social Pseudo-Sciences* (West Sayville, N.Y.: Veritas Foundation, 1964) also documents the interconnections of the hundreds of socialist organizations in America. Says *The Great Deceit,* "There is never

any fundamental disagreement between communists and socialists about the fact that socialism is the ultimate aim of both movements. . . . Both socialists and communists face the same enemy, the system of individual freedom and private enterprise" (p. 16).

18. Dobbs, op. cit., 16.
19. Ibid., 327.
20. Chambers, op. cit., 27.
21. Ibid., 28.
22. See William Donohue, *The Politics of the American Civil Liberties Union* (Piscataway, N.J.: Transaction Books, 1985).
23. Chambers, op. cit., 65.
24. Ibid., 84–85.
25. Ibid., 85.
26. Ibid.
27. See Allen H. Ryskind, "DNC's Radical New Political Chief," *Human Events* (14 May 1999): 1.
28. See Dixy Lee Ray with Lou Guzzo, *Trashing the Planet* (Washington, D.C.: Regnery Gateway, 1990) for an excellent antidote to Gore's position, which she says is "radical environmentalism" (p. 170). The radical environmentalist call for world government pleases the humanists. Enforcing global measures to protect the environment is another way of spelling "world government." Another work exposing radical environmentalism is Michael S. Coffman, *Saviors of the Earth? The Politics and Religion of the Environmental Movement* (Chicago: Northfield Publishing, 1994).
29. See Al Gore, *Earth in the Balance: Ecology and the Human Spirit* (New York: Houghton Mifflin, 1992), 62. "Scientists are sketching out the influential roles played by climate and ecology in shaping human evolution" (p. 62). "The new discoveries [global cooling] relating the emergence of *Homo sapiens* to global climate changes have solved one of the mysteries in the human story by providing, at least in ecological terms, the missing link in the history of evolution" (p. 62). Vice President Gore does not mention the fact that there are millions of missing links, not just one. Yet,

he is using junk science to justify human evolution and world government. The humanists could not be happier!

30. See *The Prager Perspective* (1 January 1999) for Rabbi Prager's war with the Levi Strauss company over the Condom Christmas Tree. Says Prager, "Perhaps the most widely believed untruth in America is that big business is a conservative force in American life. . . . With regard to social issues, big business is far more leftist than rightist. Big businesses are in the forefront of promoting 'diversity' and 'multicultural' training, in avoiding politically incorrect practices as Christmas parties, in sponsoring leftist conferences, think tanks, television shows, and so on. The Levi Strauss Company, although more activist than most companies, is no aberration. Indeed, President Bill Clinton awarded Levi Strauss a presidential 'Company of the Year' award in 1997 precisely for its leftist, often radical, social work."

31. See Michael Levin, *Feminism and Freedom* (New Brunswick, N.J.: Transaction Books, 1988) for a summary of feminism in action—academically and politically.

32. See David Horowitz, *The Politics of Bad Faith: The Radical Assault on America's Future* (New York: The Free Press, 1998) for a look at the names and faces of those involved in this assault.

33. A homosexualist is a heterosexual who advocates the homosexual agenda. Bill Clinton, for example, is an excellent example of a homosexualist. From homosexuals in the military to appointing homosexuals to high government positions, including ambassadorships, Clinton has done everything in his power to advance their agenda.

34. If you find this difficult to believe, we direct you to *The Weekly Standard*, 17 June 1996, for a ten-page article by Mary Eberstadt on the subject of pedophilia. Also, the 8 May 1995 issue of the *New Republic*, which contained "the most overt attempt by a hip Journal to give pedophiles a place at the table."

35. Andrea Billups, "Pro-Gay Booklet for Schools Draws Ire," *Washington Times* (24 November 1999): 4.

36. Ibid.

37. David Barton, *Original Intent: The Courts, the Constitution, and Religion* (Aledo, Tex.: WallBuilders Press, 1997), 229.

38. Ibid.
39. Ibid.
40. Ibid., 230.
41. Paul Johnson, *A History of the American People* (New York: HarperCollins, 1997), 229.

CHAPTER 10

1. Robert L. Cord, *Separation of Church and State: Historical Fact and Current Fiction* (Grand Rapids, Mich.: Baker Book House, 1988), 51.
2. Ibid., 3.
3. For a Christian critique of this humanist ploy, see Michael Bauman, "Dispelling False Notions of the First Amendment: The Falsity, Futility and Folly of Separating Morality from Law," *Christian Research Journal* 21 (1999):20–23, 36–41.
4. N. T. Wright, *The New Testament and the People of God* (Minneapolis: Fortress Press, 1992), 225: "The high priest, who was in charge of the Temple, was as important a political figure as he was a religious one." "The Temple combined in itself the functions of all three—religion, national figurehead and government."
5. N. T. Wright, *What Saint Paul Really Said: Was Paul of Tarsus the Real Founder of Christianity?* (Grand Rapids, Mich.: Wm. B. Eerdmans Publishing Co., 1997), 157.
6. Ibid., 154.
7. David A. Noebel, *Understanding the Times: The Religious Worldviews of Our Day and the Search for Truth* (Eugene, Oreg.: Harvest House, 1991).

   This work is currently being used as a textbook in a thousand Christian schools and home-school associations, and Moody Bible College is publishing a college course of study based on the textbook. It is also being translated into numerous foreign languages. It explains that within the creative order we find all the major categories of a worldview: theology–Genesis 1:1 (in the beginning God); philosophy–Genesis 1:1 (in the beginning); ethics–Genesis

2:9 (knowledge of good and evil); biology–Genesis 1:21 (after their kind); psychology–Genesis 2:7 (a living soul); sociology–Genesis 1:28 (be fruitful and multiply); legal–Genesis 3:11 (I command thee); political–Genesis 9:6 (whoso sheddeth man's blood); economic–Genesis 1:29 (it shall be for food); and history–Genesis 3:15 (seed of the women vs. seed of the serpent).

Within the redemptive order we find that Jesus Christ is the foundation stone of all these worldview categories. That fact alone makes them sacred. Christians have been quick to judge these categories secular and thus assure their capture by the humanists. Notice the titles of deity associated with each of the categories that make up the biblical Christian worldview: theology–Colossians 2:9 (Christ is the fulness of the Godhead); philosophy–John 1:1 (Christ is the logos of God); ethics–John 1:9 (Christ is the true light); biology–John 1:4 (Christ is the life); psychology–Luke 1:46–47 (Christ is the savior of the soul); sociology–Luke 1:30–31 (Christ is the son of Mary); legal–Genesis 49:10 (Christ is the lawgiver); politics–Revelation 19:16 (Christ is King of kings and Lord of lords); economics–Psalm 50:10–12 (Christ is owner of all); and history–Revelation 1:8 (Christ is the Alpha and the Omega). The work develops the Christian worldview in all ten categories as well as presenting the secular, Marxist, and New Age worldviews in all ten areas.

8. Charles Colson and Nancy Pearcey, *How Now Shall We Live?* (Wheaton, Ill.: Tyndale House, 1999), 15.
9. Wright, *What Saint Paul Really Said,* 154.
10. Ibid., 163.
11. Ibid., 182.
12. Kenneth L. Woodward, "2000 Years of Jesus" *Newsweek* (29 March 1999): 54.
13. Wright, *The New Testament and the People of God,* 135. Wright develops an interesting Christian worldview centered around four key questions: (a) Who are we? (b) Where are we? (c) What is wrong? and (d) What is the solution? He says the answers to these four questions "constitute an articulated ground-plan of the mainline or traditional Christian worldview" (pp. 131–32).

14. Colson and Pearcey, op. cit., 17. Every preacher of the gospel of Jesus Christ should read the Colson-Pearcey book in its entirety. It is a call to informed action and responsibility.

15. Unless, of course, you are the Reverend Jesse Jackson, who was photographed taking offerings in black churches for his political campaign for president. The staid and courageous liberal news media met the situation with deafening silence.

16. Rick Scarborough, *Enough Is Enough: A Call to Christian Involvement* (Lynchburg, Va.: Liberty House, 1996), 201.

17. Ibid., 205.

18. Ibid.

19. Ibid.

20. Dr. Paige Patterson, former president of the Southern Baptist Convention, and Dr. Jimmy T. Draper, head of the Southern Baptist Sunday School Board, wrote the preface.

21. Daniel Lapin, *America's Real War* (Sisters, Oreg.: Multnomah, 1999), 43

CHAPTER 11

1. George Barna, *The Second Coming of the Church: A Blueprint for Survival* (Nashville: Word, 1998), 67: "Seven out of ten Americans view themselves as religious. Most of us—86 percent—describe our religious orientation as Christian; a mere 6 percent claim to be atheist or agnostic."

2. Ibid., 148.

3. Ibid., 67.

4. Tim LaHaye, *The Battle for the Mind* (Old Tappan, N.J.: Fleming H. Revell, 1980), 184–85.

5. Diane Winston, "Gallup Says America Has a Shallow Faith," *Dallas Morning News* (11 December 1999): G1.

6. Barna, op. cit., 23.

7. Ibid.

8. Ibid., 120–21.

9. Ibid., 122.

10. Ibid., 123–24.

11. Charles Colson and Nancy Pearcey, *How Now Shall We Live?* (Wheaton, Ill.: Tyndale House, 1999), 17.
12. Dennis Prager, "Levi Strauss and the Condom Christmas Tree," *The Prager Perspective* (1 January 1999): 3.
13. Ibid.

CHAPTER 12

1. Our definition of a patriot is one who can read America's founding documents (the Declaration of Independence, the U.S. Constitution, the Northwest Ordinance Treaty) and endorse them.
2. Our definition of a Christian is a believer in the Lord Jesus Christ as Savior or Redeemer of our souls (1 Corinthians 15:1–4) and called unto good works (Ephesians 2:8–10).
3. David Horowitz, *Hating Whitey and Other Progressive Causes* (Dallas: Spence Publishing, 1999), 153.
4. Charles Colson and Nancy Pearcey, *How Now Shall We Live?* (Wheaton, Ill.: Tyndale House, 1999), 339.
5. Jennifer Harper, "A Lockhart Moment," *Washington Times* (31 December 1999): A5.
6. Ibid.
7. Justin Torres, "TV As a Religion-Free Zone," *The Weekly Standard*, 24 January 2000, 22.
8. Robert H. Bork, *Slouching Towards Gomorrah: Modern Liberalism and American Decline* (New York: HarperCollins, 1996), preface.
9. Remember, it was Barbara Walters who said, "The real crisis is one of character. Today's high school seniors live in a world of misplaced values. They have no sense of discipline. No goals. They care only for themselves. In short, they are becoming a generation of undisciplined cultural barbarians." Quoted in Charles Colson, *Against the Night: Living in the New Dark Ages* (Ann Arbor, Mich.: Servant Books, 1989), 80.
10. Deuteronomy 23:17: "There shall be no ritual harlot of the daughters of Israel, or a perverted one of the sons of Israel."

11. Jeff Jacoby, *Colorado Springs Gazette* (5 January 2000): M6: "Ted Forstmann and John Walton, two donors to the Washington Scholarship Fund raised $170 million—$100 million from their own pockets—to create the Children's Scholarship Fund, and invited low income families to apply for 40,000 scholarships that would defray part of the cost of private school tuition. To their astonishment, nearly 1.25 million applications came flooding in, representing almost 1 out of every 50 schoolchildren in America."

12. Tim and Beverly LaHaye, *A Nation Without a Conscience: Where Have All the Values Gone?* (Wheaton, Ill.: Tyndale House, 1994), 110: "Fathers are all but nonexistent in too many families. Democratic Senator Patrick Moynihan has been a welcome spokesman against the dangers of the escalating illegitimacy among the black population. As he well stated, 'Either there is a rebirth of moral responsibility in this area, or we are on the way to ruin.'"

13. John Godfrey, "Money Trail Marks Rise of Government," *Washington Times* (26 December 1999): C1: "As the 20th century opened, local, state and federal governments consumed $1 out of every $15 generated by the nation's economy. As the century closes, the federal government alone will take $1 of every $5 from the gross domestic product. All levels of government combined will take nearly 30 percent of GDP. . . . The vast majority has been in the area of income transfers, 'robbing Peter to pay Paul,' said Stephen Moore, economist with the CATO Institute."

14. "The American Century," *Washington Times* (31 December 1999): A18: "During the early part of the 20th century's first decade, the United States surpassed Great Britain as the world's wealthiest major nation. . . . Due to dramatic increases in productivity during the 20th century, per capita income, adjusted for inflation is now nearly seven times higher than it was at the beginning of the century. Meanwhile, the average work week for a full-time employee was slashed from 60 hours to about 40 hours. Whereas more than 40 percent of American workers labored in agriculture in 1900, today only 3 percent do. Just as it requires far

fewer workers to produce the nation's food supply today, the percentage of personal consumption expenditures devoted to food is much smaller now (15 percent) than it was at the beginning of the century (44 percent). The average worker needs seven minutes of work time today to purchase a half-gallon of milk, compared to 56 minutes at the beginning of the century. A three-pound chicken requires 14 minutes of labor today, compared to 2 hours and 40 minutes 100 years ago. Not only are Americans living much better. They are living much longer. The annual death rate from infectious diseases has plummeted from nearly 800 per 100,000 population in 1900 to less than 60 today. Meanwhile, average life expectancy at birth during the past 100 years has increased from 46.3 years to 73 years for men and from 48.3 years to 79.7 years for women. Today, 66 percent of families own their own home, 99 percent of families have running water, flush toilets and electricity, compared to 24 percent, 15 percent and 3 percent, respectively in 1900. In 1900, 5 percent of families had telephones; today 94 percent do. In 1900, only 1 percent had an automobile; today 83 percent do." Is it any wonder why the dispossessed of the world risk all to get here in spite of the humanist left telling them how evil America is and how socially unjust its lifestyle?

15. Aleksandr Solzhenitsyn argued that art is an accurate indicator of what is to come and that art in Russia foretold the most physically destructive revolution of the 20th century. See Solzhenitsyn's article "How the Cult of Novelty Wrecked the 20th Century," in *American Arts Quarterly* (spring 1993). All of the controversial art sponsored by the National Endowment for the Arts involved desecrations of Christian images (Mapplethorpe, Serrano, etc.). And today the Virgin Mary is draped in elephant dung at a New York museum. Tomorrow it will be Jesus Christ draped in condoms or Jesus and John portrayed as homosexuals. We believe Christians should not be silent and that senators and congressmen need to hear that no more taxpayers' monies will go to such blasphemy. Also, see *Commentary* magazine, January 2000, 61–62 for an update on where art is today, including the scandal surrounding the Brooklyn Museum of Art.

When artists sell cans of their own excrement as art, someone should surely notice that "art has lost her soul."

CHAPTER 13

1. Daniel Lapin, *America's Real War* (Sisters, Oreg.: Multnomah, 1999), 54.
2. See Alvin J. Schmidt, *The Menace of Multiculturalism: Trojan Horse in America* (Westport, Conn.: Praeger Publishers, 1997) for an exposé of the anti-Western civilization bias being taught under the guise of multiculturalism.
3. Charles Colson and Nancy Pearcey, *How Now Shall We Live?* (Wheaton, Ill.: Tyndale House, 1999), 376.
4. Lapin, op. cit., 52.
5. Stephane Courtois, ed., *The Black Book of Communism: Crimes, Terror, Repression* (Cambridge, Mass.: Harvard University Press, 1999), 15.
6. R. J. Rummel, *Death by Government* (New Brunswick, N.J.: Transaction Publishers, 1994), 9.
7. Courtois, op. cit., 752.
8. Ibid., 750.
9. Kurtz actually says he tries to abide by the Golden Rule. See Paul Kurtz, "Humanist Manifesto 2000: A Call for a New Planetary Humanism," *Free Inquiry* (fall 1999): 10.
10. B. K. Eakman, *Cloning of the American Mind: Eradicating Morality Through Education* (Lafayette, La.: Huntington House, 1998), 109.
11. See Zygmund Dobbs, ed., *The Great Deceit: Social Pseudo-Sciences* (West Sayville, N.Y.: Veritas Foundation, 1964), 144.
12. Quoted in Cal Thomas, *The Things That Matter Most* (New York: HarperCollins, 1994), 113.
13. Author unknown; read on Dr. Laura Schlessinger's radio show, 3 December 1999.

CHAPTER 14

1. Daniel Lapin, *America's Real War* (Sisters, Oreg.: Multnomah, 1999), 246.

NOTES

2. Malachi Martin, *The Keys of This Blood* (New York: Simon and Schuster, 1990), 261.

3. Charles Colson and Nancy Pearcey, *How Now Shall We Live?* (Wheaton, Ill.: Tyndale House, 1999), xii.

4. Ibid., 17.

5. George Barna, *The Second Coming of the Church: A Blueprint for Survival* (Nashville, Tenn.: Word, 1998), 135.

6. David A. Noebel, *Understanding the Times: The Religious Worldviews of Our Day and the Search for Truth* (Eugene, Oreg.: Harvest House, 1991). For example, theologically, biblical Christianity is theistic; Secular Humanism is atheistic. Philosophically, biblical Christianity is supernatural or logocentric; Secular Humanism is naturalistic or materialistic. Ethically, biblical Christianity maintains moral absolutes; Secular Humanism maintains moral relativism. Biologically, biblical Christianity is creationistic; Secular Humanism is evolutionistic. Psychologically, biblical Christianity accents soul, spirit, mind; Secular Humanism accents physical-chemical brain. Sociologically, biblical Christianity defends three social institutions—family (father, mother, child), state, and church; Secular Humanism defends trial marriages, world government, and ethical culture churches. Legally, biblical Christianity bases positive or man-made law on biblical and/or natural law and an objective moral order; Secular Humanism defends positive law. Economically, biblical Christianity defends the concept of private property, work, inheritance; Secular Humanism has had a love affair with socialism (until some of Ayn Rand's disciples joined their ranks). Politically, biblical Christianity recognizes the state as a God-ordained institution necessary to curb the wickedness of man; Secular Humanism believes that mankind can now control his future evolution through the function of the man-made state. Historically, biblical Christianity is the outworking of God's plan through His people from Adam and Eve to the return of Christ and beyond; Secular Humanism sees history as the outworking of a blind, random evolution.

7. Barna, op. cit., 148.

8. See David Barton, *Original Intent: The Courts, the Constitution, and Religion* (Aledo, Tex.: WallBuilders Press, 1997), 111.
9. Those interested in a free "Key 16" card may write Concerned Women for America, 1015 15th Street NW, Suite 1100, Washington, D.C. 20005 or call (202) 488-7000.
10. Colson and Pearcey, op. cit., 139.
11. The programs are based on David's best-selling *Understanding the Times* text and provide Christian teens with some of the best teachers in the country, including J. P. Moreland, Frank Beckwith, Michael Bauman, Norm Geisler, Ron Nash, Del Tackett, Mark Cahill, John Mark Reynolds, Phillip E. Johnson, Jobe Martin, Chuck Edwards, Jeff Myers, Chuck Asay, and Kevin Bywater.

Listen to what James Dobson said about these programs: "One of the best programs for teaching the concepts I've described is called Summit Ministries, located in Manitou Springs, Colorado. Run by Dr. David Noebel, it is designed to prepare 15- to 25-year-old students to deal with the Secular Humanism they will certainly encounter in high school or college. It is an economical, two-week program each summer that 'pops open' the eyes of teenagers and young adults." (James C. Dobson, *Children at Risk: The Battle for the Hearts and Minds of Our Kids* [Dallas: Word, 1990], 268.)

Charles Colson: "Summit Ministries in Colorado is pointing the way. Perched high in the Rocky Mountains, every summer Summit packs in high school students who want to learn how to defend their faith against the ideological trends of the day. Founder David Noebel has developed a curriculum that gives Christian kids a crash course in apologetics, teaching them how to deal with the intellectual challenges they face in high school and college. They learn how to analyze and critique the New Age movement, humanism, Marxism, feminism, evolutionism, and whatever other 'ism' happens to be gaining a foothold in contemporary American culture. Churches and Christian schools ought to take a page from Summit's book (or use Summit's own book *Understanding the Times*) and begin preparing young people to face an increasingly hostile culture" (Colson and Pearcey, op. cit., 339).

Because space is limited for these summer programs, Summit Ministries offers a series of curricula based on them for junior high, senior high, and Sunday Schools. These materials are used in hundreds of Christian schools and home-school settings. The organization is also developing a course on the Christian worldview for grades 1–6. This curriculum should be available in a few years. Summit Ministries may be contacted at P.O. Box 207, Manitou Springs, CO 80829 or (719) 685-9103.

12. If you wish to help identify campus groups or distribute books or assist the project financially, contact Students for America at P.O. Box 649, Manitou Springs, CO 80829.

13. Andrea Billups, "Christian Group Fights Ouster at Tufts over Gay Student Flap," *Washington Times* (20 April 2000): A3.

14. Frank York, "Public Employees Teach Kids 'Gay' Sex," World Net Daily, 9 May 2000.

15. Barna, op cit., 4.

16. Ibid., 6.

17. See David A. Noebel, *Understanding the Times,* chapter 21, for a summary of how the humanists subverted American Constitutional law.

18. Ibid.

19. James C. Dobson, *Family News,* February 2000, 3.

20. Ibid.

21. Ibid.

22. Nancy R. Pearcey and Charles B. Thaxton, *The Soul of Science: Christian Faith and Natural Philosophy* (Wheaton, Ill.: Crossway Books, 1994), 19.

23. Robert Bork, *Slouching Towards Gomorrah: Modern Liberalism and American Decline* (New York: HarperCollins, 1996), 339.

24. Ibid.

25. Ibid.

26. Ibid., 336.

27. Barna, op. cit., 102.

28. Ibid., 210.

CHAPTER 15

1. God judged nations severely for destroying their sons and daughters (cf. Genesis 15:16; Deuteronomy 2; and Deuteronomy 12:31). God judged both Israel and Judah for the same sin of destroying their sons and daughters (cf. 2 Kings 17:17; 2 Chronicles 28:3; 33:6).

APPENDIX B

1. "The unique message of humanism on the current world scene is its commitment to scientific naturalism. . . . Nature is basically physical-chemical at root. . . . We decry the efforts of a few scientists, often heralded by the mass media, to impose transcendental interpretations upon natural phenomena." Paul Kurtz, "Humanist Manifesto 2000: A Call for a New Planetary Humanism," *Free Inquiry* (fall 1999): 8–9.
2. Francis A. Schaeffer, *How Should We Then Live?* (Old Tappan, N.J.: Fleming H. Revell, 1976), 134–35.
3. Dr. Donald B. DeYoung, "Creation Scientists, Part I," Institute for Creation Research, September 1978, radio transcript no. 345.
4. *Encyclopedia Britannica,* 1975 edition, vol.3, 97.
5. Ibid, 96.
6. Ibid, 97.
7. Schaeffer, op. cit., 135.
8. Ibid., 136.
9. DeYoung, op. cit., no. 346.
10. Ibid.
11. See Nancy R. Pearcey and Charles B. Thaxton, *The Soul of Science: Christian Faith and Natural Philosophy* (Wheaton, Ill.: Crossway Books, 1994) for a defense of Christianity's role in science. Also, see Stanley L. Jaki, *The Origin of Science* (South Bend, Ind.: Regnery Gateway, 1978) and *The Savior of Science* (Washington, D.C.: Regnery Gateway, 1988).
12. Schaeffer, op. cit., 132–33.
13. Ibid., 134.

14. Balint Vazsonyi, "The End . . . of What?" *Washington Times* (21 December 1999): A19.
15. Ibid.
16. Daniel Lapin, *America's Real War* (Sisters, Oreg.: Multnomah, 1999), 157.
17. See Dan Graves, *Scientists of Faith: Forty-Eight Biographies of Historic Scientists and Their Christian Faith* (Grand Rapids, Mich.: Kregel Resources, 1996).

THE BATTLE FOR YOU MIND HAS BEGUN

PERFECT FOR GROUP AND INDIVIDUAL STUDY,
Mind Siege IS ALSO AVAILABLE IN THESE FORMATS

· WORKBOOK
· LEADER'S GUIDE
· VIDEO CURRICULUM

WORD PUBLISHING
www.wordpublishing.com

R